THE NEW BROADCASTING REALITIES

Real-life Strategies, Insights, and Issues for Broadcast Journalists,
Aspiring Journalists, Production Executives, and Broadcasters
in *The New Age* of Broadcasting, Cable, and the Internet

KEN LINDNER

LIVE OAK
BOOK COMPANY

Published by Live Oak Book Company
Austin, TX
www.liveoakbookcompany.com

Distributed by Live Oak Book Company

For ordering information or special discounts for bulk purchases, please contact Live Oak Book Company at PO Box 91869, Austin, TX 78709, 512.891.6100.

Design and composition by Greenleaf Book Group LLC
Cover design by Greenleaf Book Group LLC

Publisher's Cataloging-In-Publication Data
(Prepared by The Donohue Group, Inc.)

Lindner, Ken.
    The new broadcasting realities : real-life strategies, insights, and issues for broadcast journalists, aspiring journalists, production executives, and broadcasters in the new age of broadcasting, cable, and the Internet / Ken Lindner.—2nd ed.
        p. ; cm.
    First edition published as: Broadcasting realities : real-life issues and insights for broadcast journalists, aspiring journalists and broadcasters.
    Issued also as an ebook.
    Includes bibliographical references.
    ISBN: 978-1-936909-23-0
    1. Broadcast journalism—Vocational guidance. 2. Broadcast journalism—Technological innovations. 3. Broadcast journalism—Moral and ethical aspects. 4. Television broadcasting of news. I. Title.
PN4797 .L562 2011
070.4/023   2011939278

eBook ISBN: 978-1-936909-24-7
Second Edition

No matter what form the carriage of content takes [now or in the future], we will always need [charismatic and compelling] talent to deliver it.

—*Jim Bell, Executive Producer,* Today

Dedication

This book is lovingly dedicated to my dad, Jack Lindner, who has been my teacher by example, and to my mom, Betty, who has instilled within me a love of learning and psychology. You are my best friends. While my dad taught me so very much about how to artfully *Choreograph*, nurture, and truly appreciate a highly successful and tremendously gratifying career, my mom has taught and continues to teach, enrich, and inspire me with her wide-ranging insights, brilliance, and humaneness.

I love you as much as—if not more than—any child could possibly love his parents. Thank you so very much for everything that you have been and have given to me.

This book is also dedicated to the following very special individuals:

To all of the exceedingly talented and loyal KLA clients, who trust us to protect and enhance their precious careers;

To my cherished KLA staff members: Karen Wang-Lavelle, Susan Levin, Kristin Allen, Rob Jordan, Melissa Van Fleet, Jill Walter, Lexi Strumor, Tom Ragonnet, Nick Goeringer, and Eric Moreno;

To Shari Freis, who, with a warm smile, enables me each and every day to multitask and somehow get it all done;

To Clint Greenleaf, Justin Branch, Natalie Navar, Alan Grimes, Neil Gonzalez, and the wonderful people at the Greenleaf Book Group for all of their help, guidance, and support;

To our KLA alumni, such as Babette Perry and Rick Ramage, who through their wonderful talents have helped make KLA what it is today;

To Edward Miller for his extraordinary typing and proofreading services and for being such a supportive, bright light through the whole process;

To Shelley and Bill Berman, Jack Hartley, Dr. Charles Masterson, Sam Weisbord, Lee Stevens, and Richard Scheer for their unconditional love and support through the decades;

To my sweet aunt Sylvia, whom I love and who loves the news;

To Ben Cammarata, Don Browne, Thomas Dingman, and Phil DiPicciotto, who continue to show me in every way that you can be a huge success and remain truly humane and higher-value-based;

To Phil Liebowitz, Norman Brokaw, Lou Weiss, Art Fuhrer, Len Hartman, and Don Aslan for being so kind and nurturing during the early years;

To *Broadcasting & Cable* and its writers for their excellent articles and for keeping the broadcasting community informed;

To Joel Cheatwood and Rich Sanchez for taking the time to make exceedingly valuable contributions to this book;

To the wonderful media writers at the *Los Angeles Times* and the *New York Times*; and

To Jennifer, Elie, and Sean at the Juan Juan Salon; Junior's Deli; and all of the Coffee Beans in the West Los Angeles area for allowing me to sit in their wonderful establishments and write for hours at a time.

Additionally, this book is written in loving memory of Ron Tindiglia, Don Fitzpatrick, and Jon Petrovich, who truly loved on-air talent and inspired and taught all of those who came in contact with them. I love you all, and I thank you for all of the gifts that you have shared with me.

Kenny

Contents

SECTION I

Your Introductory Information

Your Glossary

Programming: This term shall include all forms of programs, such as talk shows (e.g., *Oprah, Ellen, Live With Regis & Kelly*), game shows (e.g., *Jeopardy, Deal or No Deal, Wheel of Fortune*), magazine shows (e.g., *Entertainment Tonight, Inside Edition, Extra!, Access Hollywood, Showbiz Tonight*), competition shows (e.g., *Survivor, Wipeout, The Amazing Race*), reality shows or docu-soaps (e.g., *Big Brother, Family Jewels, Keeping Up with the Kardashians, The Real World*).

For our purposes, *programming* shall mean shows with hosts, narrators, facilitators, reporters, interviewers, contestants, personalities, and/or an ensemble of individuals who discuss a topic or various topics. These programs are not produced under the auspices of a network's or local station's news division and are not meant to be "hard" newscasts or shows.

Broadcasting: For the purposes of this book, *broadcasting* shall mean all newscasts and news shows, as well as all programming shown on any network, local station, cable network, the Internet, or other means of carriage that currently exists or will in the future be devised. We will use this term to mean what it implies: the carriage of content in the *broadest* and most all-encompassing sense possible.

Talent: Throughout this book, I use the term *talent* to mean and include newscasters, anchors, hosts, reporters, contributors, etc.—essentially anyone who renders on-air services. Additionally, there will also be times when I use the term *talent* to refer to on-air individuals, as well as to producers and executive producers.

Career Choreography™ **and** *Career Choreographer*™: *Career Choreography*™ is a proactive, calculated set of logical steps that an individual takes in order to put the percentages in his or her favor to successfully achieve career goals. The individual who devises and takes these steps shall be referred to as a *Career Choreographer*™.

Multi-Platforming: This term shall mean that a talent, producer, or news or program executive is or will be rendering services *on more than one show* and/or for more than one employer *at the same time.*

The New Age of Broadcasting, The New Age, **or** *The New Economic Reality:* These terms shall refer to the current state and *Stage* of broadcasting, and to the influence that the economic downturn, program exhibition fragmentation, and the Internet have had on broadcasting.

The New Age **Broadcasting Realities,** *The New Age Realities,* **or The New Realities:** These are truths, strategies, realities, insights, and thoughts that will enable you to constructively and successfully navigate through *The New Age of Broadcasting.*

Network: *Network* shall refer to the broadcast networks, such as ABC, CBS, NBC, and FOX, and not to any cable networks.

Transcendence: Transcendence occurs when a talent has an expertise, a specialty, or fame in a particular area, which we will call their "power base," and the talent then uses that power base to achieve even greater success in other areas. An example of transcendence is Rachael Ray evolving from a food expert to a talk-show host, and thereafter, to an owner of a thriving international business. What she has done is transcend her (original) power base of food expertise.

Owned Stations or O&Os: These are local stations that are owned and operated by one network. For example, WABC (New York City), KABC (Los Angeles), and WLS (Chicago) are three O&Os of the ABC Network.

Affiliated Stations or Affiliates: These are stations affiliated with, but not owned by, a particular network. For example, WSVN in Miami is affiliated with the FOX Network and carries FOX Network programming, but it is not owned by FOX. WSVN is owned by the Sunbeam Television Corporation.

Syndication or Syndicated Shows: *Syndicated shows* are programs that are essentially sold or distributed, station by station, in each market. Therefore, a syndicated show can appear on an ABC affiliate in one market or an NBC-, CBS-, FOX-, or CW-affiliated station in another. When a network or a station group buys a particular show that will run on all or many of its owned stations, this is often called a "group buy."

Gold Ring Dream: This is your ultimate, long-term dream job or position.

"It" or the "It" Factor: "It" is composed of those qualities that certain extraordinarily gifted on-air individuals have that engage viewers in such a positive, irresistible, and/or "magical" way, such that viewers are drawn to watch them, like them, feel comfortable with them, and connect with them. As a result, employers are always in search of talent who have "it."

Block Shooting: *Block shooting* occurs when multiple shows are shot during a defined period of time (a day, a week, and/or a month), so as to be cost- and time-effective.

Ratings: The term *ratings* is an estimate of the percentage of the public viewing a particular television program or newscast.

Demographics or Demos: Essentially, the term *demographics* or *demos* is used to identify what types of viewers are watching a particular program or newscast. For example, "demos" identify whether the viewers of a particular newscast, program, etc., are male or female, and/or their age (range).

DWTS: *DWTS* will be shorthand for the ABC Network prime-time show *Dancing with the Stars*.

GM: *GM* will be shorthand for *general manager*.

GMA: *GMA* will be shorthand for the ABC morning news program *Good Morning America*.

FOX or FNC: *FOX* or *FNC* will be shorthand for the FOX News Channel.

MS: *MS* will be shorthand for MSNBC.

E!: *E!* will be shorthand for E! Entertainment.

KLA: *KLA* will be shorthand for my broadcast journalist representation firm Ken Lindner & Associates, Inc.

***Carpe diem* (car-pay dee-im):** *Carpe diem* is Latin for "Seize the day!" (i.e., make the very most of the moment at hand). For us, *carpe diem* will also encompass the passion and positive energy that catalyze and motivate you to make the very most of your particular gifts, strengths, and skill sets, so that you will fulfill your greatest potential.

This spirit is the rock-solid foundation of this book, and it is in this self-empowering spirit that the following material is presented.

Introduction

Over the past five years, all on-air newscasters, hosts, and broadcasters have unquestionably had to deal with and successfully adapt to many new and tremendously impactful *Broadcasting Realities*. What were once tried-and-true norms, strategies, and actions during a very different economic time may well no longer be relevant or appropriate today.

The economic downturn created *The New Economic Reality* in broadcasting, as the recession had a tremendous negative impact on the advertising revenues received by broadcasters. It also played a major role in almost all news and programming decisions made by management regarding news gathering, talent salaries, new hires, firings, pay cuts, layoffs, unpaid furloughs, and "voluntary" or forced retirements. Additionally, declining advertising revenues have been one of the main reasons why local stations, networks, and producers are opting to purchase and/or create their own inexpensively produced programming. For the past five years, local stations, networks, and programmers have been striving to do much more, with much less and far fewer—and when it has been time for employers to offer new contracts to current employees, in many instances, 10- to 20-percent pay cuts have become the new raise. The current economy has also put the onus on the networks to re-purpose and re-package as much of their existing material as possible.

There is also a *New Reality* regarding what is expected from one's on-air performance, depending upon whether the talent appears on broadcast TV or cable, on network or on local television, and whether the talent renders their services during morning drive time, daytime, early evening, or prime time.

The pervasive use of the Internet, social media, and multimedia journalism has become one of the major *New Age Realities* for all newscasters, hosts, networks, local stations, producers, and production executives. As we will discuss later, *The New Age* is a time of huge digital growth and integration. Being able to write, shoot, and edit your own material is now, in many cases, a prerequisite for on-air individuals to be hired and for veterans to retain their positions. As salaries decrease, it is crucial for on-air talent to be able to *multi-platform* their careers, as increased visibility and career-enhancing on-air opportunities can well result in increased income—sometimes exponentially so.

Additionally, by strategically increasing your visibility, you may add significant value to your persona and "brand," which may well enhance your value to current and future employers. As a result, now, as never before, *on-air individuals must brand themselves and take ownership of their careers and business, as opposed to just being employees for hire.* This is imperative in *The New Age of Broadcasting* and a *Career Choreography™ Commandment.*

Essentially, what *The New Age* requires of newscasters, program hosts, and reporters, executives, and producers is that they develop a set of far more broadbased, long-range strategies for successfully navigating a new, ever-changing landscape. The material in this book will give you much of the requisite information to help you accomplish this.

By the by, as we will discuss, the information presented here is equally applicable and beneficial as we recover from our financial downturn, as the models that stations, networks, and programmers have put into place as a matter of survival are now *The New Age* models that they will fervently strive to maintain in order to increase profits as the economy rebounds. So, in almost all instances, these *New Age Realities* are here to stay!

The major goal of *The New Broadcasting Realities* is to supply you with the necessary information from which on-air talent, as well as news and programming executives, can make enhancing short- and long-term career and work-related decisions. This book will also give valuable information and perspectives to all those who want to learn about news and programming.

The material that follows offers a wealth of strategies that will help you to wisely grow your career vertically, as well as to expand it horizontally. It explains how to effectively *Choreograph* the steps of your career, so that you can logically and strategically put the percentages in your favor to attain your career goals.

This book will also meld *The New Broadcasting Realities* with those from years past that remain valid and relevant. Many of these past and still current *Realities* were discussed in my first book, *Broadcasting Realities*, published 12 years ago.

In this *New Age*, individuals in broadcasting are operating in a world of reduced revenues and budgets, smaller staffs, and significant media[1] and ad spending[2] fragmentation. Yet never before have more newscasts, as well as entertainment, pop-culture, magazine, reality-based, and game shows been produced. And notwithstanding that this is a tremendously challenging time to be an on-air talent, executive producer, producer, or production executive, it is also a time to create as many highly beneficial *Multi-Platforming* opportunities as possible for yourself. For broadcasting, the following cliché rings absolutely true: With great changes and challenges come new needs, niches, and opportunities to seek out, fill, and seize. Regardless of what many say, *The New Age* presents an abundance of new and great opportunities to grow, create, and re-create yourself, your brand, and your business. You just need to be equipped with the right and most forward-thinking information, understanding, and mind-set in order to make the very most of these opportunities. My aim is to give all of this to you.

About the Author

For the past 29 years, I have had the pleasure and honor of working with and helping to develop the careers of many of the most well-respected, most well-liked, and most watched national and local newscasters and program hosts. Matt Lauer, Lester Holt, Dr. Sanjay Gupta, Mario Lopez, Maggie Rodriguez, Robin Meade, Megyn Kelly, Shepard Smith, Tom Bergeron, Samantha Harris, Sam Champion, Liz Claman, Nancy O'Dell, Ann Curry, Elizabeth Vargas, Lisa Gregorisch-Dempsey, Rob Marciano, Betty Nguyen, T.J. Holmes, Paula Zahn, Greg Kinnear, Natalie Morales, Rick Sanchez, Shaun Robinson, Brooke Baldwin, Deborah Norville, Brooke Anderson, Giselle Fernandez, Leeza Gibbons, Tamron Hall, John Saunders, Joel Cheatwood, Martha MacCallum, Jenna Lee, Melissa Francis, Christi Paul, Lonnie Quinn, Susan Hendricks, Chip Reid, Jill Wagner, Kimberly Caldwell, Lisa Guerrero, Michelle Kosinski, Janet Shamlian, Jodi Applegate, Christina McLarty, Lynn Berry, Jackie Johnson, Sharon Tay, John Ireland, Steve Mason, Lauren Sanchez, Kristina Guerrero, Thea Andrews, Julie Moran, Lisa McRee, Dayna Devon, Terry Murphy, Tucker Carlson, Maria Sansone, Shibani Joshi, Kris Gutierrez, Phil Keating, Isha Sesay, Jim Moret, Shannon High, Trace Gallagher, Courtney Friel, Gigi Stone, Mike Hill, Cindy Brunson, Pat Harvey, Sibila Vargas, Daryn Kagan, Diane Macedo, Brooke Burns, Victoria Recaño, Jason Carroll, Jackie Nespral, Diane McInerney, Terrell Brown, Monica Novotny, Jill Arrington, Dr. Wendy Walsh, Linda Stouffer, Sophia Choi, Dr. Cynara Coomer, Dorothy Lucey, Jillian Reynolds, Michelle Gielan, Lisa Dergan, Larry Mendte, Dawn Stensland, Emily Smith, Suzanne Rico, Jerry Penacoli, Mark Thompson, Teresa Strasser, Leeann Tweeden, Virginia Cha, Nancy Glass, Beth Ruyak, Rolanda

Watts, and Dana Fleming are just a few of the nationally recognizable in als with whom I have worked.

I have also had the great privilege to work with many of the most talented and compelling local TV anchors, hosts, and reporters throughout the country; however, because my career spans more than 29 years, there are too many local news talents to mention here. But please know that local news—and the individuals who shine there—is the lifeblood of my talent representation firm, and I spend a big part of my day *Choreographing* the careers of our stellar local news clients. *Choreographing* local news careers has been and will continue to be one of the very most strategic and enjoyable components of my work.

In many instances, I found my clients during the early stages or at pivotal points of their broadcasting careers and helped them to *Choreograph* their career-enhancing steps, so that they were able to secure their dream positions. As a *Career Choreographer*™, I believe that there are certain logical, well-conceived, strategic steps that individuals can take in order to put themselves in the very best position to do great and fulfilling things with their particular set of talents and gifts, and their career. The material in *The New Broadcasting Realities* is a distillation and collection of what I have learned over the past 29 years as a talent representative, *Career Choreographer*™, and broadcasting attorney who has worked on nearly five-thousand news, hosting, producing, and other forms of television contracts.

While at Harvard University, I wrote a thesis on decision-making that received a great deal of positive attention. This work contributed significantly to my graduating magna cum laude. After Harvard, I attended and graduated from Cornell Law School, where I focused on contract law and conflict resolution. Upon leaving Cornell, I took and passed the New York State Bar and began working for the William Morris Agency as a business-affairs attorney. Two years later, I became a news agent, and then vice president in charge of news for the William Morris Agency's Beverly Hills office. Four-and-a-half years later, I left William Morris and founded Ken Lindner and Associates. For the past twenty-two years, it is certainly arguable that KLA has been the most successful and well-respected news and hosting agency in the United States.

During the past few years, Ken Lindner and Associates has formed what we call "Strategic Alliances" with various major theatrical agencies, and thereafter with Octagon. These relationships allow us at KLA to co-represent certain clients when it comes to "packaging" them in television shows, and to expand these clients' careers into the commercial, digital, literary, speaking, television-production, and acting areas. This *multi-platform* representation has given me a much fuller big picture, and a far more sophisticated perspective as to how to effectively design and implement multimedia *Career Choreographies*™ for broadcast journalists, producers, and production executives in this *New Age of Broadcasting*.

Twelve years ago, my first book, *Broadcasting Realities*, was published. Since that time, broadcast journalism, both in front of and behind the camera, has materially changed—and I have grown tremendously in both my knowledge of and my appreciation for what I do and the world in which I do it.

Seven years ago, my book *Crunch Time: 8 Steps to Making the Right Life Decisions at the Right Times*[3] was published. This book focuses on the cognitive component of and strategies for making enhancing life and career decisions. *Crunch Time* was inspired by an *Oprah* producer who heard me speak about *Broadcasting Realities* at a broadcasters' convention.

The New Broadcasting Realities combines my knowledge of and love for broadcasting with my lifelong interest in decision-making. Through the years, I have learned and advised my clients that you cannot make great career decisions on any consistent basis without the requisite knowledge and understanding of the issue(s) before you. However, I have also learned and counseled that you can know and understand *everything* about the issue before you, but if you are unable to or choose not to use this information and understanding in a beneficial way because your best judgment is clouded or crippled by your emotions, all of your knowledge can be rendered useless.

My goal is for this book to be important, because broadcast journalism and the functions that it serves are profoundly important. I have done my very best to do justice to the subject.

This book is imbued with my opinions and perspectives, which are based upon my experiences. These opinions and perspectives are not in any way meant to be hurtful or harmful, just illustrative and informative. I do not profess to be perfect or to suggest that I am always right. I am neither. But I do have a great deal of experience in connection with many of the subjects about which I have written, and I truly love equipping and empowering individuals to achieve their most cherished goals. This is one of my most dearly held life missions.

In many instances, I may well focus upon the careers of my clients significantly more than those of others. This is because I know more about them and have a deeper and fuller understanding of the steps that they have taken to achieve their goals, since I have often helped them *Choreograph* their steps. This focus is by no means meant to diminish what other individuals whom I do not represent or have the requisite knowledge of have accomplished.

Infused throughout this book is my passion for news and hosting from a pure talent and production-executive perspective. I also love being *strategic* in connection with careers and their growth. Therefore, *The New Broadcasting Realities* is highly strategic.

Finally, the Latin phrase and concept of *carpe diem* pervades this book. As I mentioned earlier, there are *still* many wonderful and exciting opportunities in news and programming to seize, so I want the tone of this book to be constructive and hopeful.

Okay, let's get to the meat of the material so that you can create, seize, and enjoy your potentially fulfilling and highly rewarding career!

SECTION II

The Aims of News and Broadcasting during Four Key *Stages* of Broadcasting History

News

Quality, relevant, well-researched, and accurately reported news is of the utmost importance to every one of us! The nature and quality of the information that is imparted to us can materially impact our opinions, our ideas, and our life decisions. We rely on news programs and the individuals who work on them to equip and thereby empower us to make informed decisions regarding such topics as: Who is qualified to represent us? What should our laws and policies be? What is the very latest information regarding new and established drugs and medical procedures? What are prudent ways to invest and maximize our income? How can we raise the quality of our lives?

The press not only informs us, it also protects us. Through investigative and other reports, it unearths wrongdoing, corruption, and/or other questionable practices. It provides "essential checks and balances."[4] The press is our watchdog, shining its glaring light on those who would much rather do their deeds in the dark shadows and back alleys, free of any scrutiny.

In times of crisis, the press is there for us to rely on. It lets us know what is going on, how the event at issue affects us and others, and how we and others can proceed with our lives—in the short and long terms. It can be our lifeline.[5] At its best, the press can skillfully knit the elements of a major story together, give the viewers an informed and experienced perspective, and put events in their proper context.[6]

In the United States, we live in a democracy run by the people. Implicit in the effective functioning of a democracy is that the people—you and I—receive the necessary information to make enlightened and wise decisions. Often it is the press that supplies us with that enlightenment and wisdom.

For a myriad of compelling reasons, truly meaningful and important news is one of our greatest and most essential day-to-day allies.

The News Continuum

L et's begin our study by very briefly discussing the history of news, and then examining what the main objectives of broadcast news and broadcasters were/are during the following four *Stages* of broadcast news:

Stage One: The infancy of news

Stage Two: The 1970s until the economic downturn

Stage Three: 2008 through mid-2010

Stage Four: *The New Age of Broadcasting*—mid-2010 through today

By understanding the aspirations of the *Stage One*, *Stage Two*, and *Stage Three* broadcasters, as well as their news dissemination goals, you will be better equipped to understand *The New Age*, and thereby make decisions and take steps that will enhance you and your broadcasting career.

Stage One: The Infancy of News and Its Lofty Aim—To Serve the Public

During *Stage One*, when television news was in its infancy, news divisions were non-profit-making entities. Their noble goal was to serve the public interest by supplying individuals with important and relevant information so that they could make informed life decisions.

While in law school, I learned about the legislative history of a law—that is, the modification and edification processes that a law goes through in the Senate and House of Representatives before it is finally passed. By studying the legislative history of a law, we can ascertain the "why," the "what," and the "how" of the law. In essence, we can learn how to correctly interpret and apply the law by understanding why the law was originally introduced and ultimately passed; why it is drafted as it is; what the law is supposed to accomplish; and how the law is intended to be administered.

Similarly, if we can truly understand some of the initial and integral whys, hows, and values of broadcast journalism, we will better understand how and why we have arrived at where we are today. Therefore, it is worth spending a moment or two reviewing a bit of *Stage One* broadcasting history.

In 1925, more than 10,000 radio stations were in existence in the United States.[7] As these stations competed for listeners, they were constantly switching frequencies and increasing their power. According to Edward Bliss, Jr., the huge number of stations and the unrestricted competition brought chaos.[8] As a result, Congress recognized the need for more effective regulation and passed the Federal Radio Act of 1927. The words "public convenience, interest and necessity" appear in that act,[9] which referred to the Federal Radio Commission's requirement that as a condition of granting a license to a station, that station must "take care" to meet the all-important obligation of informing the public.

Later, Congress passed the Communications Act of 1934, and the Federal Radio Commission (FRC) became the Federal Communications Commission (FCC). That act required stations to broadcast in "the public interest, convenience and necessity." Interestingly, the meaning of this mandate is not found in the act.[10] Therefore, it has been left up to the FCC, through its rulings, to distill, as well as to enforce, the letter and the spirit of this now well-known phrase.

Similarly, the judiciary continues to interpret and protect the First Amendment guarantee that Congress shall make no law (abridging) the freedom of the press. Below are excerpts from three of the numerous United States Supreme Court decisions citing and reinforcing the public's strong interest in being informed.

In the 1972 case *Branzburg v. Hayes*, Justice Douglas, in his dissenting opinion, writes:

> Today's decision will impede the *wide-open and robust dissemination of ideas and counter thought*, which a free press both fosters and protects, and which is *essential to the success of intelligent self-government.* 408 U.S. 665 (1972) (emphasis added)

Justice Douglas, in the well-known 1974 case *Pell v. Procunier*, writes:

> In dealing with the free press guarantee, it is important to note that the interest it protects [is] the right of the people, the true sovereign under our constitutional scheme, to *govern in an informed manner. The public's interest in being informed…is thus paramount.* 417 U.S. 817 (1974) (emphasis added)

In *Houchins v. KQED*, Justice Stevens, joined by Justices Brennan and Powell, maintains:

> *The preservation of a full and free flow of information to the general public has long been recognized as a core objective of the First Amendment. 438* U.S. 1 (1978) (emphasis added)

The Radio & Television News Directors Association (RTNDA) states in its constitution that its goals are "[the] achievement of high professional standards of electronic journalism and the fostering of principles of journalistic freedom to gather and disseminate information to the public."[11] The preamble of the RTNDA's *Code of Ethics* states: "The responsibility of radio and television journalists is to gather and report information of *importance and interest to the public accurately, honestly and impartially.*"[12]

It was the near-sacred and noble obligation and mandate to supply viewers with information of importance that the *Stage One* broadcasters fulfilled and sought to protect, respectively. Making a profit from news dissemination was not a *Stage One* goal.

Stage Two: To Attain and Maintain Maximum Profitability

Stage Two of broadcast news began when broadcasters discovered that huge sums of money could be made in news. As a clear result of this realization, in lieu of a competition for journalistic excellence and achievement, TV journalism became a fierce competition for viewers, demographics, and ratings. Thereafter, news began to be treated as a business—a *Big Business*! The original end of serving the public interest with information that people *needed* to know often placed a distant second to the end of giving viewers what they wanted to see and hear—that which would entertain and titillate them˙ so as to attain the new and almighty end: *ever-growing profitability*.

For example, years ago a local news manager said to me that he has the ratings of his local newscasts broken down into three-minute segments. This way, he can compare one day's news ratings with the next day's, and thereby specifically identify which particular stories resulted in viewership increasing or decreasing. With this information, he can then decide which stories to continue to run in a later newscast, or the next day. For this television station executive (who is now the president of a major cable network) and for many others, the defining factor was not the importance of the story to the community that the station was serving, but which stories provided the highest ratings. During *Stage Two*, the goal of broadcasters was to establish and/or to increase their huge profit margins.

Michael Gartner, former president of NBC News, wrote the following during *Stage Two*, about the network evening newscasts clearly focusing on what viewers want to see, not what they need to know:

> The [O. J.] Simpson trial chewed up more time than the next two coveted events combined—the continuing war in Bosnia and the tragic bombing in Oklahoma City. The networks have spent five times as many minutes reporting on, obsessing

---

* It would appear that *Stage Two* broadcasters, when they read the RTNDA *Code of Ethics* regarding the broadcaster's responsibility "to gather and report information of importance and interest," chose to report and disseminate information of "interest" to their viewers, but often ignored what was "important" to them.

about, and analyzing the Simpson trial on nightly newscasts, as they have spent covering the debate over Medicare and welfare, issues that truly affect our lives.[13]

Edward Bliss, Jr., echoes Gartner's sentiments, when he writes:

> To a large extent, marketing researchers, not editors, determine the content of local newscasts. Since consultants have warned against the sin of boring anyone, pictures have become increasingly important, the more graphic the better—in traffic accidents, blood on the pavement; in homicide cases, bodies being removed in bags. No one argues that automobile accidents and murders should not be covered; the question is what priority to assign them. To quote John Hart, "*Too many producers select stories because they may seize an audience, instead of offering coverage designed to serve the audience.*"[14] (emphasis added)

Richard M. Cohen, former senior producer of *CBS Evening News*, shares the following *Stage Two* broadcast news observations in his caustic essay, "The Corporate Takeover of News":

> Television news has an important job to do and, I believe, it has become an institution that fails America everyday...what is the purpose of news in America today? To enlighten and edify, perhaps? *No.* The purpose of news is to make money, to generate corporate profits.[15]

So, just like separated parents competing with each other for popularity with their children, *Stage Two* broadcasters, in order to maintain viewership, in many instances gave viewers what they thought we wanted—not what we needed or what was intellectually, emotionally, and spiritually beneficial and healthy for us.

While there was a tremendous ideological shift between *Stage One* and *Stage Two*, there was no such blatant change between *Stage Two* and *Stage Three*. For example, it is easy to substitute the exhaustive and exhausting *Stage Three* TV news coverage of pop icon Michael Jackson's death and the war in Iraq for the *Stage Two* news coverage of the O. J. Simpson criminal trial and the war in Bosnia, respectively, which were discussed in the aforementioned excerpt from the former NBC News President, Michael Gartner's article devoted to the shortcomings of *Stage Two* broadcast news. In fact, it is arguable that due to the desperate need for broadcasters to increase/maintain viewership and revenues, they pander even more in *Stage Three* and *The New Age* to what the viewers want to know. Is there any greater example of this than the amount of time our national morning shows, newscasts, cable newscasts, and local stations spend on covering the brain-numbing exploits of such pop-culture staples as Lindsay Lohan, Britney Spears, or Charlie Sheen? Or the scandal or fall from grace of the day? And who would have thought that *TMZ* would be *Stage Three's* Associated Press and/or Reuters?! Therefore, it is arguable that *Stage Three* broadcasters have not only carried on *Stage Two's* aim-to-please content, but that they have ratcheted it up a couple of notches.

Stage Three: To Survive Financially and to Not Become Irrelevant

During *Stage Three*, which coincides with the worst times of our economic downturn, broadcasters were understandably trying to survive financially and remain relevant. During this dark and exceedingly challenging period:

1. Local stations, network news divisions, and syndicated shows laid off as many on- and off-air employees as was feasible as they produced barebones newscasts; pooled helicopters, photographers, etc.; requested or forced individuals to take "early retirement"; asked staff members to take substantial pay cuts; requested or mandated that employees take unpaid days or weeks off ("unpaid furloughs"); terminated employment contracts whenever they were able, so they could negotiate down talent or producer agreements and have them work "freelance," so as to save as much money as possible in salaries and health benefits; and/or renegotiate employment contracts, so that they could terminate these

contracts at much more frequent intervals, "without cause," should the broadcasters' economic plight worsen.

2. Several stations and station groups filed or considered filing for Chapter 11 bankruptcy protection, reorganized their debt, made wholesale layoffs of on- and off-air talent, sold off assets, or went out of business entirely.[16]

3. Stations and station groups defaulted on their payment obligations to producers who licensed major syndicated shows to those stations, because at the time when these stations negotiated the rich license agreements (*Stage Two*), their corporate incomes were substantially higher.[17]

4. Stations and national news divisions that once were cash cows either became far less profitable or no longer made profits at all. Witness the many local stations and network news divisions that cut every cost possible—big and small—in order to remain financially viable.

5. Some shows and newscasts re-created their formats, making them (far) cheaper to produce. For example, one well-known syndicated magazine show significantly reduced its fine complement of field reporters, as it became much more studio- and pod- (individuals giving their news from their desks) centered. During *Stage Three*, many production companies, when they were able, terminated correspondent contracts and instead offered to use the correspondents on a freelance basis, if and when they were needed.

6. There were many instances of (mid-contract) forced retirements of longtime "franchise," highly paid anchors and correspondents, and of off-air individuals as well, by their employers. (Apparently, by paying these talents off in a lump sum, the employer was able to receive favorable tax treatment.) In many other instances, highly paid popular hosts, anchors, and reporters lost their jobs as soon as the employer was contractually able to implement the change. Employers then substituted in their places talents who were happy to earn a fraction of what their predecessors had been paid.

Such are the *Stage Three New Broadcasting Realities.*

Let's briefly consider some of the factors that contributed to how we arrived at the highly precarious *Stage Three*:

1. For years, network TV was the only alternative for television news, so it flourished. However, with the success of cable and so many other viewer-compelling choices, network television viewership began to dwindle. And, as viewers found and flocked to cable as a viewing option, advertisers began to see cable as a very viable advertising vehicle. This was the case for a number of reasons, but one reason was especially compelling and made great strategic sense for advertisers: Conventional broadcast TV meant just that—its goal was to appeal to the broadest, largest audience possible. The concept was that the biggest audience meant that the network show could command the largest amount of advertising revenue per 30- or 60-second advertising spot. However, cable television presented a very different concept for advertisers and offered the means for them to reach a very specific, highly desirable "target" audience: Cable brought them narrow- or niche-casting. For example, if we look at *Stage Three* cable fare, there were (and continue to be) cable networks that focused strictly on sports, gardening, cooking, science, animals, and so on. Therefore, advertisers knew exactly what audiences their ads were reaching. So not only did viewers migrate from broadcast television to cable in order to watch some of their favorite shows, newscasts, and sportscasts, but substantial advertising revenues migrated as well.[**]

2. Then, during the past few years, the Internet began to siphon off viewers—especially younger ones—from broadcast and cable television. So, for many individuals who have grown up with the Internet, as well as for those who have become Internet-comfortable, it was quite natural

---

[**] In fact, it was announced that in the 2011 "upfront market," which is the period when advertisers commit to buying the bulk of their commercial time for the upcoming TV season, that "for the first time, the cable upfront take will be greater than the broadcast upfront" (Meg James, "Cable Channels Pull in More Ad Revenues," *Los Angeles Times*, June 18, 2011, B3). James goes on: "Of course, it is slightly unfair to compare ad revenues of scores of cable channels with that of the five major broadcast networks. But cable being poised to take in more (total) ad revenues is nevertheless a symbolic moment for the industry" (ibid.).

to receive most of their news, sports, financial information, and some entertainment from the Internet—not from TV.

3. And, finally, the economic downturn caused local stations and networks to lose tremendous amounts of already dwindling advertising dollars.

So, what, in essence, led to *Stage Three* was a confluence of things taking place that created, as one of my clients put it, "the perfect, devastating economic storm." Once again, here are the components of that "storm":

1. Broadcast television received major competition for viewers and advertising dollars from cable TV and other attractive viewer options.

2. Broadcast TV (and cable) viewers began getting their news, sports, and entertainment via the Internet.

3. Our economic downturn resulted in broadcasters' suffering very real, precedent-setting economic challenges and losses. In some cases broadcasters filed for bankruptcy or were on the verge of filing for reorganization relief.

Thus *Stage Three* broadcasters had two main aims:

1. To survive financially during this crippling economic time.

2. To remain relevant and viable for the future.

Two other influences also had a significant impact on news and programming during *Stage Two* and *Stage Three*: Voyeur TV and the Joel Cheatwood/WSVN influence.

Voyeur TV

The memorable televised O. J. Simpson Ford Bronco chase materially changed television news and, in some cases, reality programming even more. During that fateful day, viewers were riveted to their TV sets, as they watched a real-life superstar, O. J. Simpson, attempt to evade arrest by the police. There was no script. No safety net. No predetermined outcome. It was just a lot of "Who knows what's gonna happen next?" as we watched news and pop-culture history unfold before our eyes.

Because of "the Chase," there is now a huge viewer/voyeur appetite for and expectation of seeing all things "live." As a result, news executives now strive to bring as many news events as possible to the viewer/voyeur "live." As we have seen, however, it can be a risky undertaking to do so with such stories as car chases and/or attempted escapes. For example, in one unfortunate and unforgettable instance, a man shot himself, live on TV, while children watched, many of whom became traumatized. (This station broke into after-school cartoon programming to bring the chase live to its viewers.)***

In the reality-programming world, we watch shows such as *The Real World*, *Cops*, and various docu-soaps, such as *Keeping Up with the Kardashians* and *The Real Housewives of New York City/New Jersey/Beverly Hills/Atlanta* because we love having a seemingly uncensored window into other people's worlds, their crashes and burns, and their dramas, dreams, and chaos. When it comes to stars and other public figures, we're exponentially more curious and voracious voyeurs. This is one of the main reasons why entertainment and pop culture shows, such as *TMZ*, *ET*, *EXTRA*, *Access Hollywood*, *Showbiz Tonight*, and *The Insider* remain viewer/voyeur staples.

To a lesser degree, we can be voyeurs during such shows as *Dancing With the Stars*. We can watch the stars' practice sessions, as they reveal their thoughts and fears, and oftentimes fall over themselves as they practice their routines. On *American Idol*, we crave seeing the audition process. We're excited to see individuals suffer heartbreaking embarrassment and disappointment, or, conversely, be discovered. Watching the auditions also gives us valuable texture, context, connection, and traction with the contestants who do make it onto the show. It gives us a rooting interest.

Voyeur TV is based upon exposing the wizard by pulling away his curtain. It can be real, true, exciting, and often raw. It was a *Stage Two* and *Stage Three* staple and is now an integral part of almost all newscasts and programs.

*** This and other regrettable live events gave rise to the practice of delayed broadcasting by local stations and networks, so that broadcasting executives can decide whether they want to stop the airing of highly sensitive, upsetting, and/or offensive material.

The Joel Cheatwood/WSVN Influence:
The Creation of "Miami Vice News"

The other major influence came when WSVN, owned by the Sunbeam Television Corporation, lost its NBC affiliation in 1989 because of NBC's purchase of WTVJ, the CBS affiliate in Miami. WSVN became a news-intensive Independent with Fox programming three nights per week. The station's owner, Ed Ansin, and its executive vice president and general manager, Bob Leider, then hired a visionary young maverick named Joel Cheatwood. He was told to produce a non-traditional newscast with strong production values. Joel then created a totally new kind of news product. Stacey Marks-Bronner was the creative service director during that time, and she, along with Joel, was responsible for WSVN's cutting-edge look. For lack of a better term, I have always referred to it as "Miami Vice News."

WSVN decided to counter-program against all of the traditional Miami station newscasts with a hot, sexy, and flashy news product that grabbed you visually, audibly, and viscerally. It sizzled with eye-riveting anchors, striking graphics, dramatic music, and grisly/bizarre stories. This news engaged you and demanded your attention! It was voyeur delight, as viewers were bombarded with all sorts of sensory-captivating stimuli.

WSVN anchors Rick Sanchez, Sally Fitz, Penny Daniels, Jessica Aguirre, Kelly Mitchell, and Joan Lovett, among others, sold their copy like no other, as they presented rock 'n' roll, crime-laden news. Thoroughly compelling reporters, such as Shepard Smith, Michael Williams, Jeff Michael, and Craig Stevens, to name a few, walked and talked in the field, as they impactfully brought every visual element of their story to the viewer.

Undeniably, the WSVN anchors and reporters owned their stories. Eye-catching and exceedingly talented weathercasters such as Jackie Johnson, Jillian Reynolds, and Amy Murphy were captivating and compelling. Morning anchors such as the current HLN megastar Robin Meade, Shaun Robinson, John Turchin, and Julia Yarbrough grabbed and held your attention as they conversationally communicated every story.

No doubt, the WSVN newscasts were a feast for the senses. However, from my perspective, during the Joel Cheatwood years, WSVN's news coverage was also significantly better than that of any other Miami station. So not only did

WSVN push the stylistic envelope—big-time—but it also had many of the best reporters in town.

Through the years, I have clearly witnessed that almost every local newscast has taken some or many key elements from the WSVN playbook. The same can be said for all cable network and broadcast network newscasts, as well as all of the national morning shows. Some of the signature WSVN elements that almost every local and national news entity has adopted are its active, walk-and-talk reporting style (which is now a reporting staple); its higher energy and faster pacing; its edgy music; its bold, hot graphics; the conversational style of the anchors; and their attitude ("the Fox attitude").

Joel Cheatwood, maybe more than any one individual, and WSVN, perhaps more than any other news station, have influenced today's newscasts in a most pervasive and profound way.

Stage Four: To Develop and/or Implement an Appropriate Profit-Enhancing New Business Model

Here are three *Broadcasting Realities* of *Stage Four* (*The New Age*):

1. During the very bleak days of *Stage Three* (the economic downturn), many draconian cost-cutting business models were developed and implemented by broadcasters in order for them to survive financially. Now, at a time of increased prosperity,**** broadcasters are fervently

---

**** This new prosperity is largely the result of more available advertising dollars flowing to broadcasters. For local stations, specifically, *The New Age* prosperity is in large part due to income derived from retransmission consent fees (fees paid by cable companies to run local station/network programming); the return of automotive advertising; new technologies, such as mobile broadcasting and social media; and "a return by marketers to local broadcasting advertising after a period of experimenting with other platforms" (Paige Albiniak, "Broadcasters Look Forward to Better Times Ahead," *Broadcasting & Cable*, January 31, 2011, 7). However, regarding retransmission consent fees, at the time this book is being completed, the networks are aggressively seeking to be paid a significant portion of the money that their affiliates receive, as consideration for the networks' supplying valuable retransmitted content. For example, CBS says that it will receive a billion dollars in re-trans and reverse compensation from TV station negotiations (John Eggerton, "Spectrum: What Is It Good For?" *Broadcasting & Cable*, June 6, 2011, 12). As a result, stations may no longer make as much money as they have regarding retransmission fees (Michael Malone, "Affiliate (Dis)agreements," *Broadcasting & Cable*, March 21, 2011, 8).

striving to keep their *Stage Three* business models intact—with some modifications—in order to increase and maximize *Stage Four* profitability;

2. Broadcasters will continue to make great efforts to incorporate and make the very most of new technologies, as a means to stay relevant, maintain/increase viewership, and maximize profitability; and

3. *Stage Four* (*The New Age of Broadcasting*) brings with it a new set of *Broadcasting Realities*—rules, issues, norms, and strategies, that everyone in broadcasting must know, understand, and be able to adapt to in order to survive and thrive.

For your review, here are our Four Key *Stages* of Broadcasting History, and what broadcasters' aims were/are during each *Stage*:

Stage One	*Stage Two*	*Stage Three*	*Stage Four* (*The New Age*)
The infancy of news	1980 through 2007	2008 through mid-2010	Mid-2010 through today
To serve the public	To maximize and maintain profits	To survive financially and remain relevant	To develop/implement appropriate new post-economic downturn profit-making business models

SECTION III

The New Age Realities, Insights, and Strategies on Which to Base Your Career Decisions

The Enhancing Niche

It is a *Career Choreography™ Commandment* that as you go through the process of deciding whether or not to accept a particular broadcasting position, you strongly consider how enhancing and/or beneficial that job or position will be in helping you to achieve your career goals and dreams. With this *Commandment* in mind, let's study the various components of *The Enhancing Niche*.

The Enhancing Venue

> Treat a man as he is and he will remain as he is.
>
> Treat a man as he can and should be and he will become as he can and should be.
>
> —Goethe

My take on Goethe's insight is that if you are in a non-supportive, negative, and diminishing environment, you are less likely to flourish as a performer than when you are in a nurturing, supportive, and enhancing one. For example, I know that I performed far better as a tennis player for coaches who believed in me and expected the best from me. This was absolutely the case with my freshman coach at Harvard. During my competitive tennis career, I may have had more accomplished coaches, but I never played better than I did for that freshman coach. He thought I was great, and he never expected me to lose—and I never lost for him. His belief in me inspired me and lifted my performance.

Because I felt safe with him and supported by him, I was never afraid to take a risk on the court and push the envelope in order to improve and grow.*

Anchoring, hosting, and reporting are all in great part about *performance*. Therefore, you almost always will perform better, and will more quickly and easily hit your on-air comfort level after joining an organization, when you work for individuals who support, promote, and enhance you.

For example, Ann Curry rarely anchored at KCBS, the station at which she worked before she joined NBC News. Matt Lauer didn't enjoy great, consistent on-air success until he joined WNBC and NBC News. But when Ann and Matt worked for an organization that "got" them and their great on-air gifts, appreciated them, and promoted them, their careers and career satisfaction were tremendously enhanced. By the by, I could certainly make the same case regarding Katie Couric joining NBC News.

In my experience, when on-air talent feel that they are not supported by key managers or executives, they can suffer from various levels of *performance anxiety*, which is damaging to everyone. In most instances, these feelings of anxiety are manifested by the on-air talent appearing tight, timid, stiff, studied, or angry on air. *Performance anxiety* can preclude talent from achieving on-air comfortability, ease, and a light, breezy, conversational manner. Essentially, on-air talent suffering from performance anxiety, in many cases and to varying degrees, are in *lock-up mode* and therefore are unable to be the comfortable, open, and real communicators that they can be and their employers need them to be.

With this *Reality* clearly in mind, you must do your homework and seek out companies and individuals who have a reputation for being supportive of their talent. This is not always easy, because there is so much management change in broadcasting. One of the keys to your success in this area is to identify companies that are known for staying the course with their management and talent—ones that do not make changes every year or so. If managers feel more supported and less vulnerable, they are apt to be more supportive of others. As a journalist, you must do your potential-employer research.

---

* I remember an interview conducted years ago, after tennis star Lindsay Davenport defeated Martina Hingis to win the 1998 U.S. Open Women's Singles title. In discussing her road to success during her post-victory CBS interview, Davenport said, "There are many who said I couldn't make it, but I stuck with the people who believed in me." Once again: Great things can happen if you surround yourself with people who enhance you.

I have heard it said that you "shouldn't worry about the guest list until you're invited to the party." This approach may work well for parties, but when it comes to potential employers, if an employer isn't right or appropriate for you and/or what you aspire to accomplish in your career, it is *imperative* that you know this *before* you accept a position with that company. Therefore, it is essential to do your potential-employer homework *before* you apply for a job there, as your findings may tell you whether being invited to that (employer) party would be career-enhancing or career-inappropriate, career-retarding, and career-damaging.

Strategically Choosing or Creating Your "Enhancing Niche"

They say that no two snowflakes are alike, as each is unique. So, too, is every on-air talent. What this means is that depending upon what your unique set of gifts, strengths, experiences, and skills are—or what you at this point in your career need to develop, experience, improve upon, or polish—it is critical that every position that you consider accepting takes these essential data into account. Therefore, it is arguable that there is no more enhancing *Career Choreography*™ strategy than artfully choosing the right position for you and your unique skill set.[**]

So, no matter the stage of your career, it is imperative to objectively and accurately assess what your strengths and gifts are, and what makes you and your work effective and special. During the early stages of your career, you would be wise to focus on those areas of your skill set that need developing

---

** A beautiful illustration of this occurred when the exceedingly talented and likable morning show anchor/host Robin Meade and I were about to commence negotiations with *Headline News* for a contract extension for Robin. At the time, three other network news divisions had expressed serious interest in Robin. However, after giving all of the positions thorough consideration, she told me that she would happily stay at HLN, because her show, *Morning Express with Robin Meade*, had been carefully constructed and had evolved into a perfect showcase for her, and it would be nearly impossible to duplicate its magic. (Robin also truly liked and respected HLN management, who had treated her wonderfully and had allowed her to host appropriate career-enhancing outside projects.) As a result, Robin signed a highly beneficial contract extension with HLN.

and/or polishing. Seek out positions that will allow you to grow or polish the areas that you want to concentrate on later in your career (for example, anchoring, packaged reporting, live reporting) along with those that will also shore up your skill-set foundation ("live shots," writing, shooting, producing, editing, and so on).

On the other hand, when you move to a larger market or on to a national stage, the key is to find a position that highlights and showcases your gifts and what makes you special. The thought here is that once you secure one of your dream jobs—or at least a big and/or highly visible position—you must go with your "A game" and "what brought you to the dance," so that you can be successful and continue to grow. A bit of minor tweaking in "the majors" will be allowed in some cases, but it is expected that all talent who are fortunate enough to work in highly coveted, major positions, *will not* face a major learning curve that they or their employer will have to suffer through. Essentially, if you are going to play on the center court of Wimbledon, it's the time to *bring it*, not wing it! The stakes for both you and your employer in these venues are way too high—especially in this *New Age*.

Okay, let's go to the psychology behind why securing the enhancing niche is so crucial.

The goal for you here is to identify, seek out, and secure positions that are highly beneficial for *you*. Once again, you want to accept positions that will help *you* grow and/or showcase *your* gifts—not negate them.

Would Oprah Winfrey be nearly as successful if she had remained a news anchor in lieu of becoming a host? Would Matt Lauer be as successful or as fulfilled if he had remained a news anchor? I don't think so. Did Katie Couric ever enjoy the success or popularity, or have the audience traction, as an evening news anchor that she did when she was a host of *Today*? Absolutely not! No matter how many fortuitous Sarah Palin–type career-enhancing interviews came her way.

Why? Because Oprah, Matt, and Katie all have unique *hosting* gifts that allow them to showcase what makes them extraordinarily special. These individuals are so very comfortable in their own skin, and they have a unique chemistry and connection with the viewer and with those individuals on set with them. They are compelling interviewers and respectful listeners. They are blessed to have tremendous range and the great ability to change gears, as well as to ad-lib on a second's notice. The loose format of their shows allows them to organically engage you like very few others ever have. Would these individuals be able to use and showcase their unique skills if they were just reading tightly written scripts to prompter, as Brian Williams and Diane Sawyer do; and as Dan Rather, Peter Jennings, and Tom Brokaw did? Not a chance! The format of the shows that Matt and Oprah host showcases and accentuates their unique gifts and talents, and has enabled them to enjoy unprecedented success. Therefore, for you, it is all about *finding the appropriate, enhancing niche.*

The Enhancing Skill-Developing Niche

It is also important, when you are considering a potential employment position, that you understand what that particular position will and will not do for your skill development and career.

For example, if you want to learn to report and to anchor, make sure that you will at some point be guaranteed to do both. If you desire to work on one skill specifically, make sure that your management understands this and that your employer is on the same page with you—spiritually and contractually. For example, if you desire to do packaged or long-form reports, as well as live reporting as a steady diet, be sure that your preference has been made verbally and contractually clear with your employer.

Certain stations or programs, with specific philosophies and formats, will allow you to accomplish certain goals better than others. Before accepting a position:

1. Know which skills you want to develop and focus upon.

2. Know which employers and venues will allow you to develop those skills on a regular basis.

3. Make sure, with management changes being as prevalent as they are, that you have something in writing to protect you and your position in case your management allies or your management's news philosophies change.

NEW AGE STRATA-GEM

One key to correctly *Choreographing* your broadcasting career is to know what you want to learn, to experience, and to accomplish in connection with each position that you accept.

Highlighting Your Strengths

As you grow in broadcasting, it is also important to know what your strengths are, what makes you special, what kinds of venues will allow you to truly shine—and what kinds will not. As we have discussed, your goal is to then find positions that showcase and amplify your strengths. For example, some individuals are more effective reporters than they are anchors. Somehow, they look and/or perform better in the field. At some point you may want to focus on positions that strictly play to your superior reporting strengths. However, there are caveats and nuances here. Some individuals who are not effective local anchors because they do not ad-lib or chitchat well may make very effective network and cable news anchors, as some of these anchor positions require only solo anchoring and little or no on-set interaction with others. Therefore, it is important to very carefully define your strengths and *non-strengths*, and to find which particular venues positively highlight what you do well.

Here is an example of an individual who did not know his non-strengths and/or weaknesses and thus did not understand why he had been a very successful weeknight anchor at his prior station.

After a number of years of anchoring one newscast at his top-rated, large-market station, "Bob" entered into a deal for more money to anchor two newscasts at a competing station in his market. When I asked the news director of the station that Bob was leaving if he thought Bob's departure would hurt his station, he told me that he sincerely believed that Bob wouldn't be nearly as successful "across the street." He explained that Bob was a very poor ad-libber and that his station had taken that weakness into account by very tightly scripting and carefully producing Bob's newscasts. Therefore, Bob almost never had the opportunity to expose his weakness. During Bob's debut week, I happened to be in the town where he worked, and I saw firsthand what his former news director meant. Bob's newscasts at his new station were loosely scripted and allowed him to ad-lib and chitchat away. I agreed with the former news director's assessment: Bob didn't ad-lib well. Within one year, one of Bob's weeknight newscasts was canceled because of very poor ratings. Thereafter, he was taken off weeknight anchoring altogether and reassigned to anchor on weekends. Since then, his salary has been cut twice, and he has never been as successful at his new station as he was at his old one. In this case, Bob's former station's news format amplified his strengths and minimized the impact of his weaknesses. Neither he nor his new station management understood this—to his and his new station's detriment.

In Bob's case, the astute manager who knew him was far better (for him) than the one who, in essence, didn't. This is an important insight. When talent is thinking of switching or leaving a successful situation, they must take into account *why* they are successful at their current station or program, and whether the reasons for this success can be duplicated or improved upon at a potential new station or program. (Similarly, potential new employers should do their best to understand *why* someone is successful at their current venue, and then try to duplicate that environment and improve upon it.)

Here's another example of the importance of *niche awareness*: I know a sports talent who is far, far more comfortable in the field—without a suit and tie on—than he is in the studio. If I were this talent and his management, I would make every effort to ensure that he is anchoring and reporting from the field, where he shines, rather than appearing on the studio set, where he loses his charisma and seems to lose his passion and accessibility.

Another *Reality*: Some individuals are better hosts than they are anchors. Some people have a great presence, comfort level on camera, a sharp mind, a quick wit, and an ability to compellingly engage not only the viewer, but also all of those on the set with them. As we will continue to discuss, they somehow can make the sum of the on-air chemistry more than its individual parts. In contrast to hosting, anchoring—for the most part—is a very structured and tightly scripted assignment, which often doesn't allow for one's warmth, sense of humor, wit, and on-the-spot analytical skills and interviewing abilities to come to the fore on any regular basis. For example, Matt Lauer, Katie Couric, Robin Meade, Megyn Kelly, and Jodi Applegate are *great* hosts. They have a wonderful mix of talents and warmth that naturally work on morning television—which requires a softer touch. While these individuals are also very talented anchors, arguably they are more successful as hosts because that venue allows their special qualities to shine more brightly. Years ago, Matt Lauer was interviewed by Larry King. At one point in the interview, Larry asked Matt what other kinds of shows he could picture himself doing. His response in essence was, "Larry, I think that I am on the perfect show for me. Early in my career, when asked about what I aspire to do, I always responded, 'I'd like to host the *Today* show or be Larry King.'" Matt understands what makes him special. I, too, agree that the *Today* show is the perfect, enhancing venue for him, and he is perfect for it.

Conversely, there are extraordinary on-air talents who will not be as good, likable, or effective in hosting venues as they are as anchors. An instance of this comes to mind. Years ago, someone who was a very successful news anchor was given the opportunity to become a host of a very prominent morning news show. When I asked the very insightful individual who had discovered and mentored her how he thought she would fare in her new position, he—to my surprise—(in essence) said, "I don't think she'll do well. She doesn't have the depth, soul, and life experience to pull it off. She's great at reading copy. But when she needs to dig down deep and find empathy, sympathy, and honesty, it won't be there." He was right. The host's stint was short-lived.

Of course, there are some individuals—Charlie Gibson, Diane Sawyer, Lester Holt, Maggie Rodriguez, Megyn Kelly, Martha MacCallum, Liz Claman, Brooke Baldwin, Betty Nguyen, T.J. Holmes, Jenna Lee, for example—who are excellent anchors *and* hosts, because they possess exceptional and diverse communication skills.

Here is a local-news example of what being in the enhancing niche did for someone. Years ago, a wonderfully talented and totally out-of-the-box weathercaster, then named Jillian Warry and now named Jillian Reynolds, came to Los Angeles to be the weeknight weathercaster at KTTV. Jillian, who was very attractive, sexy, facile, and charismatic, made, from my perspective, a fairly uneventful debut on FOX's 10 p.m. newscast. This was the case because she was given very little time to deliver the weather and no opportunity to show her extraordinary personality in this exceedingly straightforward, tightly scripted newscast of record.

But then one day, Mark Thompson, the very talented morning weathercaster at KTTV, asked to be reassigned to weeknights, as it fit better with his internal clock. That gave the wise news manager, Jose Rios, the golden opportunity to flip-flop Mark and Jillian. Being on the very loosey-goosey, personality-driven KTTV morning show allowed Jillian to showcase her often wild but very real and compelling personality. And she *broke through*—BIG TIME!—especially when she did her "Style File" segments. Long story short, the tremendous difference between Jillian's performance on the 10 p.m. newscast and that in the mornings was literally career-making! She went from noticeable on the evening newscast to a local megastar in the mornings. As a result of Jillian being put in the most enhancing niche *for her*, she wound up hosting national shows, doing weather spots for the FOX NFL broadcasts, and appearing on national commercials for such companies as Nutrisystem.

Some other examples of careers that have skyrocketed when very talented individuals find their enhancing niches are: Ryan Seacrest hosting *American Idol*, Kelly Ripa hosting *Regis and Kelly* (and Regis Philbin hosting the original incarnation of this show), Bill O'Reilly hosting *The O'Reilly Factor*, and of course, the mother of all moves, Oprah Winfrey becoming the host of *A.M. Chicago* and then *Oprah*.

On the subject of understanding what and how much a particular venue/format/niche contributes to a talent's or a team's success, I will always remember the extremely wise observation that one of my very astute clients made when we were discussing possible formats for a potential afternoon syndicated talk show that he might one day cohost. During our discussion, he pointed out, "Don't forget that the third star (and an important reason for my and my cohost's success) is the wonderful, talent-enhancing format of my [current] morning show."

I believe what this client implied in his observation was, "Let's just not assume that if you put some very talented female host and me on a set, we will automatically create magic. Our morning show, with its family members, guests, correspondents, concerts, outside interview area, etc., gives us the right assorted stimuli to react to and play off of, in a way that enhances all of us. It is an excellent vehicle and format for us to be relevant, be informative, and have fun. If we are to duplicate our morning show success, we must find/create a vehicle/format that works for us and our audience. We cannot minimize the importance of identifying the right vehicle/format/niche for us."

Creating Your Own Enhancing Niche

Throughout this section, we have discussed seeking out and identifying positions that will most help you to grow and shine. Here is one other thought: Once you have accepted a position, do all that you can to make it the most enhancing one possible. Here are four suggestions:

1. If you are a reporter, do your best before each show to tell the anchor who will be tossing to you and to your story some of the interesting things about your piece. This way the anchor may be able to make an informed and compelling introduction, and when appropriate, will thereafter be able to ask intelligent questions and/or engage you in an interesting dialogue. This will give you and the anchor more of a *connection* and (hopefully) chemistry. It will enhance you both.

2. As we discussed, if you are an anchor of a newscast, do your best to make everyone on the set look good and appear to be an integral part of the product. Good group chemistry can play a material role in a broadcast's success and in the enjoyment that the participants derive from their work. Always remember: If you make everyone else on the set look good, you look good, too.

3. Be enterprising and initiate worthwhile stories. Be proactive.

4. Do your best to know your audience and what it is that they expect and want from their broadcast journalists. As we will discuss, I have always believed that Oprah Winfrey, besides being a wonderful broadcast talent and an extraordinary communicator, has the rare and invaluable ability to identify what it is that her audience really wants and then to effectively and compellingly give it to them.

Regarding the highly enhancing *Choreography* of creating your own niche, one very inspiring story comes to mind. It is about a woman who was hired as a general-assignment reporter at her station. To the best of my recollection, at some point midway through her contract there, she approached station management about anchoring and reporting sports—which had become her passion. At first, station management denied her request, as they wanted to keep this woman's excellent news presence and reports on their newscasts five days a week, and they already had sportscasters to cover all of their existing newscasts. However, to her credit, the woman suggested that she *work an extra day* each week so that she could anchor sports on one of her station's new weekend morning newscasts. Her station news director agreed to let her try it.

The enhancing result was that this individual became so very good at sports anchoring and reporting (while at the same time working as a full-time news reporter) that upon the expiration of her station contract, she left to become a much-praised national sports anchor/reporter in her next job. Interestingly, she eventually left sports and thereafter became a very successful cable-news anchor. Unquestionably, through insightful and creative *Career Choreography* and hard, effective work, this person truly created her own enhancing niche.

NEW AGE STRATA-GEMS

1. When you are looking for and accepting a position, it is essential that the position that you take enhances and/or showcases you, your skills, and/or your on-air performance, or it must help you to develop certain skills and/or afford you necessary career-enhancing experiences.

2. When you are thinking about leaving a successful position, you must take into account those factors that have led to your success, and make sure that they can be duplicated or improved upon at your potential new position.

3. It is equally important for employers who are contemplating hiring a new talent to understand why that talent is successful at their current venue, and to duplicate or improve upon those factors if they hire the talent.

Lead with Your Strength

One very effective means of jump-starting a success-evoking *Choreography* and, as a result, your career, is to *Lead with Your Strength*. This strategy requires you to identify what your personal and professional strengths and expertise are, and to find a position that will use those strengths and that expertise to your and your employer's best advantage as you learn, grow, and shine.

One example of how I helped a talent lead with her strength occurred years ago when I was introduced to Lisa Dergan, a new client of our office. Upon meeting her, not only was I struck by her radiant, nonthreatening beauty, but I was taken with her honest, deep-down warmth, effervescence, and charm as well. Lisa also had the one quality that I look for above all others in an aspiring on-air talent. She was real! About a year or so later, Lisa's agent departed from our agency. At that point, Lisa's career was stagnant, so I decided to invite her to lunch to see if there was a way that we could jump-start her growth. Before doing so, I reviewed her "demo reel" (which we used to market her), and I realized that it was holding her back, because it showed her inexperience, and didn't showcase the many gifts and qualities that made her special. As a result, in the initial potential-employer tape-viewing process, she easily lost out to more experienced and polished females with whom she was competing for on-air positions.

As we dined, I listened intently to Lisa, and I developed a sense of her wonderful value system, as well as the emotionally intelligent way that she viewed life. Most importantly, I learned that Lisa was an exceptional golfer and that she also had a good working knowledge of pro football. I then asked her what would "make her heart sing" professionally. She said that her goal was to host syndicated or prime-time network shows. With that information in hand, I began to develop our *Choreography*. I told her that if her goal was to have a career like that of Nancy O'Dell, Mary Hart, or Leeza Gibbons, she had to start doing live TV as soon as possible. And "the way to accomplish this is by *Leading with Your Strength*, which, in this case, is focusing on your unique athletic background, both when we market you and when you interview." I told her that her athletic knowledge, when combined with her great look, would set her positively apart from others, and in some situations would make up for her lack of on-air experience.

With this in mind, the next step would be for me to call KCBS, the Los Angeles CBS-owned station, which had an open position on its weekend sports program, *Sports Central*. This job called for someone to conduct a series of fun and lively interviews with fans right after the NFL football games aired on KCBS. I knew that if Lisa could secure this position, it would be a great vehicle for her to develop her live television skills. It would also be a stellar showcase for her charismatic personality and charm. I would make a call to the general manager of KCBS as soon as I returned to my office. I would also call the Golf Channel to find out about any open positions that would take advantage of Lisa's golf expertise.

On the basis of my enthusiastic recommendation, the KCBS general manager agreed to meet with Lisa the next day. After their meeting, the GM called to offer Lisa the Sunday "Fan-Cam" position.

We were on our way!

I then explained to Lisa that our *Big Picture Choreography* was not to develop her as a sportscaster. It was to use her sports knowledge to gain on-air experience, and then little by little, to develop a much more polished and effective demo reel, which would enable her to transition into hosting.

Our *Choreography* worked. After doing ten weekends of Fan-Cam interviews, Lisa received a call from Steve Tello, an executive at the FOX Sports Network. Steve's plan was to bring Lisa to FOX, and to groom and develop her as a sportscaster. As she needed a great deal more training and on-air experience, the FOX offer was a golden opportunity for her to be able to grow and improve. So the next steps were for her to accept the offer and to make the most of the FOX situation. Which she did.

Steve and the individuals at FOX were true to their word—they worked hard to train Lisa and give her opportunities to shine. And Lisa, much to her credit, worked tirelessly and effectively to learn as much as she could. FOX's leap of faith paid great dividends, as Lisa became a very effective anchor/host in relatively short order.

After Lisa had spent a year or so at FOX, we moved to the next Step, which was for me to start sending out her new and dramatically improved demo reel to program producers. I did so with great anticipation. Within weeks, Lisa was hosting a network national prime-time show. Thereafter, she hosted a second one.

The *Choreography* strategy of *Leading with Your Strength* helped Lisa begin to fulfill her career goals and dreams in the national sports and hosting arenas.

In *The New Age*, there are abundant on-air opportunities for individuals who have an expertise—or a unique background or set of experiences—to use these strengths to secure on-air appearances, as well as to jump-start and/or further their careers. Here are some illustrations of this strategy or practice:

1. You are a chef or cooking expert, and you use your expertise to secure on-air opportunities on various cooking-related shows, or on morning or noon newscasts, where you give cooking or food advice.

2. You have a strong financial background and you use your expertise to give on-air financial advice on one of the cable business channels, such as CNBC, the FOX Business Network, or Bloomberg.

3. You are a doctor and you use your expertise to give on-air medical information or perspectives, and if you are positively impactful, you then become a host of a medical show or a major contributor to a national show.

4. The same *Choreography* certainly applies to attorneys, as well as to experts in fields like politics, fashion, pop culture, psychology, and so on.

Some other interesting advantages of beginning your career as an expert are these:

1. You do not have to start in a small market and work your way up through the conventional, vertical, market-to-market route.

2. Often, because you are an expert, at least at the beginning of your on-air journey, less on-air polish is expected of you since your profession and training are not those of a broadcast journalist. However, comfortable and charismatic experts who break through the clutter and *connect* with the viewer can have a tremendous career *runway* and one day transcend their expertise. We will discuss this strategy in the next chapter.

NEW AGE STRATA-GEMS

1. A very effective means to jump-start a success-evoking *Choreography* and your career is to *Lead with Your Strength*. This requires you to identify what your strengths and expertise are and to find a position that will make great use of them to your and your employer's best advantage.
2. One means by which you can begin an on-air career is by using an expertise that you possess (law, medicine, cooking, science, etc.) to secure invaluable on-air appearances and experience.

Transcendence

A natural evolution of the concept of *Leading with Your Strength* is the concept of *Transcendence*, which for us means going beyond your expertise, power base, or niche. A perfect example of *Transcendence* is what Rachael Ray has accomplished. Rachael began as a food expert and then used her expertise to secure various on-air opportunities, which led to hosting her own cooking show and appearances on *Oprah*. Rachael's on-air talents and successes eventually led various high-ranking executives at CBS Television Distribution to put her in a role that transcended just food—hosting her own talk show. And from this show, Rachael has been able to grow her brand and her empire, by founding a magazine, a cookware line, and so on. Essentially, she transcended her original strength and power base to build a diverse empire.

In many instances, this transcendent growth can be anticipated, visualized, and *Choreographed*. For example, among the individuals who have used their expertise to expand their base are Megyn Kelly, who began as a legal reporter at a local station in Washington, D.C., and then at the Fox News Channel, and is now a star weekday news anchor/host; Martha MacCallum and Jenna Lee, who used their financial/business expertise to work for CNBC and the Fox Business Network, respectively, before blossoming into excellent weekday news anchor/hosts; and Savannah Guthrie, who is using her legal background and reporting to become a major current and future player on the *Today* show.

On the other hand, the most unexpected *Transcendence* can also occur. This was the case when our agency put our client Greg Kinnear in E! Entertainment Network's soon-to-be hit show *Talk Soup*. This move materially enhanced Greg's career, because it showcased his wit, edge, humor, and hugely likable and engaging personality. Thereafter, Greg hosted NBC's late-night show, *Later*. While on that show, director Sydney Pollack contacted Greg, in order to learn whether he would be interested in transitioning into acting. At the time, Mr. Pollack was looking for someone to play the role of the younger brother of Harrison Ford in Pollack's remake of *Sabrina*. Greg was only too happy to take this role and successfully transcend hosting by acting in, and then starring in, major films.

At the writing of this book, I have the honor and pleasure to be working with Dr. Sanjay Gupta of CNN. Obviously, since Sanjay is CNN's Chief Medical Correspondent, his power base is his medical expertise. However, I sought out the opportunity to represent Sanjay because every instinct that I have told me that Sanjay has the intellect, warmth and depth of soul, and "it" factor to host a network morning show or a nationally syndicated show. I believe that many individuals in the highest places share my vision of Sanjay transcending the areas of medicine and wellness, and moving into the role of a major host.

NEW AGE STRATA-GEM

A natural progression of the strategy of *Leading with Your Strength*, is the concept of *Transcendence*, which for us means going beyond your expertise, power base, or niche to a bigger, broader platform and in all likelihood a longer career runway.

Some Key *New Age* News Employers: What They Are Looking for and What Makes Them Special/Different

What are *New Age* employers looking for? On the one hand, this is a somewhat tricky question to answer, because as what broadcasting executives*, consultants, research, ratings, and successful competitors do changes, what a particular news employer looks for from its on-air talent can also change. On the other hand, there are certain constants that almost all employers want and seek out.

Let's start with the constants. Here is what I perceive and have been told by the highest news and programming executives to be *Broadcasting Realities*, regarding what they want and need from talent in *The New Age*:

1. *Employers need to get more with less and fewer.* What this means is that employers want to spend less money and do everything with fewer staff members. Therefore, they want to hire and employ only "A players," who will bring their best efforts and talents to their jobs every day. They want employees who will initiate stories, develop sources, secure valuable and/or hard-to-come-by interviews, etc. They also want employees who will be happy—or at least willing—to work harder and smarter, and take on more job real estate.

2. They want employees who will blog, Tweet, and market/publicize their stories, newscast(s), and/or show(s) on the Internet, as well as in any

---

* As this book is being completed, CBS News has a new chairman, Jeff Fager, and a new president, David Rhodes; ABC News has a new president, Ben Sherwood; CNN has a new president, Ken Jautz; and NBC News is now owned by Comcast.

and all other appropriate ancillary media. In many markets, they want their on-air staff to write, edit, produce, and shoot as well. We will discuss this in depth in the area devoted to *Multimedia Journalism*.

3. Employers want talent who have on-air traction, engage the viewer, are compelling and impactful, and who break through the clutter. They want on-air individuals who have "it."

Obviously, there are many different ways to have on-air traction or to be compelling. In Matt Lauer's case, it is his intellect, warmth, accessibility, likability, credibility, quick wit, compassion, and emotional intelligence. For prime-time cable ratings magnets such as Bill O'Reilly, it is their edge, intelligence, wit, credibility, opinions, and huge personality. Oprah Winfrey, through her unique on-air gifts and background, as well as her intuitive brilliance (which we will discuss later), has achieved unprecedented viewer acceptance and loyalty. All of these individuals have their own ways of achieving viewer traction and garnering high viewership. The point to remember here is that different individuals have different styles and talents that engage and resonate with viewers.

Similarly, different venues require different kinds of performances from talent. For the most part, especially in cable news and programming, gone are the days of the plastically perfect, sweet female anchor/host. Or the plastic/mechanical deliveries of the Ted Baxter–type male anchors of the '70s and '80s (and, in some instances, the '90s). Perfect and plastic are no longer in, sought after, or effective. The success of certain local stations, such as WSVN, edgy magazine shows, and the FOX News Channel has led to varying degrees of ramped-up energy levels, as well as a visual and visceral connection that viewers now want and expect. The qualities of being real/authentic, conversational, edgy, quirky, unique, and comfortable in your own skin are what most cable viewers and employers seek out. The key questions for talent are which of these qualities are most appropriate and success-evoking for a particular venue and to what degree they are appropriate. We will discuss these concepts below. A key point to remember is that what employers want and need is for their on-air talent to establish and maintain a positive and lasting connection with the viewer. This all-important connection, in time, should lead to increased and sustained high viewership, which should translate to higher advertising revenues and profits for the employer.

Some Thoughts Regarding What Many News Employers in *The New Age* Are Looking For

It is almost always essential to know what specific broadcasting employers want from their on-air talent. This is true both when the talent is applying for a position with a particular employer and when the talent is already working for an employer and wants to keep his or her job and continue to grow and flourish with that employer. Therefore, talent must do their focused homework in order to learn or confirm what a particular network or station of interest's vision is regarding its news product and talent.

Once again, it is important to keep in mind that just as every individual has a unique on-air style and feel, *every broadcast network, cable network, local station, and program tries to distinguish itself by its brand, content, talent, feel, and tone.*

As a means of illustrating how various employers differ in connection with their on-air vision, tone, feel, and talent performance style, here are some thoughts, observations, and perspectives regarding what some very prominent and top-tier cable news employers, at the time that this book is being completed, want in connection with their talents' on-air performance.

Cable News

Generally, cable on-air talent—especially those who host prime-time shows—need to have *Big* personalities (or bigger than those of conventional network news talent). For example, there is little similarity between the performance styles of Charlie Gibson, Diane Sawyer, Brian Williams, and Scott Pelley and those of Bill O'Reilly, Keith Olbermann, Glenn Beck, Shepard Smith, and Nancy Grace. Yet all of these individuals have ascended to great heights and hold or have held very prominent positions anchoring or hosting evening news programs. The key is to understand that to varying degrees, cable newscasts generally are higher-energy, more conversational, more loosely scripted, and edgier than their network counterparts. And depending upon the particular part of the day and the specific cable news network's philosophy, cable news can also be (highly) opinionated.

Neither style is "better" or "worse" than the other. The broadcast and cable venues are just different, so there are very different performance expectations. The *Reality* here is that generally—with CNN being the exception—cable newscasts, especially those in early evening and prime time, have a far different feel, tone, and sensibility than do the NBC, ABC, and CBS network newscasts. Therefore, talent must recognize these material differences, and their performance must fit the particular employer's style, sensibility, and feel.

I view CNN as an exception to the general edgy/high-energy/often opinionated cable news performance norms, since I perceive that for the most part, CNN talent are far closer in performance feel and tone to those on the broadcast networks ABC, NBC, and CBS, than to those on FOX and HLN. For example, look at the stark difference in performance tone, style, and sensibility between past and present CNN anchors Anderson Cooper, Wolf Blitzer, Campbell Brown, Paula Zahn, and John Roberts; and those of the FOX News Channel, Shepard Smith, Bill O'Reilly, and Glenn Beck; or HLN's Nancy Grace or Jane Velez-Mitchell. Additionally, compare the feel, tone, and content of CNN's *American Morning* with that of *FOX & Friends*. They are often worlds apart.

Because cable news is so loosely scripted, free-flowing, and conversational, radio hosting experience has given many individuals the foundation to become great cable news hosts. Larry King, Rachel Maddow, Glenn Beck, Dr. Drew Pinsky, and Brian Kilmeade are just a few radio personalities who have successfully taken their talents to cable news.

What I have gleaned through observation and my conversations with cable news executives is that what cable networks such as MSNBC and HLN would like to do is find compelling, break-through-the-clutter on-air talent around whom they can build shows. A prime example of this *Reality* is HLN building a four-hour weekday morning show around the very appealing, accessible, and oh-co-comfortable-in-her-own-skin Robin Meade. *Morning Express with Robin Meade* is a ratings and demographic winner. During this show, Robin, along with her cast of engaging and credible on-air teammates, talk to and with the viewers, reach and connect with them on many levels, and thereby compel them to gladly return to watch *Morning Express* each day. The same can be said for Megyn Kelly and her FOX News Channel show, *America Live with Megyn Kelly*; MSNBC's signature morning show, *Morning Joe*; and Brooke Baldwin's two-hour weekday *CNN Newsroom* show.

Essentially, the goal of these network executives is to create highly coveted *appointment viewing* and a differentiated, appealing brand. The huge advantage of successfully creating appointment viewing is that even on a slow news day or during a slow news period, people tune in to watch their favorite hosts/shows. Appointment viewing leads to invaluable viewer traction and loyalty, which is broadcaster gold. So if you as an on-air talent want to be successful in cable news, in many instances you will work to be perceived by cable executives as someone whom they want and need to build a show around. And these executives will, in all likelihood, see you in this light only if you are real, smart, likable, comfortable in your own skin, an "original," and "own" your copy and your on-air performance. Mere newsreaders won't cut it! So be *real,* likable, and smart on air!

Your Cable News Network Review

What the above generalization of on-air personas and feels is meant to show is that different cable news networks have different talent feels and performance expectations. As a result, if you plan to work for a particular cable news network or already work for one, it is essential for you to understand the network's vision of what it wants from its talent so that you can effectively execute that vision. So let's review some very important cable news *Realities* in *The New Age of Broadcasting*:

1. In many instances, cable network newscasts and news programs have a very different feel, tone, content, and energy level than those of network news.

2. In cable news, talents often have higher energy and more edge, voice their opinions, etc. These *Realities* vary depending upon the cable network, the talent, and the part of the day in which the talent appears.

3. In most cases, it is necessary to have a big, or at least a more emotive on-air personality to be successful in cable news.

4. Being a "character" in cable news can be a huge asset.

5. A wonderful training ground for many cable stars is radio.

6. Be real, smart, comfortable in your own skin, and unique on air; this way you have the very best opportunity to be successful in cable news and possibly have a show built around you.

Network News

In network news, you need to be credible, impactful, and, in many instances, likable. And, as we discussed earlier, your performance, while compelling and engaging, needs to be dialed down, less edgy, and more scripted than what is required in cable news—especially prime-time cable news. Additionally, in almost all instances, your delivery of the news must be objective—not opinionated. In most cases, network news requires anchors to report far more often than many cable anchors/hosts do. Of course, some cable news anchors do go out into the field and file reports; Anderson Cooper, Shepard Smith, and Brooke Baldwin are three who come to mind. But by and large, the level of a network anchor's live and packaged-piece reporting skills can count far more in the network-news interviewing process and in connection with a talent's day-to-day job success.

In many ways, NBC News has a tremendous advantage in the area of talent development, because it has MSNBC and, to a lesser extent, CNBC and the Weather Channel. For example, such NBC news stars as Brian Williams, Lester Holt, and Natalie Morales received valuable grooming at MS. CNBC stars such as Carl Quintanilla and Maria Bartiromo also continue to receive valuable cross-exposure on *Today* and *Weekend Today*. What this means is:

1. Comcast/NBC News has a number of outlets on which to groom and grow talent.

2. Comcast/NBC News has a long and diverse *runway* for talent to grow and secure valuable, diverse on-air experiences and visibility.

3. Comcast/NBC News very effectively cross-pollinates the talent from its local stations, MSNBC, CNBC, the Weather Channel, and their other owned properties.

For the past fifteen years or so, I have felt that NBC News has focused on and has been highly successful at hiring on-air talent with "star" quality. Recently I have noticed a strong push to hire more on-air individuals of color at NBC. All in all, NBC News is talent-rich and ratings-strong.

Since the days of Roone Arledge, ABC News has always had megastar news talents, such as Barbara Walters, Peter Jennings, Diane Sawyer, Charlie Gibson, and Ted Koppel, as well as excellent correspondents. However, the era of the aforementioned superstars is rapidly giving way to finding/anointing the next generation of ABC News stars. Over the next few years, ABC News should have a number of major opportunities for talent hires and talent growth. It also appears that ABC News is on its way to staffing *Good Morning America* (*GMA*) with some excellent new hires. From early returns, Josh Elliott, the new *GMA* newsreader, has already enhanced *GMA*'s on-air chemistry. I expect that *GMA*'s hiring of Lara Spencer will be very positive as well.

With new executives running CBS News, there is an exciting new playing field there for CBS News talents and those who aspire to join CBS News. From what I can glean from both the few moves that the new CBS News executives have made so far and their backgrounds, top-tier reporting and excellent storytelling will be on full display on all CBS News broadcasts—as it has been with great consistency on CBS News' stellar newsmagazine show, *60 Minutes*.

For years, I have wondered why CBS executives haven't tried to counterprogram against the traditional morning shows with a different kind of early morning format, such as HLN did with *Morning Express with Robin Meade*. In other words, breaking the mold and creating their own morning niche/show and appointment viewing, rather than reproducing the same old show with different hosts. That time may well be here! From my perspective, there are indications that a new form of CBS morning show may well be in the mind's eye of the new CBS News executives.

If you are a student of network news, this is an incredible time for you. With Comcast acquiring NBC News, with a new chairman of CBS News, and with new presidents of ABC and CBS News, it certainly will be interesting to see what impact these management changes will have on the various news divisions and their newscasts. It should make for a fantastic watch and study!

Local Stations

This is a very exciting time for local stations as well! It appears that advertisers and ad revenues are returning to local stations and that there is renewed enthusiasm regarding the health and future of local news.

Under the stellar leadership of ABC executives, the ABC-owned stations have for years been the most successful and stable station group. I fully expect that their great success and their brilliant strategy of maintaining stability of management and talent will continue.

The result of combining exceedingly strong CBS prime-time programming with excellent CBS-owned and -operated management, is that for the first time in decades, the CBS O&O newscasts are enjoying significant ratings success (especially the late-evening weekday newscasts). There is now management and talent stability, along with a new, positive CBS O&O news pride* and energy. All of this is great to see.

It is also an extremely exciting time for NBC-owned stations. Along with Comcast's acquisition of them has come a Comcast commitment to reinvest in and thereby revitalize its station group. From all indications, this sincere commitment to its stations is in full swing. This is a very positive *Reality* for everyone in broadcasting.

As I will discuss throughout this book, if talent can find personality-driven vehicles in which to showcase their range, gifts, personality, and wit, they will reap huge career dividends. The personality-driven morning shows at many of the FOX- and Tribune-owned stations are just such vehicles. If you aspire to host a national show one day, or you just want to have (more) fun on air, these morning shows can well be career-makers and true joys to host and report for.

When it comes to talent trying to identify a particular anchoring, hosting, or reporting style that a local station (a potential employer) embraces, your best bet, if you cannot see a newscast live, is to watch online, record it, or have someone record it, in order for you to see and emulate the styles of the main players. For example, when my client Dayna Devon was anchoring in Memphis and was about to be auditioned by *EXTRA* for its weekend anchor position, she taped ten shows of Maureen O'Boyle anchoring its weekday shows.

since Maureen embodied and reflected the hosting style, cadence, and script interpretation that *EXTRA*'s executive producer envisioned and wanted, after reviewing the ten shows, Dayna had a great feel as to how to deliver her audition copy (while integrating the gifts that made her unique). Dayna's audition was a home run, and she secured her *Gold Ring Dream* job of being a host of *EXTRA*. Unquestionably, Dayna accomplished this partly because she effectively studied the performance style that her prospective employer wanted.

The key here is that stations, newscasts, and programs often embody performance styles that

    a. have worked for them in the past;

    b. reflect a key executive's vision;

    c. reflect some new research; and

    d. reflect what a successful competitor is doing.

It is therefore crucial for any talent pursuing a position with any local news employer to make sure that he or she is intimately acquainted with that particular station's style, feel, and production values *before* interviewing or auditioning with the prospective employer. This is an essential step in the process, because local stations, in different local markets, can be completely different in style and feel when compared to their sister stations in other markets. Therefore, a talent, producer, or an executive aspiring to be hired by that station should be careful not to make general assumptions about a station's style, tone, or content. Effectively doing your research in this instance is necessary.

NEW AGE STRATA-GEM

Every broadcast network, cable network, local station, and show has a unique feel, sensibility, and brand. Whether you are applying for a position or are already working at one of these venues, be sure that you understand what makes the particular newscasts or programs at issue different, as well as what the executives there expect and need from their talent.

Making the Sum of Newscasts and Programs Even More Compelling Than Their Parts: A Call to All *New Age* Anchors and Hosts

Years ago, when I was a business-affairs attorney for the William Morris Agency, I met Ernie Anastos at a Long Island pro-celebrity tennis tournament. At the time Ernie had recently joined WABC-TV in New York City as an anchor, having left WPRI in Providence, Rhode Island, where he had enjoyed great success.

Prior to the tournament, I had seen Ernie on TV a number of times. As a lay viewer, I was incredibly impressed with how he, as an anchor, brought everyone together on the set in an extraordinarily enhancing way. He was like a great basketball point guard in that he made everyone else on the set (or court) shine their brightest. He seemed to know just enough about each reporter's story to intelligently and respectfully set up the report and debrief the reporter. Ernie knew exactly what to say to his on-set team members regarding weather, sports, and even traffic so as to bring out the best in them and make their material (even more) compelling. He had also developed the warmest and most respectful chemistry with his co-anchors. Additionally, Ernie was (and is) an incredibly gracious, warm, and giving person who established a rock-solid rapport and connection with the viewers. As a direct result, watching the newscasts that Ernie anchored was not only a very enjoyable informational experience, it was a chemical and visceral one as well.

Here is what I mean by "chemical and visceral." Many of us have watched programs such as *Seinfeld*, *Friends*, *Law & Order*, and *NCIS*. In these shows, we not only enjoyed the material being presented, but we also *felt* the chemistry between the cast members. And this chemistry made the experience incrementally and possibly exponentially more enjoyable. So viewers would return for the material and the chemistry each week. I viscerally felt that Ernie did this for every one of his newscasts.

At the tennis tournament, I approached Ernie and shared with him my thoughts about his work. I also explained that although his job was to anchor, he had a *host sensibility*, in that his warmth, sense of humor, conversational style, and humaneness radiated through the TV set, unlike that of most anchors, who just read to me in an unfeeling, antiseptic, *me-centric* manner.

Two days later, Ernie called me at William Morris and said that he would like me to represent him. I told him that I was incredibly flattered, but that I was a business-affairs attorney and couldn't directly do so. However, I would introduce him to my mentor, Lee Stevens, who ran the New York William Morris office, and to Jim Griffin, who ran the news department. A day or two later, Ernie became our client, and I was soon jettisoned from business affairs to work under Jim in the News Department. That was more than 29 years ago; Ernie and I are still agent/client, and we will remain lifelong close friends.

Because of Ernie's faith in me, I not only owe him my start and career in news representation, but I also thank him for at least one other gift: Ernie showed me how being emotionally intelligent, gracious, giving, and respectful on set makes the parts of a newscast or program a much more compelling, cohesive, and successful *collaboration*. Because Ernie, in our conversations, explained in detail about his big picture perspective and goal of enabling everybody on the set to look their best, I was able to identify this great quality in a few select others as I grew as an agent. It is unquestionably why I called Matt Lauer about representation when he was at WWOR in New York City. I recognized the same big picture, on-set emotional intelligence and grace in Matt. Anyone who watches *Today* understands what I saw in Matt—and I would argue that one of the biggest assets that positively separates *Today* from its competitors is its wonderful on-set chemistry. *Today* just *feels* more fun and cooler than the other morning shows.

Sometime thereafter, a Boston-based client and friend told me about a very talented individual named Tom Bergeron, who was hosting *Evening Magazine* and a radio show in Boston. Upon seeing Tom's work, I knew that Tom had the same kind of big picture, collaborative gifts. Anyone who has watched Tom through his FOX *Breakfast Time*, game-show, and competition-show incarnations knows what a respectful and skillful host he is. My point in all of this is that in *The New Age*, when competition for viewers is at an all-time fever pitch, broadcasters can effectively make the case that differentiated content will bring viewers into the tent. They can say that the right format can make all the difference and that compelling on-air individuals can have a very positive impact on ratings. However, if broadcasters can have all, or many, of these assets, along with *great on-air talent chemistry*, they have a tremendous chance to be a ratings winner, year after year—and remain relevant and profitable.

As a talent, always remember: If everyone else on-set looks great, you look (and may well be perceived as) great too! At a time when broadcasters desperately need "A players" on their air, by having the big picture mind-set of graciously enabling everyone else on-set to look and perform at their best, you may become the superstar talent that your employer needs and that you aspire to be. It has certainly worked well for Ernie, Matt, and Tom.

NEW AGE STRATA-GEMS

1. One of the most career-enhancing skills an anchor or host can have is the ability to make the sum of their newscasts or show bigger than the parts. This calls for the anchor or host to make sure that everyone on the set performs at their best.
2. Always remember: If everyone on your show looks great, you exponentially increase the likelihood that you will look great as well!

Tone, Pitch, Connection, and Understanding: *Performance* and *Communication Intelligence*™

R ecently I had a conversation with Lester Holt, and we discussed how a particular individual has a wonderful interpersonal connection with others. During our discussion, Lester said that the individual whom we had been talking about has "perfect pitch and tone." (Just like Lester!) Because these words and concepts are so meaningful, let's examine them.

Some on-air individuals are so natural and comfortable in their own skin, as well as *performance-intelligent*™, that they connect and resonate with almost everyone. Oprah Winfrey is one such individual. Matt Lauer and Lester Holt are two others. Regardless of one's political views, I would also argue that Presidents Clinton and Obama, *as communicators*, draw people to them in a very positive way. All of these individuals have a tremendous sense of pitch, tone, and understanding of the art of communication, or, to put it more succinctly, great *performance intelligence*™.

For example, as an interviewer, you need to know when to have soft hands and a gentle touch, when to ask hard questions, and then when to let up. There is a line between being a strong, focused, and even ferocious interviewer and being offensive and overbearing. Some individuals get it. Some do not.

Additionally, timing—that is, when to ask a particular question—is an art. For example, I will always remember the terrible response that accomplished sports reporter Jim Gray received when he asked Pete Rose about Rose's alleged gambling before an audience of millions at an All-Star game.

This was a disaster for Jim, because it was the wrong time and place to ask such a highly sensitive, negatively charged question—a question that would have been perfectly acceptable, and even required, at another time, in another forum.

It is also important for individuals to correctly read and understand their viewership. I would argue that Oprah is the master of this. When she began to host a national talk show, Oprah covered and discussed many of the same topics that other talk-show hosts did. But her take on these subjects and her tone were neither tabloid-like nor sensational. She adopted a more positive, high-road, and uplifting approach, which appealed to her audience. As I recollect, Oprah also spent a great deal of time focusing on relationships, on reading worthwhile books (and her book club), and on products that she liked—much more than the other shows and hosts did. And because Oprah and those who ran her show had a better feel and excellent insight for what to include in her show, along with the tone and pitch with which to do it, she and her show connected and resonated with viewers in an unprecedented positive way.

As someone who is an avid student of on-air performance, I believe that Oprah has been truly brilliant at understanding the needs and wants of her viewers, as well as what the content and tone of her show should be. She also possesses or has developed a communication demeanor and delivery that have engaged and kept her viewers coming back for more, year after year.

On the subject of tone, pitch, and *performance intelligence*™, I would like to discuss two interviews that Matt Lauer conducted, which I will always remember. They are the memorable and much-discussed Tom Cruise *Today* show interview and a *Today* show interview with a well-known author.

During the interview with Cruise, I recollect that at one point Cruise told Matt that he was being "glib" and appeared to try to goad Matt into going down with him to an uncomfortable and unprofessional on-air place. Throughout the interview, however, Matt kept his cool, kept his soft hands—yet firm approach—and guided the interview to the softest landing possible. With the passing of time, I have identified four memorable things about that interview:

1. Cruise handled himself poorly and, as a result, materially tarnished his public persona.

2. Through Matt's even-tempered approach, he did his best not to escalate a potentially image-tarnishing situation for himself. Essentially, he kept the interview focused on Cruise and his beliefs, and not on himself.

3. Matt handled things well enough that he was able to have Cruise come back on *Today* at a later time, so that Cruise could attempt to repair his tarnished image while promoting his latest film, *Valkyrie*.

4. When you are interviewing, there is no safety net, so you must be able to keep your inner calm, razor-sharp intellect, and *performance intelligence*™ in great working order.

Regarding the author interview, my recollection is that the author was extremely unhappy and irked that her *Today* interview, about her new book, had been pushed back from the preceding day. Allegedly this delay was necessary because *Today* had to allocate appropriate time to cover a major news story that broke the day before. When Matt interviewed the author, it appeared that she came on with more than a highly contentious attitude. Throughout the interview, she verbally attacked the production executives of *Today*, implying that they didn't want individuals with her particular beliefs to appear on *Today*. As I remember, Matt continued to take the high, gracious road, explaining that there was a clear reason for the delay of the author's interview and reiterating that she was always welcome on the show. Watching the author for those few minutes was like watching and listening to someone run their tremendously strong nails down the world's longest chalkboard. She and her highly antagonistic approach irritated me beyond articulation.

As the author continued to voice her displeasure with *Today*, Matt took firm control of the interview, essentially saying to her, "You're here now; let's talk about your new book." Thereafter, thank goodness, the interview moved to its conclusion.

Once again, Matt showed his incredible on-air emotional and *performance intelligence*™. He didn't let the author tweak him or let his emotions cloud his brilliant on-air judgment. Instead, he let the author's barbs roll off him, like water off a duck's back, until he was ready to firmly rein in the author and bring the interview back on track. Once again, Matt wouldn't let himself *be* the news. The news was about what was in the author's new book.

When I first closely watched Matt, he was hosting a morning show on WWOR-TV, titled *9 Broadcast Plaza*. On that one day, I recognized that he had a great on-air comfort and feel, he was a respectful listener and host, and he had an extraordinary rapport and connection with those individuals on set, as well as with the viewers. What I didn't know until I worked with him is how stone-cold smart and *performance intelligent*™ he is. Matt is blessed to have perfect on-air pitch and tone. I do not know whether he has these skills through great instincts, learned them through experience, or possesses them through a combination of these means. But he, like Oprah, thoroughly and *organically* understands and intuits who he is, what his role is, what his persona is, and where he wants and needs to go with every on-air move.

I feel that a few other key talents, such as Lester Holt, are blessed with the same gifts. As is the case with Oprah and Matt, Lester conducts himself, and delivers and reports the news, in a way that encourages viewers to highly respect, like, and trust him.

All talent can learn a very important lesson from Oprah and Matt:

1. Know your audience and what they want and expect.

2. Clearly understand what your role is. (For example, ask yourself, Am I the story? Or, am I someone who facilitates the articulation and flow of information?)

3. Know who you are, your objectives, your specific gifts and skill sets, the persona you want to portray, and be true to yourself—even during the most trying of circumstances.

4. Do not let others' on-air agendas or bad behavior cause or incite you to act inappropriately.

5. As important as intellect is, emotional intelligence can in many instances be just as important, or more so. This means that you must maintain your most appropriate on-air pitch and tone through the effective use of your emotional and *performance intelligence*™.

NEW AGE STRATA-GEMS

1. It is an invaluable asset for a talent to understand and master the appropriate tone, feel, and pitch of the particular moment, story, interview, or conversation.
2. It is also important to have a keen sense of timing and appropriateness when deciding how to conduct yourself on-air.
3. An essential component of this skill set is a clear understanding of who your audience is and what their expectations are.
4. As an on-air information facilitator, not only do you need to find your voice, but you also need to know what you want your voice to be.

Why Take a Particular Job?

There are many compelling professional reasons to take a particular position. Let's review some of them:

1. The position is your *Gold Ring Dream* position, and it will make your heart sing!

2. The job will showcase a particular set of your gifts and strengths. For example, if you have a wonderful on-air personality, a loosely scripted morning show may be perfect for you. A lighter early-afternoon show might also be enhancing.

   Conversely, if you are a hard-nosed investigative reporter, a position with a news organization that has a committed investigative unit and a long history of breaking investigative stories would seem to be ideal. Additionally, in *The New Age*, it is important for you as a potential staff member to research and consider the financial health of the company that owns the station for which you intend to go to work. For example, if you are going to a station specifically to be a member of its investigative unit, be aware that in *The New Age,* this unit may one day be discontinued because it is perceived as a luxury that is no longer affordable.

3. The position will:

   a. develop or polish a particular skill of yours or set of skills;

   b. prepare you for more and better career-enhancing opportunities; and/or

c. put you in contact with accomplished organizations and individuals that can teach you, enrich you, enable you to grow, and give you valuable experiences from which to grow. Such experiences might include covering certain kinds of stories and being assigned to particular highly interesting, provocative, and/or famous individuals, such as a political candidate, or a "beat" (a specialty such as finance, health, investigative, or entertainment.)

4. The position resonates and is consistent with who you are. Essentially, in this instance, you, your potential employer, and the position "feel especially right" to you.

5. The position or the organization for which you will work has a long runway on which to develop your career.

Years ago, one of my clients met with a very wise and successful NBC news executive when she was interviewing for a position there. During their talk, I am told that the executive explained to my client that one of the very attractive things about her accepting a job with NBC News was that NBC would provide her with a long and exciting runway. The idea that I believe the executive was communicating was that NBC News, unlike other news organizations, offered many diverse platforms from which to grow: MSNBC, network news, the various NBC-Universal-owned cable networks (such as USA, Bravo, Syfy), NBC Productions (which produces *Access Hollywood*), Peacock Productions, and others.

This particular client did join NBC News, and within two short years, she had anchored and hosted a myriad of shows for MSNBC; hosted and anchored *Weekend Today*; reported for *Today* and *Weekend Today*; reported and hosted some segments for *Dateline*; and hosted various cable shows. Her growth has been varied and great, and so has the growth of Lester Holt, Brian Williams, and Natalie Morales, all of whom began their NBC News careers at MSNBC.

As an astute *Choreographer* of your career, it is essential that you understand what relationships a particular employer has, and how you might take advantage of them. You thereby can envision and *Choreograph* the potential growth runway that a particular employer can provide for you and decide whether accepting a particular position with that employer is the very best growth option for where you presently are—or want to someday be—in your career.

NEW AGE STRATA-GEM

There are many compelling reasons to take or be in a particular position. The key is to know or to correctly intuit, at the time when you are making your decision, what reasons are the most important to you in the short term and in the long term.

Understanding What Different Positions Do and Do Not Offer

Weekend Versus Weekday Anchoring

We have all heard the term "weekend warrior," which refers to someone who gives a sport their all on the weekends only. Not only can this be dangerous for one's physical health, but such a schedule also makes it hard to maintain one's skill level, and even harder to improve it. For instance, I have always found that when I play Extreme Tennis or tennis on Saturday after a five-day layoff, I am often stiff and do not play as well as I play on Sunday. The reason is that by Sunday, I have one day of play under my belt, and I have found my rhythm. If I play on Monday, after two days of practice, I almost always play better than I do on Sunday. If I play five days a week, I have my best chance to reach my potential.

The same applies to on-air skills. I cannot count the number of weekend anchors who have complained that they feel out of sync when anchoring on Saturdays after not having anchored for five days. By Sunday evening, they begin to find their groove, only to once again not anchor for five days thereafter.

The point is this: If you want to grow to be the best anchor possible, anchoring five days a week will generally be more beneficial than anchoring only two days a week. This repetition will allow you not only to maintain your anchoring skills but also to enhance them. But please remember: The optimal five-days-a-week anchor position should not in any way diminish your reporting growth. Just report before or after you anchor. Preferably you can report after you anchor; as a result, you can be fresh for your anchoring and thereafter focus effectively on your reporting.

Obviously if you are a fill-in anchor or host, it is even harder to develop your skills and style and thereby grow to be a great anchor or host. To emphasize this point, let me share my experience of representing a young, enormously talented client of mine.

When I secured "Kevin's" representation, he was a general-assignment reporter and fill-in anchor. Knowing that a major anchoring or news hosting position was squarely in his future, I realized that it was imperative for Kevin, in his next move, to develop his anchoring skills, style, and groove—along with his reportorial skills. The concept here was this: I so respect Roger Federer, the already legendary tennis champion, because he has a great all-around game, and, as a direct result of this, he has won on any and all court surfaces. With this thought in mind, I explained to all of Kevin's prospective employers that I want Kevin, like Federer, to be an all-round talent: a great anchor/host *and* a great reporter. Therefore, we *had* to have regular anchoring, along with regular reporting, as part of any offer for Kevin that we would seriously consider.

Fortunately for us, the perfect prospective employer so appreciated Kevin and his gifts that, as I understand it, the management at his station and the network executives created a new weekend morning co-anchor position to offer to Kevin, which he gladly accepted. A true win/win for everyone. Now Kevin can grow concurrently as an anchor and as a reporter at a wonderful station in one of the very finest news markets in the country.

The Morning-Anchor Shift

Make sure that you work out your reporting schedule ahead of time. Most producer and assignment desk employees come into newsrooms around 9 a.m. They often do not realize that the morning anchor has been in since 3 or 4 a.m., and as assignment desks look for "the first warm body" that they can send out on a story, they may collar you. (By the by, in *The New Age*, the body may no longer need to be warm—or alive!) As a result, you may not be done with your story (or stories) until 4 or 5 p.m. or later each day.

One way to work this out is to have an agreement with your management that you will have two or three reporting days each week and be given two days when you leave right after anchoring your newscasts.* You can also try to make Friday a short day, so that you can have a reasonable amount of turnaround time on the weekend.

Long-Form Reporting and Finding a Venue That Gives You More Opportunities to Hit the (Reporting) Home Runs

If you aspire to be a network correspondent one day, then along with perfecting your live shots, you must develop your skills in writing, crafting, and packaging compelling long-form pieces. In order to do this, you can suggest sweeps pieces, and you should initiate your own stories. Sweeps pieces may well be reports that will afford you the time and the resources to show your employer your very best work. They can also produce some very compelling demo-DVD material with which to market yourself. Be aware, however, that if you can secure a sweeps piece assignment in this *New Age*, you are fortunate, as resources and individuals to cover the all-important day-to-day stories are becoming more and more scarce!

Format-Driven Versus Personality-Centered Newscasts

During my years representing talent, I have seen the whole spectrum of how news executives have perceived and promoted their broadcasts. On one end is the format-driven broadcast, where *format* is king. WSVN in Miami is an example of this. Up until the past few years, CNN Headline News adopted this philosophy. In format-driven situations, management finds talent to fit the format. And as a result of building a product this way, on-air individuals are, for the most part, perceived as interchangeable. Therefore they will never

---

* Of course, if there's breaking news, all such agreements are off.

earn great amounts of money, because management doesn't perceive the talent as that which brings in the viewers. Additionally, these entities promote the product, not the talent, so talent often doesn't show up as strongly in research as it otherwise might.

On the other end of the spectrum are managers who believe that people watch programs because they like and establish a connection with the on-air talent. In these instances talent are often promoted, show up more prominently in research, and make more money. Why? Because they are perceived as being more important to management's financial success, so they have more leverage. I see this *Reality* (management's high valuation of talent) reflected in how Roger Ailes brilliantly constructed and runs the FOX News Channel. Of course, many managers fall somewhere in the middle of the format/talent spectrum. Also, stations and programming philosophies change depending upon what the competition is doing and how well they are doing it.

The point is that if you work for a strictly format-driven employer, you probably will not receive much individual promotion; you will have to fit into the format, as opposed to having an employer that showcases your strengths; and in all likelihood, you will not earn as much money as in other, more talent-focused operations. But there may nevertheless be some very compelling reasons why working for a format-driven news operation or program is the most enhancing option at a given point in your career.** Just be sure to weigh the pros and cons.

Health/Medical and Consumer News Reporting Franchises

If and when my clients are looking for a reporting franchise that will enhance them and their careers, I often suggest such areas as medical/wellness, financial, consumer, and investigative. I believe in the power of these franchises for a number of reasons.

First of all, these franchise reporters supply valuable information that the

---

** For example, I believe that the format-driven WSVN in Miami is an ideal station at which talent can develop and sharpen their live-performance skills.

viewer can use to better the quality of her or his life. The act of giving this valuable information can endear the reporter to the viewer and help to develop positive equity between them. Because of this, and the fact that such franchises are frequently highly promotable and promoted, an effective franchise reporter's on-air research will in all likelihood be materially enhanced.

In addition, medical/wellness and consumer reporters often do "set" pieces and have set debriefings. The beneficial result of this is that these reporters get a good deal more on-set airtime than other reporters. This can contribute to positive research.

Furthermore, whereas management can argue that there is no real way to equate ratings success with individual reporters' contributions, that is not so with good franchise reporters. Ratings jumps and positive research can definitely be tied to an effective franchise reporter's day-to-day appearances and contributions. Therefore, compelling franchise reporters should—and generally do—earn more money than other reporters.

Also, for an expert on finances or the economy, highly visible and rewarding national positions on one of the cable business networks or on one of the network morning shows would be a natural next step in a *Career Choreography*™.

Finally, supplying news and information that can better people's lives can also result in the reporter's feeling good and positive about his or her work. This certainly can bolster and/or raise one's self-esteem and self-image.

Entertainment Reporting

Generally speaking, if you aspire to be an investigative or hard-hitting general assignment reporter, you would be better off not expecting to gain valuable experience in those areas by working for most syndicated and cable entertainment shows. Why? Because, for the most part, it pays for these shows to be celebrity/guest/interviewee-friendly. If they are, their sought-after guests will want to make return visits to the show and maybe even give the show an all-important "exclusive." However, if you criticize the guest and/or his or her work, or ask uncomfortable or "off-limits" questions, you risk alienating the guest, as well as the publicist, manager, and/or agent. This is a Hollywood no-no.

So you play ball—softball!

You lob an enhancing question to guests about their latest movie, TV series, or CD, and they hit it out of the park. There is nothing wrong with this, since all of the individuals involved—the guest, the interviewer, the executive producer of the show, and the viewers—expect nothing more and nothing less and are all happy.

If You Leave News and Go into Reality-Based Programming—Know the Risk

Notwithstanding the fact that many news programs look more and more like shows such as *ET* and *Inside Edition*, be aware that there will be stations and networks that will be reluctant to hire hosts of these shows to anchor their newscasts. However, with the line between hard news and entertainment news blurring more and more in *The New Age*, I believe that in many, if not all, instances, hosts and correspondents for syndicated magazine shows can make their way back to news. For example, at the time that this book was being completed, Lara Spencer had just left her position as host of *The Insider* to become the "Lifestyle Anchor" on *Good Morning America*. It wouldn't surprise me in the least if she eventually becomes a cohost of *GMA*.

Some Reasons Why Anchors or Hosts Do Not Succeed

Years ago, when I was driving home (from where I had been writing), I turned on the radio to hear the host of a sports show discussing the All-Pro San Francisco 49ers quarterback, Steve Young. That host said that Young, during the early part of his career, had spent two horrible years at Tampa Bay before coming to the 49ers. The host then observed that as bad as Tampa Bay's *system* and *culture* were for Young, San Francisco's team system had been equally great.

This reality is analogous to one so often found in broadcasting. There is no question that the most talented broadcasters can have the world's worst ratings and an incredible lack of success if they are not used correctly, not promoted, have horrible lead-ins, or have management that just does not see it or get it when it comes to them. Conversely, I have seen people hit incredible strides and enjoy wonderful successes when they are put in the right places, with the right people, and have the right programming in front of and/or behind them. Witness Katie Couric's huge success on *Today*, after she was allegedly told by an executive early on in her career that she was not good enough to anchor or host (in a big market). It is amazing how someone can be so unsuccessful in one situation and be a superstar in another. Or vice versa. Below are some other sobering *Broadcasting Realities*:

> If your station doesn't put you in the right position (the most enhancing set of duties or show)...you may not be successful.
>
> If you are not presented by your station in your best light...you may not be successful.
>
> If your station is poorly rated for any reason...you may not be successful.
>
> If the lead-in programming to your newscast is poor...you may not be successful.
>
> If your station doesn't promote you...you may not show up in the research as positively as you should or can, and you may be perceived by your station as not being successful.

There are many, many reasons—totally out of your control—why you do not research as well as possible, why your ratings are not as good as they might be, and why you are not deemed to be as successful as your station and you would like. It is important to understand this.

Along the same lines, talent often ask whether they can use the fact that they have good ratings at one station as a compelling reason for a different station in another market to hire them. Generally, prospective employers will not be significantly influenced by one's past ratings success—especially if the success is achieved in another market—for the following reasons:

1. Just because one is successful in one market doesn't mean that one's success will necessarily translate to another market.

2. One's ratings success can be attributed to good lead-in programming or being at an already successful station.

3. Ratings success can be attributed to factors other than one's anchoring, hosting, or reporting presence and impact.

NEW AGE STRATA-GEM

When assessing the advantageous and non-advantageous points about a particular job or position, make great efforts to truly understand what different venues do and do not offer you, your skill set as currently con-stituted, and your career. Essentially you must ask and assess: "What do the particular positions that I am considering offer? Which one will most enable me to attain my *Gold Ring Dream*?"

Primary Versus Secondary Reasons

Throughout my career as a talent representative, I have found that individuals all too frequently make dissatisfying career decisions because they are driven by secondary reasons as opposed to primary reasons. In order to define primary and secondary reasons, let us take a moment to examine the reasons why some individuals whom I know or I have heard about apparently got married. For example, one of my friends confided that the only reason she married her first spouse years ago was that it allowed her to move out of her toxic home environment at the young age of seventeen. Three years later she was divorced. Others have shared the fact that they wound up getting married upon completion of college or graduate school because they had "always planned it that way," because their friends were married by that time, or because that was the way their parents had done it. Years ago, I was told about a woman who was so intent on getting married during the month of her college graduation that when her fiancé broke off the engagement in late April, she met another man and quickly became engaged to him. She allegedly sent out an amendment to the original wedding invitation, substituting the current fiancé's name for the original one. (However, it was a bit embarrassing when she and her printer forgot to delete the names of the original fiancé's parents from the revised invitation.) So, except for the new groom, everything about the ceremony remained the same. Same day. Same time. Same reception hall. The facile change of grooms certainly made for some spicy conversations in the church pews—but not for a lasting marriage. I was told that this woman and her husband were divorced soon thereafter.

I can compellingly argue that a marriage to either of these men (the starter or the pinch hitter) was a means towards meeting the woman's predetermined marriage schedule—which was the real "end" of her marriage (figuratively and literally). I would label the desire to get married to just *anybody* by a predetermined date or at a set time as a *secondary* reason for marriage. In this case, wanting to enter into a marriage for the *primary* reasons of love or mutual respect—with a real intent to spend the rest of one's life with someone—never played a part in the decision-making process. When something or someone is pursued without true love, passion, excitement, or enthusiasm—and is instead sought for possibly related, albeit tangential and non-essential reasons, such as pleasing one's parents, doing what one thinks is socially acceptable, or something similar—the reason for the pursuit can be deemed secondary.

An example of someone making a professional decision based upon a secondary reason involved a friend who took a job (against my counsel) as a field reporter in a particular city because she had heard that the city was beautiful and that it had lots of single men. The problem was that the new position's job description did not include any regular or fill-in anchoring. Up to that point in her accomplished career, my friend had been a very successful news anchor, and she loved anchoring. From the moment that she started the new job, she worked as a reporter about fourteen hours a day, six days a week. After about three months, she called to tell me that she was miserable at work. She was feeling that she should not have taken a job that she was not truly excited about as a way to possibly meet "Mr. Right" or to enjoy a skyline. Because of her heavy schedule, she barely had any time to do either. When she did have some time, she was either too unhappy or too tired to enjoy much of anything. She concluded that she should have taken or declined the job based solely upon the consideration of whether this was the *right job* for her.

Eventually the newscaster extricated herself from her station contract, and she is now happily anchoring in another city. She is married, and I have sent her posters of skylines of beautiful cities.

Earlier I discussed the concept of finding positions that will enhance you. This practice involves honestly knowing what your strengths and non-strengths are and trying to ascertain as correctly as possible what positions, with which employers, will afford you the best opportunity to grow. It also requires you to know or learn *what will truly make your heart sing!*—which is an amazing primary reason to accept a job or position. Therefore, this chapter is devoted to asking you to honestly discern what positions will make you *truly happy* and excited to go to work each day. My dad worked until he was almost 99 years old. He traveled all over the world as a marketing coordinator and negotiator for T.J. Maxx and Marshalls. In his eighty-year career, he almost never missed a day of work. He said that his longevity and success were attributable to his extraordinary genetic constitution, to the disciplined way in which he exercised and valued his physical well-being through the years, and to the biggest factor of all—he absolutely *loved* his job!

When you are deciding what positions to accept and remain in, do not forget about or minimize the value of passion and happiness. Working for the networks or anchoring in a large city may not be for everyone. For example, I have plenty of clients who have at one time or another said to me that they no longer enjoy the 150 to 200 days of traveling that they do for their network. In fact, they now perceive it as a big emotional and physical drain. They long for a geographically stable, good-paying local anchor or reporting job. Many also miss the daily reporting "fix" that local news provides, which you may not get at a network when you are one of two or three correspondents in a bureau or work on pieces or assignments that can take days or even weeks to complete.

Just remember, it's nice to receive kudos when you get to the network or you land a big-market job, but the applause dies quickly. Then you are left with your good or bad decision. You only live once, and you spend a great many of your waking hours working. Do not play for the crowd or for the validation of others. At the end of the day, do what makes *you* happy and what *you* are passionate about. If you do this, I am willing to bet that you will enjoy your work a lot more, you will be a great deal more effective at what you do, and you will be physically and emotionally healthier.

NEW AGE STRATA-GEMS

1. Everyone who aspires to achieve their life goals generally has to perform some tasks that they may not like doing. This comes with the territory. However, when and if we make significant life-goal decisions based upon secondary instead of primary reasons, we usually do not enjoy the goal-attainment process much, if at all, and the ultimate payoff is more often than not hollow. Conversely, when individuals pursue activities for true primary reasons, they tend to feel congruent and in harmony with their heartfelt passions, values, and beliefs; they usually have more fulfilling and satisfying experiences; and they are much more likely to achieve gratifying results.

2. When making significant career decisions, follow and honor *Your Truth*. This means making decisions that are consistent with who you are and who you aspire to be.

Discerning and Pursuing What You Really Want

If you want to know what lies deep inside,
You must drop your defenses and no longer hide,
And become the most effective sleuth,
By searching your heart and discerning the truth.
Don't take a job 'cause you think it's expected,
As your emotional well-being can be negatively affected.
Don't aspire to positions just because they're in fashion.
Make your heart sing! And follow your passion.

Seize a career that will make you happy and proud,
Make the most of your life, don't play for the crowd.
'Cause in life there are few greater sins,
Than ignoring the dreams you've repressed deep within.

Just Because Management Thinks You Should Assume a Particular Position Does NOT Mean That It Is the Right or the Best Move for You and Your Career

Many employment contracts provide that employers have total or partial right of talent assignability. Therefore, talent is often left with no contractual control over what services they will render should their management decide to change course and assign them to a position other than the one that they contemplated accepting when they entered into their employment agreement. There are numerous potential problems for talent when this situation arises. By way of example, let's discuss some of the most prevalent ones.

Here are two very similar stories regarding individuals who, because of their natural gifts and on-air success, were reassigned to positions that had the potential to be career-threatening.

1. Weekend anchor "A" was so successful and had so much natural personality that his management wanted to integrate him into the weekday news lineup. So one day the GM came up with the idea to make that anchor his weeknight weathercaster. There were three big problems with this idea:

   a. This talent had never done weather before.

   b. This was a top-five market, and the weathercasters at all of the competing stations were very talented, very polished, and had years of experience. Many of them were also experienced meteorologists.

c. This talent had absolutely no interest in doing the weather.

Notwithstanding the fact that this talent expressed the above stated very valid concerns to his general manager, the GM countered that:

a. he wanted to find a weekday vehicle for the charismatic weekend anchor so that the talent would get five days per week of high exposure;

b. he had a "role to fill" (a job open as a weeknight weathercaster) that would be a great fit; and

c. in order to keep the talent's anchor skills sharp and his news credibility intact, the station management would let the talent fill in for the weeknight male anchor when that anchor was off.

At the end of the day, the GM was not to be dissuaded. He went to the talent and said, "I can, by contract, force you to take this job, but I'd much rather you be a team player, be excited about this, and set the right tone in the newsroom and on-set."

Against the talent's best judgment and the advice of his representation, he embraced the change of position. After three two-hour coaching sessions, station management threw the talent on-air as a weeknight weathercaster. To be as kind as possible, the talent looked exceedingly awkward in his new position.

Within a few weeks, the GM of the station was fired (for reasons totally unrelated to this event). When new management came in with fresh eyes and saw the amateurish weeknight weathercaster, their negative first impression of this talent stuck. And no matter how many individuals explained that the newly positioned weathercaster was really a great anchor and was just being a team player, because that individual dutifully followed his former GM's wishes (orders), his news credibility in the new management's eyes was shot. He was immediately demoted to a general-assignment reporter position, and when his contract expired, it was not renewed.

I am aware of a very similar story of a willing talent who was pushed by his management to become a sportscaster, even though he had very little knowledge of sports. The career-derailing result for this individual was equally as bad as that for the aforementioned anchor-turned-weathercaster.

At least two key points must be made here, and talent should keep them in mind:

a. Your career is precious, and the way you are showcased can mean everything! If you are put in a non-enhancing or inappropriate situation, especially in a major market or in a national newscast or program, your lackluster, awkward, and/or poor showings can derail or kill your career. So even if your management doesn't know or get what your gifts and strengths are, it is imperative that you do! And you must somehow make sure that you do not take a position that risks your career, visibility, brand, security, or well-being. Always remember that if a significant mistake in your positioning takes place, you will be terminated or demoted, but, in all likelihood, the station, newscast(s), or program(s) on which you appeared will continue.

b. When a manager has a "role to fill" and decides to change the course of your career, as discussed above, be very careful. In our immediate-gratification world, do not become a "Band-aid" if the move is too risky, if it doesn't make career sense, or if you do not feel good about it. Always remember that using you or your skills to "fill a role" is about solving a problem for the employer. *It is not based upon the new role's being a wise and organic evolution of your growth path.*

2. A wonderfully talented morning anchor is sought after by many top-market stations because he lights it up in the mornings and because in each of the last three markets in which he has worked, the morning shows he has hosted have enjoyed huge ratings success. Although this anchor has many options, he chooses to move to Los Angeles to anchor the morning show for a popular station there. He does this despite the

fact that he has an offer to anchor mornings in New York City, where his family is, and in Chicago, where his fiancée lives. The reasons for his choice of the L.A. station are that the show he will host is a personality-driven vehicle, and he wants to be seen by L.A. producers in hopes that he will one day receive opportunities to host Los Angeles-based national shows.

This talent signs his L.A. station contract while he is finishing up his services to his current station employer. However, between the 60-day period when he enters into the L.A. contract and when he is due to start work in L.A., the GM who hired him is fired, and a new one arrives, bringing with her a new news director.

As soon as the new management has a few days to catch its collective breath, they contact the incoming host to reassure him that all is stable and well at the station and that there is nothing to worry about. Relieved, the talent is reassured that he made the right decision to go to the L.A. station. However, two months after the host goes on-air in L.A., the new GM is told by the head of the station group to remove the current main evening anchor and put in the "new morning guy you just hired."

Obviously, the new GM needs to please her boss, so the first thing she does is to have the station's corporate attorney review the assignability language in the talent's contract. It reads that the anchor will be *initially* assigned as a Monday through Friday morning anchor/host, but that the station thereafter has the right to assign him to any anchor position it chooses, including weekends.

Being armed with that very broad talent assignability provision, the GM tells the talent that because he has done so incredibly well in the mornings, the head of the station division wants to make him the main evening anchor. The talent, who came to the station solely for the opportunity to host its rock 'n' roll morning show, explained this to the GM. He also told her that his talents and passion are "all about" personality-driven morning shows, that he has great morning sensibility, and that he has a personality-based connection with the audience, which is why he consistently has had tremendous morning ratings success. He then ended his plea with this compelling argument: If you had

Matt Lauer hosting your morning show, why would you move him to evenings, which isn't his best venue?!

The GM answered, "We're sure you'll be as successful in the evenings as a solo anchor." The talent somewhat sarcastically countered, "You mean, like Katie Couric moving to the evening news?!" The talent then explained that his strength (much like Katie Couric's) is ad-libbing, having fun, and playing off of and with morning ensembles—not being a solo anchor who simply reads from a script.

The GM, sensing the great resistance from and unhappiness of the talent, told the talent that she would think about it and would again talk to her boss. Three days later, the GM came back and said, "Look, my boss will make you the solo anchor for the 5, 6, and 11 newscasts. We'll promote you up the wazoo. We can find another morning anchor. As of next week, you're our new solo week-night anchor. Congratulations!"

Reading to a prompter, away from fiancée and family, and not in any way showcasing his great personality, the anchor quickly became miserable and barely noticeable. This was a lose/lose/lose scenario for the talent. To add insult to career injury, he never made any impact in the market as an evening anchor.

There are three other related instances that I would like to raise. The first one involves Matt Lauer, who at the time was the newsreader on *Today* and the fill-in host for Bryant Gumbel. As I will discuss later, Matt's work experience, prior to coming to WNBC-TV and then to the *Today* show, was in the essentially lighter fare of hosting and/or reporting for *PM Magazine*, entertainment shows, and local morning and afternoon programs. Because of this, Matt worked incredibly hard at WNBC to build up his news experience and news persona. Notwithstanding all of his hard work, some executives at NBC News, even after Matt became *Today*'s newsreader, still questioned Matt's "news chops." Yet, with everything going so well for him on *Today*, a high-ranking executive of NBC Network asked Matt to leave *Today* and move to cohost NBC's new syndicated show, *Access Hollywood*. This individual even told Matt that if Bryant should ever leave *Today*, Matt could come back and host it. However, Matt and I both knew that if he were to once again host lighter fare, his *Today* career would be all but over. So we decided, notwithstanding the fact that one of the heads of NBC personally asked Matt to become the host of *Access* and that Matt's salary would have as much as tripled if he accepted that position, to respectfully decline the opportunity. Obviously, this was the right decision. What is also crystal-clear is that management isn't always right!

Here's a similar story: "Glenn" was the very talented host of a successful national weekend morning show, and he was flourishing there. He was doing so well, in fact, that his management gave him the cohost position on a new program that would air on weekday mornings. Although Glenn had strong reservations about leaving the weekend show, which was such a great fit for him, the network had the right to assign him to host its new weekday morning show—and it did. Before the show's debut, many individuals at the network told Glenn that the new show would be great! It would be a cross between *Today*, *The View*, and *Live with Regis & Kelly*. It sounded like a tremendous opportunity on paper! However, in reality the show didn't know what it wanted to be, and it never found its voice or caught on. As a result, it was canceled.

When Glenn asked the network executives to once again assign him as the cohost of the weekend morning show that he had left at their direction, they regretfully declined, as the position was already filled. Furthermore, he was told that there was no longer any appropriate hosting position for him in the news division, so his contract would not be renewed. It appeared that because Glenn was so much the public face of a show that was such a ratings flop, he had lost his heat and allure. It took years for him to once again find the right position for him.

Always remember: Success has many fathers and mothers, but failure or non-success is an orphan. Because Glenn was a team player and followed the career course that his management set for him, he went from a rising star to a forgotten talent who had to resurrect his career.

One more illustration, with a bit of a different twist: Years ago, "Carol" joined a top-tier market station as its main female anchor. From my vantage point, few anchors have come into a market and been as positively received and accepted as was the exceedingly smart, talented, and attractive Carol. A few years later, with a major broadcast network needing to find a replacement for its longtime beloved female host, they sought out Carol. At the time that the network executives contacted her, she was enjoying tremendous success at her local station. Life was great! But, the great allure of cohosting a major network morning show, coupled with being paired with a tremendously well-respected and popular male host, was too good to pass up. So she accepted the network's offer. It all seemed very well conceived, until Carol learned that the network executives had decided that the iconic male host wouldn't be her cohost. That position would be given to a young, popular anchor on the show. The profound problem was that the anchor may well have been great in that position, but he didn't have the same credibility, gravitas, folksy demeanor, appeal, and established-over-time audience equity that the original host had—so his shortcomings significantly changed, much for the worse, the on-air chemistry and feel of the show. Instead of Carol slowly settling in as the established cohost's partner, with that host welcoming and anointing her, she immediately became the senior host of the show, having replaced the beloved longtime female host, the sum of which was a *Choreography* disaster!

I truly believe that if the iconic male host had remained as Carol's cohost, or if Carol had had the opportunity to be hired by *Today* and work with Matt Lauer and had been brought along and integrated slowly, because of the built-in credibility, likability, and acceptance of a Matt, Carol would still be hosting a network morning show. Instead, the pairing of the newbies, Carol and the anchor, apparently didn't work, and they were replaced.

Please remember: No one in management meant any harm to anyone's career in these stories. Quite the contrary! Everyone sincerely wanted Glenn and Carol to be on a successful vehicle; but when the vehicles didn't work, management just didn't or couldn't find another appropriate spot for them. The lesson to be learned here is that you need to be exceedingly careful as to how and with whom you make your career bed, because ultimately you are the one who will sleep in it, regardless of what management tells you and how very well intentioned they are.

NEW AGE STRATA-GEMS

1. Just because your management, with all good intentions, believes that you should assume a particular position does *not* mean that it is the right or the very best move for you or your career. Manage-

ment often is compelled to make a change for reasons other than those that make organic, developmental sense for *you*, *your* skill set, and *your* personal career goals.

2. It is essential for everyone in the broadcasting business to make moves or changes for primary reasons such as: the move makes sense in the big picture of your long-term career path; it feels right in your gut and/or heart; and it will not put your career in any jeopardy.

3. As talent, you need to be absolutely careful as to how and with whom you make your career bed, because ultimately you are the one at the end of the day who will be left to sleep in it!

The Skills of Being a Respectful Listener and a Confident and Relaxed Interviewer

O ne of the skills that I look for and greatly appreciate when I watch someone conduct an interview is whether the interviewer truly listens to what the interviewee gives her or him, and whether the interviewer then organically and appropriately responds to it.

I have found that the very best interviewers are respectful listeners. However, sometimes one isn't an effective interviewer, not out of disrespectful listening, but because he or she is focused on other things and as a result is barely listening at all. For instance, this can happen when one is so scripted with prepared questions to ask that once the interviewee finishes an answer, the interviewer immediately, mechanically, and unthinkingly goes on to ask the next prepared question—regardless of the interviewee's response. As a sad result, a wonderful nugget of information, which needs further examination and/or elucidation, is dismissed or glossed over. Not only does this tightly scripted interview feel lifeless to the viewers, but it feels vacuous and pedestrian to the interviewee. Oftentimes a very non-memorable interview for everyone is the end result.

In a *Los Angeles Times* article, Mary McNamara eloquently describes the truly organic interview:

> *Moments of truth and beauty are never scripted* ... they exist between the items on the checklist; come up through the cracks in a conversation; rarely look anything like you thought they would.[18] (emphasis added)

It is the truly confident and relaxed interviewer who lets an interview breathe and then respectfully seizes those moments of truth and beauty and makes the very most of them.

There are a number of reasons why someone can appear to be a disrespectful listener and an inartful interviewer. Here are a few prevalent ones:

1. The interviewer is nervous and/or scared, so she or he rigidly sticks to the prepared set of questions as a safety net.

2. The interviewer is so uninvolved or dispassionate about some component of the interview that this lack of interest in the interviewee or the interview's subject matter is reflected by the interviewer's lack of respectful listening or non-responsive questions.

3. The interviewer is so self-absorbed in himself and/or his own agenda that he isn't focused on being a giving and respectful listener and/or interviewer.

An example of this third reason for non-respectful listening occurred years ago with a quick-witted host named "Chris." Chris's career got off to a relatively slow start, but he received a great deal of positive attention when he became the host of a groundbreaking new entertainment show. On that program, his razor-sharp wit made him stand out as he delivered the entertainment news of the day. As a result, he, in the best of all ways, broke through the clutter of "vanilla," highly forgettable entertainment hosts and reporters.

A couple of years later, Chris was given the coveted position of hosting a major network late-night interview program. The problem was that Chris was used to playing everything for the laugh as an anchor of his entertainment show, and he just assumed that the same strategy would work for his interviews. It didn't. When his guests would attempt to answer one of his questions, Chris would often interrupt them and interject a joke or a sarcastic remark—before the guest had finished answering. In essence, Chris was so intently focused on making each moment his own, instead of his guest's, that he was perceived by many to be a selfish and self-indulgent non-listener. Obviously, neither quality is attractive or endearing both on-air and in real life.

By sticking to his always-go-for-the-joke-at-every-opportunity strategy, which worked for him as an anchor/host but was totally inappropriate in the role of an interviewer, Chris found that things quickly began to go south for him. I believe that this destructive behavior served as a defense mechanism for Chris. By always making quick jokes and not allowing any real connection to be forged, he avoided developing any real intimacy with his guests. But it was not until a couple of months after he had become the host of the network interview show—and "A-list" guests and viewers began to dwindle at a precipitous rate—that Chris finally got the message: If you want to connect with someone, show them that you respect them and that you truly desire to hear what it is that they are telling you. The key is to be an open, objective, and active listener.

Another way to respect an interviewee is for the interviewer to show that she or he has done the necessary research and homework regarding the interviewee by asking questions on the basis of the relevant information gleaned and secured from that research—rather than relying solely on the cheat sheets provided by a show's producer or researcher. This extra effort may go a long way toward the interviewer's establishing an extra-special rapport and connection with the interviewee and thus being able to elicit far more personal information from the interviewee than would otherwise have been the case.

A striking example of this beneficial extra effort took place when *The Early Show* host Harry Smith interviewed actress Amanda Peet. Obviously, when one is on a pre-film-release press tour, the interviewee expects to be asked questions focusing on the new film. But instead of asking questions that Ms. Peet had either heard ten times before or that she had anticipated, Harry took a different path. He analogized and compared her role in her new film to that in one of her early films, which he had obviously taken a good amount of time to personally research and watch. As a direct result of Harry's offbeat but highly informative and insightful questions, the Amanda Peet interview turned into a magical experience for Peet, Harry, and the audience. Literally, Ms. Peet appeared to be tickled pink that Harry knew so much about her early work. It made for a truly insightful conversation and interaction to listen to and watch.

When I remarked to an *Early Show* staff member that I thought Harry's interview with Ms. Peet was great, that staff member shared that "Harry always tries to find something unusual about or especially meaningful to his interviewee, as a way to strike a personal chord."

What a great lesson for all interviewers! Make an extra effort to learn something more and/or different about your interviewee, in a true and honest effort to be a respectful listener as well as an artful interviewer and information facilitator. Remember, when it comes to conducting interviews, you often get out what you put in. So be an active and well-prepared interviewer and a respectful listener!

NEW AGE STRATA-GEMS

1. It is essential to be a respectful and active listener when you interview someone.
2. When interviewing, do your best to put the "internal chatter" and your defenses aside and truly listen and organically respond to the interviewee.
3. Make your interviews extraordinary experiences for the interviewee, for the audience, and for yourself by doing your research. Try to learn something unique about the interviewee or something especially meaningful to him or her as a way to draw the interviewee out and forge a connection.

The Tremendous Advantage of Proximity

We have all heard the real estate adage "Location, location, location." Obviously, the location of a home or a business can mean everything to one's happiness and success. This is also true when you aspire to take your career national.

For example, if you are a local newscaster and want to work for a broadcast or cable network, strive to secure a job at a local station in New York City. This will allow the many New York City-based network executives to watch your work on a regular basis. And if they like what they see, they will seek you out, and/or be much more receptive when you apply for a position with them. If you are at a local New York City station, you are essentially auditioning every day. If you are talented and have your skill set ready, this daily exposure can be great for you. If you are not ready, often the network executives will know it and write you off.

If you are already at a network but at a bureau not located in New York City, and you aspire to host or anchor at that network, you will want to be assigned to a position in New York City. For example, Shepard Smith and Ann Curry were both bureau correspondents for their networks. It was when they were moved to New York City that their careers as anchors and hosts took off. Why? Because they were around to fill in as anchor and host, and they had a chance to show off their considerable gifts and talents. And now, in *The New Age of Broadcasting*, with money being in such short supply, networks will be much more reluctant to spend it to fly talent to New York City and house them, just to have them fill in as anchor or host once or twice. This is especially true when news divisions have so many able and willing individuals already working in New York City who can fill in. So it is even more essential in *The New Age* to get yourself relocated to New York City, so that you are there to fill in as anchor and/or host when needed.

It can also be beneficial for talent to be in the same city and possibly in the same building as your employers. Positive contact with your employers and having them get to know you can make a very positive difference in your career.

Working at WNBC was certainly a career-making step for both Matt Lauer and Al Roker. It was there that NBC News executives realized that they needed to take Matt and Al from WNBC to the *Today* show. It was the same thing for Sam Champion. For years, Sam was WABC's main weathercaster. In time, he became the *GMA* weathercaster and environmental reporter.

Of course, when it comes to CNN and CNN Headline News, being in New York City or Atlanta can be highly beneficial. However, my feeling is that between the two, it is most career-enhancing for CNN talent to be based in New York City.

Conversely, if you aspire to one day host a network or syndicated program, you may well want to be on TV in Los Angeles, since most of the major programming executives are there. I cannot tell you how many programmers inquire about our clients, whom they watch on local TV each day, for potential hosting positions … but it is a substantial number! Obviously, if you are in Boston, Des Moines, or Pittsburgh, Los Angeles-based program executives are far less likely to know who you are, unless they have already received your demo DVD or a link to your work.

So, in *Choreographing* your career steps, location counts! If you are truly ready for the big stage, understanding what regular exposure of your work in New York City or Los Angeles can do for you and your career is essential. It can absolutely put the percentages in your favor that you will achieve your national anchoring or hosting goals.

NEW AGE STRATA-GEMS

1. You can gain tremendous visibility and career-growth advantage by working in a market where potential employers can watch your work each day.

2. However, this proximity and exposure are advantageous only if you and your work are ready to be viewed by those very important potential employers.

Know or Correctly Intuit What Your Employer's Expectations and Needs Are

O ne of the *Strategies* that I continually share with my clients is this: If you want to maximize your potential to be successful, you must know or intuit what your employer's expectations and needs are, because you are not functioning in a vacuum.

I have observed and advised my clients that more relationships go south and sour because the parties involved do not communicate, miscommunicate, or do not meet each other's expectations. Conversely, if you meet or exceed expectations, you put the percentages squarely in your favor for having a positive experience and outcome with everyone you encounter. This is a major building block of your career success and enjoyment.

Let me share an illustration of this with you:

One of my very talented and bright clients joined a local station as a host of one of its shows. About six months into her stay there, she unilaterally decided to go to New York City to get a new on-air wardrobe because she perceived that her current assortment of clothes "didn't fit" the more conservative market that she was now in. Without conferring with anyone, she went to Manhattan, bought herself a completely new on-air wardrobe, and got a new hairstyle. Three days after she had returned to her local station with her new look, I received an irate call from her general manager, who was nearly frothing at the mouth. He told me how much he "hated" my client's new outfits and "haircut," and that I should get her to stop wearing the "old lady" clothes immediately!

When I called my longtime client to delicately broach the subject and tell her that her general manager "couldn't stand" her new clothes and hairstyle, she shot back in a thoroughly exasperated tone, "I just went to the best hairstylist in Manhattan and I just finished spending a fortune at Brooks Brothers on some new clothes. He just doesn't appreciate anything!"

I let a few moments pass before I counseled her: "*Before* you get your hair cut and go clothes shopping next time, have a conversation with your GM. Ask him what *he* wants, because *he* is the person you are trying to please. Think of it this way—if you bring him Chinese food and he hates Chinese food, most of the time you will not secure the desired positive response. However, if you know what he likes and what will make him happy, and you base your decisions on those preferences, you will greatly increase the chances that your actions will be received in a positive way."

From then on, my client got to know her GM better so that she could correctly intuit what would please him. And when she was not relatively sure what he desired, she would ask him. From that day on, they developed a much stronger relationship—based upon *fulfilled expectations.*

If you want to maximize your potential, you must know or correctly intuit what your employer's expectations and needs are. Therefore, it is always worth your very best efforts to make sure you and your employer (and your managers) are on the same page regarding all that you do for them, as well as what you need from them.

NEW AGE STRATA-GEM

If you want to maximize your career potential, you must know or correctly intuit what others'—especially your employer's—expectations
and needs are.

Do Not Leave Your Job Until You Have Secured an Enhancing Position to Go to

With all of the changes that take place in broadcasting, clients often end up at places that are no longer as desirable or as enhancing as they once were.

When someone first hires you, they are excited about you, they believe you are *the* answer, or *an* answer, to their problems, and they look to use your services as much as possible. However, when management, research, goals, or perceptions change and you are no longer coveted, loved, or at the top of management's list, these changes have the potential to not only profoundly affect you professionally, but also to affect you psychologically and emotionally. When you work for someone who doesn't see your talent, doesn't believe in you, or doesn't treat you well, you can very easily lose self-esteem and confidence. It's like being in a bad or abusive relationship. You can begin to think that everything is your fault and that you are not much good at anything or to anyone.

For these and other valid reasons, you may want or need to move on to a new and healthier venue. One rule that I always share with my clients is this: If it is at all possible, do not leave your present position until you have secured another one to go to.

I say this for a number of reasons. First of all, when you are out of work and looking, you are almost always on the defensive. People ask, "What happened?" and "Why didn't it work out?" as if the departure from your job was your fault. Additionally, financially you can lose some or a great deal of leverage regarding your next contract, as employers often feel that you now need a job. So think very carefully before leaving a position without having another one to go to. For example, if your annual salary is $175,000 and you leave your job, you are now earning *nothing*. On the other hand, I have found that if you are still earning $175,000, when you negotiate a salary with a new employer and that employer asks what you are currently earning, she/he will do one of three things:

1. offer you a raise;

2. match your current salary; or

3. offer you a bit less, due to the financial exigencies of *The New Age*.

However, if you are earning nothing, the employer will not feel at all compelled to offer you a raise or match your prior salary. It is far more likely that with no current salary for you to bargain with and use as an all-important base negotiating figure, you will be offered a *substantial pay cut*—especially in *The New Age*.

Additionally, if you have any real discord or problems with your current employer that you would rather a prospective employer not hear about, then I would definitely advise you to stay at your current position until you have found a new one. I recommend this because a prospective employer will most likely not consult with your current management about you while you are still at your current job, but will ask questions of your previous employer.

A memorable example of this occurred when a very bright news director had a bitter falling-out with his new general manager. As a result of this dispute, the news director quit his job, even though he had no new position to go to. Thereafter, when he interviewed for potential positions that he was more than qualified for, he was not hired. Eventually he was forced to resurrect his career by accepting a relatively low-paying position at a station in a much, much smaller market than he left. At some point he learned why he had been shut out from positions that he should have secured: His former general manager, with whom he had the squabble, sabotaged his chances when potential employers called her to do a reference check on him. Allegedly this general manager didn't actually say bad things about the applicant; she was able to nix his chances of securing work by what she *didn't* say and how she *didn't* say it.

My advice: Keep your friends close, and keep working for your potential enemies until you have secured your next job!

However, there are times when your self-esteem is so low—when you are so unhappy and feel so underutilized and unwanted—that you just do not want to endure any more anguish and humiliation. In that kind of situation, it may well be professionally and emotionally healthier to leave your job. However, this is a last resort, as attractive alternative broadcasting positions can be scarce in *The New Age*.

NEW AGE STRATA-GEMS

1. It is always constructive to stay at a position until you have an enhancing position to go to. Conversely, there are times when you are so unhappy and/or beaten down or demoralized that your emotional, psychological, and physical health must be preserved. In that case, it may well be wise to leave a position *before* you secure another one. However, this should be a last resort, as new positions are hard to come by in *The New Age*.
2. Keep working for your potential detractors or enemies until you have secured your next job.

Effectively Managing Your Emotions in *The New Age* by Seeing the Big Picture and by Being Consequence Cognizant

With money and resources in exceedingly short supply, with colleagues all around you losing their jobs or having to endure substantial pay cuts, and with everyone in *The New Age* under tremendous pressure to survive, people's emotions are much closer to the surface and are often at a fever pitch. The potentially devastating problem with this *New Age Reality* is that when individuals act on the basis of intellect-nullifying emotions, they often make counterproductive or highly destructive decisions.

Upon reflection, I realize that some of the most valuable time that I spend with my clients is in counseling them to view their day-to-day issues in the context of the big picture of their careers. In order to accomplish this, I suggest, that they spend time going over the following *7 Step Cooling-Off Process*:

1. Step back from the heat of the moment.

2. Take a deep breath.

3. See the anger- or hurt-producing incident that we are discussing in the context of the big—long-term—picture of your career.

4. Carefully consider all of the consequences of the potential act(s) that you are contemplating in response to the emotion-evoking incident in issue (essentially, "be Consequence Cognizant").

5. Take the necessary time to identify what you truly want for your career in the long term and what your *Gold Ring Dreams* are.

6. Thoughtfully choose your most career-constructive and beneficial response.

7. Take well-reasoned actions that will preserve your ability to one day attain your most cherished career goals and live your career *Gold Ring Dreams.*

I have learned over the years that in calm, cool, collected moments—when we are in a good, positive place or space—we often recognize the right and career-enhancing responses to our day-to-day irritants, setbacks, and challenges. However, when we are overtaken by potentially sabotaging emotions, the power of our intellect can be negated, and we often make decisions or choices that do not reflect our very best judgment. In most instances, we opt for a self-destructive quick fix. We thereby can derail our career growth and potentially sabotage our career for all time. Obviously, all of these results are extremely bad.

A key step in this constructive and reflective cooling-off process is that you clearly identify what you truly want to attain in the context of the big picture of your career. By doing this, and by not allowing your potentially destructive emotions (hurt, anger, sadness, neediness) to hijack your carefully reasoned best judgment, you will be far less likely to choose the often self-sabotaging quick-fix solution in order to feel better *for the moment.* We have all seen and experienced that quick fixes are oftentimes at direct odds with and counterproductive to securing our long-term goals. By choosing the quick fix, you may well settle for career brass, and thereby preclude your chances of ever attaining your career *Gold Ring Dreams.*

Our pop culture, in many instances, teaches us to seek immediate gratification. It also reinforces the very dangerous concept of getting what we want without ever considering *the very real consequences* that will result from the actions we take. This highly flawed philosophy can absolutely lead us to make devastatingly destructive life and career decisions. In my representation career, I have all too often seen individuals act impulsively—by *unthinkingly* acting out of blinding emotion or an overwhelming urge—thereby putting their careers and their lives as they knew them in great jeopardy. In many instances, the individuals committing these impulsive acts lost their jobs and permanently destroyed their careers. Who knows the devastation that they caused to their personal lives? You want to talk about your very worst nightmare coming true? It happened for many of these urge/emotion-driven individuals!

I truly believe that if these individuals had been Consequence Cognizant—that is, if they had identified and appreciated all of the potential HORREN-DOUS CONSEQUENCES of their choices and actions—they never would have committed any of their alleged acts. Here are just a few of the potentially devastating consequences that they could have identified *before* they acted:

1. Loss of their wonderful and cherished career.

2. Loss of their great, coveted, stimulating, prestigious job.

3. Loss of substantial income.

4. Being the direct cause of tremendous embarrassment to their loving and wonderful family.

5. Living in ignominy.

6. Being accused of committing a felony.

7. Being convicted of a felony.

8. Enduring the tremendous, unhealthy stress of having to go through all of these devastating consequences; and, possibly worst of all,

9. Going to jail and serving a sentence there!!!

Once again, knowing these unfortunate individuals, I am convinced that if they had carefully gone through the *7 Step Cooling-Off Process*, it is far less likely that they would have committed the acts that derailed their careers and their lives. The key here is that whenever you are faced with making an important career choice and you feel that you are under the influence of any potentially damaging emotional influence or stress, you need to take the requisite time to go through the *7 Step Cooling-Off Process*.

NEW AGE STRATA-GEMS

1. Oftentimes our clear best judgment can be clouded by our emotions. Through the *7 Step Cooling-Off Process* that I have outlined, you may well be able to rid yourself of emotions that will otherwise lead you to act in a destructive manner.
2. Whenever you make a career decision, be Consequence Cognizant.

At the Beginning— Less Is Often More

Pushing the Envelope

Years ago, I heard about an exceedingly talented sportscaster who was very opinionated, animated, and often pushed the presentation envelope too far, too soon. The problem was that he kept securing great positions but then lost them; he polarized and alienated a significant portion of the audience so early in his tenure that his employers felt that they had to terminate their relationship with him. The employers parted ways with this talent even though they liked what he did. Apparently they felt that the early negative response was so damaging, that it was either irreparable, or it would take way too long to reverse.

After I had acquired this sportscaster's representation, a general manager at a top-rated, large-market station expressed interest in hiring my client, but only on one condition: that my client ease into the market slowly, by not pushing himself on the viewers until they were more comfortable with him. My client accepted his offer, and in time this strategy proved to be absolutely correct.

I am a big proponent of the idea that at the beginning of your tenure in an on-air position, you should let people feel comfortable with you before you start to push the performance envelope. This situation is analogous to being a guest in someone's home, in that you must show sensitivity and respect until you and your host achieve a positive comfort level. Then you may be in a position to take certain appropriate liberties.

Similarly, once you reach a positive comfort level and you develop equity and a rapport with the viewers, you can slowly begin to push the performance envelope and stretch. Often, with the right *Choreography* and sensitivity, the stretch and transition will be seamless and warmly accepted.

Publicity

During my career, I have seen situations in which so much hype and publicity preceded a person beginning a new job that she or he was doomed from the start, or as one network executive expressed it, the newcomer was "dead on arrival."

My suggestion is to keep pre-arrival and early publicity to a minimum—especially if you are just coming into a market and the individuals at whom the publicity is aimed do not know you or have not seen you before. This approach is wise, since you have not yet developed any equity with them. Here are some other reasons why early publicity should be shunned or kept to the bare minimum:

1. Very high or impossible expectations to fulfill the hype will be set—and the pressure upon you to meet those expectations will be great. You will be quickly branded a failure if you do not meet those expectations.

2. It is not unusual for people in-house to resent you if your arrival is preceded by a lot of publicity. You do not want your colleagues looking for you—or helping you—to fail. Most of them will not need any additional incentive to resent you other than the darkness of their own insecurities.

3. I have found that many individuals do not hit their performance stride in a new position until between twelve and eighteen months after they have assumed it. Therefore, if you get too much press at the beginning, you will be under the microscope and expected to be at your best at a time when it is least likely that you will deliver.

Additionally, please remember that every on-air talent sometimes has negative, hurtful things written about him or her. It is part and parcel of the business. However, you can take great comfort in the fact that in *The New Age*, most individuals have very short attention spans and memories, so the attention paid to your negative publicity is likely to wane quickly.

"Equity" Expanded

Earlier I discussed how by starting out slowly and not pushing the performance envelope too far, you can develop a comfort level and equity with viewers, and then, as these trust levels are established, you can more safely venture out and take some risks. Here is another example of this dynamic:

> A nationally known client wanted to do a new and different kind of talk show. This program would be a good deal more intelligent and spiritual than most, and would have an unorthodox format. In speaking with one of the most successful programming individuals in TV, he said, "The way that you [my client] accomplish what you want is by doing a more conventional show, with more conventional topics at the beginning. Give people what they're used to and comfortable with. Then, as time goes on, subtly begin to make some changes and slip in some of the more cerebral and spiritual topics that you want to do."[19] My client responded that she wanted to do some of the self-help and new-age topics that Oprah had discussed on her show. My wise friend responded, "It's taken Oprah over ten years to become *Oprah*."[20] Meaning that originally Oprah did many of the same interviews that others did; then, as she developed a large and loyal following, she could experiment with and interject more and more non-conventional topics and interviews into her show. It took time and the evolution of viewer equity to do this seamlessly. On the other hand, if you host a show that right from the beginning is unconventional and not what viewers are used to, you may well turn off so many of them that you are never able to recover from your bad start.

Said another way: When you take fewer risks at the beginning, this behavior is more likely to allow you to successfully do what you would like later on.

Another instance where this theory applies has to do with the components of an anchor's or a host's appearance—especially women's hairstyles. There have been times when some women have worn their hair three or four different ways during the first couple of weeks of a new on-air position. When it comes to hairstyles, clothes, makeup, and the like, it's a good idea to dress and look the part of an anchor, journalist, or host at the beginning of your tenure. Let your audience become comfortable with you. And once you develop equity with them, then begin to experiment.

One last thought. When making demo DVDs for prospective employers or consultants, dress and look the part. That is, look like what anchors, hosts, and reporters are expected to look like. The reason for this is that your demo DVD may be put into focus-group testing, where a group of individuals are asked to watch your work and determine whether they find you "trustworthy," "credible," "likable," etc. Since these respondents will probably never have seen you before, you have developed no equity with them. I believe that you will have your best shot of securing high marks with these new viewers by looking and acting like *they expect* anchors, hosts, and reporters to look. In other words, immediately tap into their expectations and what they have grown accustomed to and comfortable with.

NEW AGE STRATA-GEM

At the beginning of a broadcasting relationship, it is often wise to develop a comfort and trust level with the audience before you experiment or push the envelope very far.

You Want the Leverage in Contract Negotiations

Leverage exists when your employer believes,
That if the deal's not good, you will leave.
Leverage doesn't, in fact, have to be real,
For you to secure a really good deal.
But it's great when you can back up the talk,
That if you're not happy, you will walk!

Years ago, whenever I opened an airline magazine and saw Dr. Chester Karrass's advertisement for his negotiation seminars and tapes, I was always struck by his quotation:

"In business you don't get what you deserve, you get what you negotiate."

When it comes to broadcasting, in almost all instances, I agree with Dr. Karrass.

Whether or not a talent can negotiate a fair, good, or great deal almost always depends upon whether that talent has the leverage to do so. Leverage is comprised of (at least) four elements:

1. How much an employer or a prospective employer wants to retain your services or to acquire them (this is usually the most important element);

2. What the employer perceives your marketability or your ability to walk away from the deal is;

3. How much you want or need the deal; and

4. Whether you are willing to—or actually do—walk away from the employer's final offer.

Here are four pre-*New Age* illustrations of the impact that leverage had upon my negotiations:

1. A few years ago (during *Stage Two*), I was negotiating a deal for a well-established "franchise" reporter in a top market. The news director with whom I was negotiating told me that his station would absolutely not pay more than a 5-percent annual increase over the reporter's $150,000 salary* for a new three-year contract. When I told him that I wanted in the mid-$200,000 range as a starting point for my client, and that I thought that I could get an offer of about $250,000 at a competing station in the market, he cavalierly responded by saying, "Kenny, if he can get that kind of an offer, he should take it. But we're not going to pay more than a 5-percent raise. That's it!"

   Two days later, I received a three-year offer of $240,000, $250,000, and $260,000 for my client to work at a competing station in the market— an offer that my client would have been more than happy to accept if his current employer didn't appropriately respond. With leverage and confidence in hand, I called the news director at my client's current station to advise him that my client had decided to decline his offer of a 5-percent raise. No hard feelings. The news director (obviously shaken) nervously said that I should not do anything until he called me back. Within ten minutes, I received a call from the station's general manager, who said, in as friendly a manner as possible:

   "Kenny, my goal in running this station is to have as many [on-air] employees as possible receiving 3- to 5-percent raises."

   I replied, as cavalierly as possible, "We know that, so we're not pushing you to pay any more. My client will just turn in his resig—"

---

* The negotiation began with the news director offering a 3-percent raise.

"BUT," he interrupted, "there are times when we have to and need to keep someone, and we'll do what it takes. You've forced us to pay the [perceived] market price. Let's get this one over with. We'll pay your client $260,000, $275,000, and $300,000 for a three-year, no-cut [firm] deal."

Because we had leverage, my client received an average of over $100,000 per year more than what the news director told us his final offer was!

2. Another client of mine was offered an anchor position by a prominent network. However, this client was already a successful and well-paid anchor in her local market, where she was happy to stay. Twice she turned down the network's generous offer. However, after the second offer was declined, she decided that she would accept the position if the network would agree to the almost nowhere-to-be-found clause: "If she [my client] was unhappy for any reason, she could terminate the contract and work for someone else." Upon asking the network negotiator for the clause, he responded that he could *never* give that clause. "No how, no way." I took his reply back to my client, who was happy to forget the whole thing.

    However, two weeks later, the network once again offered her the position, along with an increased compensation package. My client once again said, "No—but thank you."

    The next day, the negotiator called and said (in a tone of half-resignation and half-admiration for my client being able to get the network to give in): "Okay. Your client can leave at any time—except during a ratings period—with sixty days' notice, and one caveat: She cannot terminate to go to another network."

    Because of the leverage derived from my client's (repeated) willingness to walk away from the network's offer, she was able to secure a truly extraordinary deal.

3. There is a middle-market station with which I have done a great deal of business through the years. Because of the high quality of both the station and my clients' work, I have been able to take three or four of their on-air people to wonderful and prominent positions. Additionally,

because of my track record, and because of how talented and market-able this station perceived a particular client of mine to be, a year and a half into a three-year agreement, the general manager called me and said, "Kenny, I know you're gonna move your client if we don't sign her now [to a new deal], so let's just double her salary and cut through the bulls—t."

I called my client, who had every intention of staying at her station for the foreseeable future—as long as she had the right contract. After hearing the offer, she told me to get whatever else I could, and then accept it. A little later, I called the general manager, appropriately improved the deal, and then closed it. My client was ecstatic.

In this instance, my perceived ability to effectively market my client and her perceived marketability gave us leverage—in spite of the fact that not one prospective employer had even been approached (so early in her contract).

4. A client of mine, who was at a network-owned station in market "A," made her wishes known that she really would like and, in fact, needed to be transferred across the country to a station owned by the same net-work in market "B." The market "B" station was willing to find a spot for her, but they could basically "take her or leave her."

When it came to her moving expenses, they stayed firm at $2,500 to move all of her belongings cross-country. She secured three moving estimates, the lowest of which came in at $3,500. When I learned that my client would have to go out-of-pocket to move to her desired sta-tion, I called to reason with the news director of station "B" in hopes that he would authorize the payment of her moving expenses. Here's how the conversation went. I began (with some tongue-in-cheek sar-casm), "My client just got three moving estimates, and the lowest one is $1,000 more than your extraordinarily generous offer of $2,500. So why don't you cover her total expenses (of $3,500), we'll call it a day, and you can feel good about yourself on your deathbed?"

"Nope. $2,500. That's it," the news director replied.

I responded, in my most humane tone, "But Steve, three months ago, you gave me $35,000 as a moving allowance for my other client to move from his home two hours away. Be fair!"

He replied, with what he perceived as perfect logic, "We *really* wanted your other client, and by giving him all that money for moving, he was able to put more in his pocket, because we couldn't pay him all that you asked for in his salary. In this client's case, *she* wants to move here; and so far as we're concerned, we're happy to have her, but we'll live if we don't. The 'deathbed stuff' was a good effort, but sorry, $2,500. That's it!"

The moral of these stories is: *You* want the leverage when you negotiate your employment contracts.

NEW AGE STRATA-GEMS

1. Leverage can enable you to negotiate and secure more advantageous assignments, security, salary, etc.
2. There are at least four elements of leverage:
    a. How much an employer or a prospective employer wants to retain your services or to acquire them;
    b. What the employer at issue perceives your marketability or your ability to walk away from the proposed deal to be;
    c. How much you want or need the deal; and
    d. Whether you are willing to—or actually do—walk away from the employer's final offer.
3. *You* always want the leverage!

Getting It Right—from the Start

Through the years, I have counseled that it is not the size of the market that you start in that counts, but how much in the long run you ultimately grow, whether you fulfill your potential, and whether you are professionally happy. On the other hand, some of the best advice that I can share with my clients, or remind them of, is this: "When starting a new job or beginning a new professional relationship, do your best to get it right the first time around." We often base our opinions on our first impressions. And it frequently takes a great deal to change our minds if individuals or events happen to get off to a bad or a lackluster start. In some cases, we may never change someone's first perceptions—even if those perceptions are inaccurate.

From my childhood, and in some instances, to this day, I have always been one of those individuals whom people underrate. Therefore, if and when I succeed, people are surprised. An example of this occurred years ago, when I played a series of tennis sets against the head pro of a well-known resort—and beat him in a number of them. Apparently, later on a few guests walked up to the pro and commented that they couldn't understand how I could fare so well against him. They just didn't get it.[*]

The pro responded, "Kenny's deceptive! You don't get it, until you play him." The other pro, whom I had also played some sets against, then added, "I said the same things when I first saw him. Then I played him. He is really good. We call him 'The Deceptor,' 'cause his playing deceives everybody."

---

[*] Interestingly, I had been playing Extreme Tennis exclusively for the past two years, and those were my first sets of tennis during that entire time. The point is that I probably would have done even better had I been playing more tennis.

Being underrated is something that I have experienced many times in my life. I have learned to understand it and to deal with it. However, I have also experienced the great advantages that can be derived from getting it right and earning people's respect from the get-go. For example, it is much easier to be highly seeded (ranked) in a big tournament: You get right into the main draw, you may not have to play a match until the second round, and you may not play another seeded (or top-ranked) player until the later rounds. This is in sharp contrast to having to play through three or four qualifying rounds just to get into the main tournament; and then if you make it, you may play a top-seeded player such as Roger Federer in the first round. If I am going to play a Roger Federer, for a myriad of good reasons I would rather play him in the finals of a tournament than in the first round.

During my freshman year of high school, I signed up to try out for the varsity tennis team. I told the coach about my Extreme Tennis successes, and he scheduled me to play a match the following week against the returning #1 varsity player, who was also the team captain. I knew that this match would be my shot to get off on the right track. It would be a *defining moment* to show that I belonged on the varsity team. During the intervening days, I practiced and mentally prepared. I wound up beating my opponent, 6–1, 6–0, in about 50 minutes. For the next four years, I was automatically given the #1 spot on the varsity team, and I never again had to play a challenge match against any of my teammates. The perception—true or false—was that I was the best player on the team and that no one was going to beat me. So as a result of my first and only intra-team match, the case was closed: I would play #1 singles.

In college, the same thing happened. My first day at the tennis courts during my freshman year, I was introduced to the #1 player (a senior) on the varsity team. He was waiting until other team members arrived, so that he could practice with them. After a moment or two, the varsity coach suggested that the number one player and I play a quick set. As the coach had never seen me play before, I (once again) knew that this could be a big opportunity for me. I focused and played the best that I could. I won the set, 6–3. We played another set. I won it, 6–2. By now, a number of varsity team members were watching, along with a now amused and excited coach. We played once more. I won, 6–4. Although, according to Ivy League rules, I had to play on the freshman tennis team, as a result of that fateful match my situation immediately and noticeably changed. From then on, I was extended the privilege of practicing with the varsity, along with attending separate practice sessions with my freshman teammates. The keener competition that I faced at the varsity level helped me to be undefeated in freshman intercollegiate match play.

A few months after I began my career at the William Morris Agency, I was given the important assignment of writing all of the contracts and being the William Morris business-affairs point person for the new morning *David Letterman Show*. This program would make William Morris a substantial amount in commissions. Upon receiving this assignment, similar to my high school and college tennis matches discussed above, I knew that it would be a defining moment for me vis-à-vis my new employers. With this in mind, I worked very hard, spending late-evening and weekend time making my very best efforts right from the start. The work paid off. David's managers were so pleased that one of them, Jack Rollins, sent a letter to one of the heads of William Morris, detailing how happy he and his client, David, were with my meticulousness, the amount of responsibility that I had assumed, and how well I interacted with the show's staff members. All of this allowed my career to get off to a very (visible) positive start, and I was immediately accorded respect for my efforts and effectiveness.

In the broadcasting arena, I have a number of clients who have been fortunate enough to begin their careers in markets that are relatively large and advanced for their early stages of development. Often this occurs when individuals begin as interns, writers, or associate producers in their hometown or college markets and work themselves up through the ranks to on-air positions. Since these individuals do not have to start out in the usual small-market setting, where they can make the expected and accepted rookie on-air mistakes, they wind up making them in markets where others are much more seasoned and polished. Therefore, their mistakes are greatly magnified and are tolerated a great deal less willingly. One problem with this situation is that news management at these stations will forever—or at least for a long time thereafter—have in their minds those rookie mistakes, and thus managers are often never able to objectively see and acknowledge the subsequent growth of these newscasters. This *Reality* is reflected in the fact that these newscasters continually make lower salaries and are promoted at a slower rate. The first impressions that they make as rookies, and the perception of their being "given a break" in being allowed to start on-air in large markets, generally stay with these managers throughout these newscasters' careers at these stations. As a result, these newscasters are often forced to leave their first station, even if they ordinarily would have been happy to stay there. Instead, they must go to a station where management's first impression of them is a more positive one and accurately reflects their advanced stage of development.

I am acutely aware of how very important it is for talent to work for people who believe in them, are excited about them, and want to enhance them. I also know that these employers will be much more likely to continue to do good things for my clients if my clients make a good first impression. It is just a fact of life.

NEW AGE STRATA-GEM

In our society, first impressions count. When beginning a new professional relationship, try to get off to the best start possible.

Career Jump-Starts

Often, when the obvious means of attaining a coveted position doesn't appear to exist, or you cannot effectively implement it, you will need to design a creative *Choreography* that will put you in the very best position to produce that means. Here are a few examples of individuals who have successfully done this.

The Christina McLarty Jump-Start *Choreography*

Earlier, we discussed how one general assignment reporter jump-started her sports career by volunteering to anchor and report sports on weekends, even though she covered news Monday through Friday. Here's another example of a creative way that one of my clients jump-started her national entertainment host/reporter career.

I found Christina McLarty at KTVT, the CBS-owned station in Dallas, Texas. As soon as I saw the exceedingly talented, radiantly lovely, and compelling Christina, I knew that she had a national entertainment hosting and reporting career ahead of her. What I didn't glean, until I got to know her, was that Christina is both very bright and emotionally intelligent, and that she has an old, wise soul.

Within a couple of months of our beginning to work together, an entertainment reporter position opened at KCBS/KCAL ("KCBS"), which are KTVT's Los Angeles-based sister stations. There was no question that this was the perfect next *Career Choreography*™ step in Christina's career, as this position would give her the big-market experience she needed. Additionally, almost all of the most important entertainment magazine shows (*ET, EXTRA, Access Hollywood*) are based in L.A., as are most of the entertainment/programming executives, so she would receive incredible, high-echelon exposure there. With these thoughts in mind, I submitted Christina to KCBS, and fortunately, they hired her. In extricating Christina from her KTVT contract a couple of months before its expiration, it certainly helped that she worked for KCBS's sister station at the time.

After she had been at KCBS for three or so years, it was time to make our next move, which was to secure a national position for Christina. The problem was that there seemed to be no appropriate position available. So Christina and I spoke, and we (mostly she) came up with the brilliant jump-start idea that would put the percentages far more in her favor that she would attain her *Gold Ring Dream* of working for *ET* and/or *The Insider*. Here it is: *ET* and *The Insider* are both CBS-owned and -distributed shows; they are in the CBS family; and they are located on the same lot as is KCBS. So why not propose to KCBS management that Christina do a sweeps series of reports about *ET* and *The Insider*? This series would feature in-depth interviews with all of the *ET* and *Insider* executives, as well as with the shows' hosts. The brilliance of this jump-start *Choreography* was that it would give Christina meaningful contact with all of the *ET* and *Insider* executives (and they would see what an exceptional talent and person Christina is). Because this was great cross-promotion for two CBS-owned shows that aired on KCBS, KCBS management approved Christina's doing the series.

As we had hoped, Christina knocked the interviews out of the park. Soon after the series aired, conversations between *ET/Insider* executives regarding Christina took place. Immediately thereafter, Christina began to report for *The Insider* on a freelance basis. However, this opportunity for Christina became a reality because KCBS management was gracious enough to give their permission for Christina to work for and serve both masters (KCBS and *ET/Insider*)—which she did, tirelessly, seven days a week, for two months.

It was then that various CBS Television Distribution executives and I discussed bringing Christina to *The Insider* full-time. As a result of KCBS management's kindness and the syndication out-clause, which I had negotiated into Christina's KCBS contract, Christina is now reporting and fill-in anchoring for *The Insider*.

The Christina *Career Choreography*™ continues. Undoubtedly, Christina's national career got a huge jump-start from her innovative strategy of creating/manufacturing meaningful and enhancing contact with the CBS Television Distribution executives who could (and did) hire her.

Another kind of jump-start is to craft a creative strategy designed to help you to secure the means (a demo DVD/link) to attain a coveted position. Here's one that involves a client of mine, Lisa Pineiro.

The Lisa Pineiro Jump-Start *Choreography*

Lisa Pineiro was an anchor in Salt Lake City when she became a single mom. At some point thereafter, she decided to leave the broadcasting business in order to more actively raise her four wonderful boys. Approximately five years later, with her boys older and things in her life more settled, Lisa decided to return to television news. The problem was that the material on her demo tape was more than five years old.

The question presented to us both was how to get some new demo-tape material in order to more effectively market Lisa. This *Career Choreography*™ conundrum was solved when KCBS management agreed to audition Lisa for a morning anchor position that they were looking to fill. At the conclusion of their anchor talent search, KCBS management decided that there was one candidate—other than Lisa—who was a better fit for the position. However, they were kind enough to let us use Lisa's extraordinarily good KCBS anchor audition material as our demo DVD. Armed with our fresh new anchoring, Lisa received interest to anchor for a network and for a few local stations. Soon thereafter, she secured what was a perfect position for her, as the Monday through Friday morning anchor at KTVT in Dallas. So everyone was ecstatic. Lisa accepted a great anchor position with a wonderful and nurturing news director. And the kindness of KCBS management was rewarded, as Lisa took a position within the CBS family.

There are many ways to come up with a fresh demo DVD. The key is to strategically and creatively *Choreograph* the best way for you in your unique circumstances to make it happen.

NEW AGE STRATA-GEM

When the means of attaining something in your career isn't available or obvious, you need to find a creative/out-of-the-box *Choreography* to identify a way to jump-start your growth.

The Three "D's" of Constructive Decision-Making: Desire, Discipline, and Delayed Gratification

Desire

It's nice to say that you aspire,
And that the goals you choose will take you higher;
But worthy goals aren't attained without the internal fire,
Of the emotional energies of want and desire.

I have learned, seen, and counseled that if you aspire to achieve a goal, "You've got to really want it," and you've got to be fully focused on attaining it. There is no question about it. If you lack either the desire or the focus, it will be too easy for you to be diverted into settling for more immediate but ultimately less-gratifying substitutes.

Desire is a powerful concept. It conjures up energized qualities such as passion, need, want, and belief. When these emotional and sexual energies are channeled toward healthy and constructive ends, they can have a HUGE positive impact upon your goal-attaining efforts. These energies can initially have a catalyzing effect upon you. Thereafter, they can help you to sustain your efforts and focus as you face problems, crises, distractions, and weak moments.

You cannot be defensive about what you want in order to hide your true feelings from yourself or from others in case you fail or fall short. To the contrary, you must clearly identify your goals and not be afraid to put yourself on the line in your efforts to achieve them.

In your quest to identify and attain your goals, you must not only identify your most important values, but you must also identify, feel, and tap into your desire and passion for goal attainment. You will need all of the desire and focus that you can muster when trying to incorporate the other two "D's" of decision-making—discipline and delayed gratification—into your behavioral repertoire.

People who are successful know what they want, and they have the drive and focus to go after it.

Discipline

Dr. M. Scott Peck, in *The Road Less Traveled*, writes, "Discipline is the basic set of tools we require to solve life's problems. Without discipline we can solve nothing!"[21]

I agree. In almost all instances, individuals who achieve their goals know that the practice of discipline in their thinking and in their actions is an indispensable element of their formulas for success.

Much of the career counseling that I have done in order to help my clients achieve their potential in one way or another involves the qualities of discipline and its soul mate, delayed gratification. For instance, years ago, one of my clients, "Julianna," called me to say that her news director summoned her to his office and asked whether she would forgo her long-awaited two-week vacation so that she could fill in for the main weeknight anchor of her station. As we often try to do, my client and I examined the appropriate values and behavioral scripts in an orderly, objective, and careful manner. We each wrote them down.

Julianna's values were that she and her husband had planned and paid for their upcoming vacation months in advance, and neither of them had taken a vacation for about a year. They both needed and wanted some time off. On the other hand, Julianna and I knew that the main anchor at her station would be leaving in the next few months and that Julianna was the front-runner to replace her. However, there was one other female anchor at the station, "Cindy," who was also a candidate for the position, and Cindy had openly made her desire to attain the position known to management. Julianna also knew that if she took her vacation, Cindy would be assigned to fill in for the two weeks.

We continued to list Julianna's values. If she did get the main anchor position, her annual income would certainly double, and maybe triple. She would also ascend to a very prestigious position in a city that she wanted to make her home for the long term. All of these values were of significant importance to her.

I then recounted the following story. Years ago, a client of mine, "Rita," left for a week's vacation. On the Friday before Rita left, the news manager of her station told us that upon Rita's return, she would be promoted from being a morning anchor to a weeknight evening anchor—a position for which she had worked hard for the past twelve years to attain. During Rita's vacation, the noon anchor, who had been at the station for a little over a year, filled in on the broadcast that my client was to be promoted to.

Allegedly, during that week, the station manager went to a gas station on his way home, and the attendant there said, "All of the guys here really like the redheaded woman you have anchoring this week." The next thing we knew, the station management had changed its collective mind, and Rita didn't get the promotion upon her return from vacation. The redheaded noon anchor did. This turn of events was emotionally and professionally devastating to Rita.

Julianna got the point. She then said, "We all know that I'm the front-runner for the job, right?" I answered, "Right." She continued, "So I shouldn't have to worry about taking a vacation and having Cindy fill in! The question is, do you think she has any chance of blowing them away while I'm on vacation?" I answered that I felt that Cindy was actually pretty good, and in reality we never know what can happen when we allow a variable that we do not have control over to enter into an equation.[*] Therefore, there was a chance, however small, that letting Cindy fill in could indeed result in an undesirable outcome for us.

---

[*] This is a strategy that I believe in. The more you can control the variables in a situation, or the more often you can eliminate variables that you cannot control or accurately predict, the more likely you are to succeed in attaining your goals.

I then ended by saying, "According to my calculation, the professional equation clearly weighs out in favor of opting to be disciplined and putting off your vacation for a while—even if it's needed and it will cost some money to postpone it. I wouldn't give Cindy the opportunity to show her stuff. However, only you can calculate the personal equation of the value to you and your husband of not taking your vacation together at this particular time. The decision depends upon how much the personal values mean to you in this instance. Do they outweigh the professional ones?"

About ten minutes later Julianna called me back after speaking with her husband. She had decided that she would fill in for the two weeks and that she and her husband would take their vacation a couple of months later. She knew that this was a defining moment for her and that she had to be disciplined, which in this case meant that she had to delay the gratification of taking her vacation as originally scheduled.

Julianna clearly made the right choice (according to her value system). Three weeks later, she was promoted to the main weeknight anchor position— and before she left on vacation, we negotiated a wonderful new deal for her that included two extra weeks of vacation each year.

Julianna has been extraordinarily successful at achieving and fulfilling many of her dreams, primarily because she has developed healthy and constructive *Choreography* strategies. She understands when discipline is required—and when and where it is appropriate, she practices it.

Most of my clients start out in small markets and move a number of times during their careers. Many of them often work six, and occasionally seven, days a week. Some of my network correspondent clients travel more than 200 days a year. Sometimes talent who ascend to the highest rung may be less naturally talented than others, but they may well be more disciplined (and have better strategies for success). They understand and accept that they have to give up things of value now (their hometowns, leisure time, the stability of their relationships) in order to attain—at some future date—something that they perceive is of greater value (i.e., the fulfillment of their dreams).

As a teenager, when I was competing in tennis tournaments throughout the country, there would usually be an exciting event or a party to attend each night. I often had to weigh whether I would go out and enjoy the festivities or go to bed early, and thereby be physically and mentally at peak condition for the next day's match. (In reaching my decision, I always had to take into account the fact that I needed more rest than many others in order to perform at my best.) With disciplined thinking, I almost always opted to get my rest. My value system dictated that I follow this reasoning: "I have traveled throughout the country, and I have sacrificed and practiced a lot to get to this point. I now have the opportunity to win a big tournament. I have put myself in the best position possible to succeed. I must not allow myself to be destructive and blow it at the end by going to the party."

I have attained many of my goals and dreams by practicing appropriate discipline.

When I entered Harvard, I knew that I would be competing for grades with some very bright individuals. I knew that if I wanted to do well academically and play on the tennis team, I would have to be disciplined about how I allotted my time. With the help of much discipline, I graduated magna cum laude and became captain and the #1 player on the varsity tennis team. I also won national titles in two sports—tennis and Extreme Tennis.

At a later time, when I left the prestigious William Morris Agency and established my own company, I knew that I would have to be twice as good and effective on my own once I didn't have the William Morris name behind me. For the first three years of my company's existence, I worked a minimum of six days a week. I put many pleasures on hold, but my discipline yielded great rewards (according to my value system).

I fully understand that not everyone desires to be as focused as I am, and not everyone has my value system. However, one thing is certain: Appropriate use of discipline in your thinking and in your behavior can be one of your greatest allies when you are trying to attain your goals and enhance your life.

Delayed Gratification

Keeping the Ball in Play Until the Right Openings and Opportunities Are Presented: Not Always Opting for the Quick Fix

In my experience of career counseling, I all too often see people who desire to attain positive ends and grab the perceived gold ring immediately. Today we live in an MTV world of quick visual bits of stimulation, a McDonald's fast-food era. We also live in an often dysfunctional society, in which many children and adults have been raised with little consistency and little or no love. They therefore want things and relationships *now*, since experience has taught them that by tomorrow these coveted things and special individuals may be gone. As a result, many people hunger for and rely upon immediate gratification—even if the gratification in the short or long term will prove to be worthless, worth little, or unhealthy. It is this kind of indiscriminate hunger and reliance on the quick fix that is likely to lead to poor and destructive decision-making.

I cannot begin to estimate the large number of bad professional and personal choices that I have seen people make because they want an inappropriate quick fix or immediate closure to a situation.

Sometimes attaining immediate gratification is possible at no great subsequent cost. But in a great many instances, we have to patiently and proactively continue to lay a solid foundation before we can achieve our most precious goals. We have to keep hanging on, winning some battles and losing some skirmishes, or vice versa—and learning from both kinds of experiences, before we can win the war. Or, put another way, with the help of a wonderful tennis analogy: With discipline, we must "keep the ball in play" until we get the right opening or opportunity—and then go for it.

I have been involved in numerous situations that have proven that there are times in life when it is best to hang in and stay sharp long enough to learn what we truly do and do not want. During this (growth) process, values, perceptions, and information may change, and with these changes our goals may be modified and reprioritized. For example, I have represented a number of individuals who initially thought that their ultimate goal was to become a network correspondent. However, after they had a taste of anchoring a newscast or hosting a program (or saw others do it)—and discovered the perks that go along with those particular positions—their aspirations changed. Also, as people's life situations change, reporting for a network can lose its allure when you are asked to be on the road 200 days or more each year. It can be great for a single person, but it might be much less attractive if you get married and/or have a family.

The key is that we often have a much better opportunity to identify what we truly do want, and secure it, if we have carefully and correctly laid the right foundation—and this, in many instances, takes time, discipline, and the practice of delayed gratification.

There are also situations when you just have to keep going, even when there is no immediate payoff in sight. This requires the greatest discipline! It is sort of like driving a car in a dense fog or through a torrential downpour. We just have to keep a careful and steady course until there is a clearing. We have to be guided by the heartfelt belief that "if I do things right and do the right things, something good will come of it." Very frequently, this turns out to be the case.

An illustration of this highly constructive strategy occurred when my dad was retired by his former employer at the age of 66. I know that my dad, in his heart of hearts, felt that he still had a great deal more to give to an employer and that he was not at all ready to be put out to pasture. As time passed and no one rushed to offer him a job, he began to realize that he might never again work in the merchandising field. Although he never shared his true feelings with anyone, I believe that he was sad and a bit dejected by and angry with the abrupt end of the career he truly loved. Nevertheless, despite the overwhelming odds against his ever again being offered a job in his field, he diligently kept himself in top physical shape—just in case a position became available. In addition, he continued to maintain his contacts with his longtime friends in merchandising and read all of the appropriate materials to keep himself relevant. Then, at age 69, he was offered a wonderful job opportunity as a market coordinator, teacher, and negotiator for T.J. Maxx. He thereafter held that position for almost thirty years!

In this instance, disciplined thinking and preparation met opportunity, and a successful professional relationship, further self-fulfillment, and an inspiring story were the fruits. Once again, if you do things right and do the right things—i.e., have faith in yourself and develop the ability to accept and wait for delayed gratification—the ultimate results may well be quite positive. Indeed, the positive results may far exceed all expectations.

Take Abraham Lincoln, for instance. Anthony Robbins, in his book, *Unlimited Power*, lists the many defeats Lincoln suffered before he accomplished his lofty goal of becoming President. Here they are:

1. Failed in business at age 21.

2. Was defeated in a legislative race at age 22.

3. Failed again in business at age 24.

4. Overcame the death of his sweetheart at age 26.

5. Had a nervous breakdown at age 27.

6. Lost a congressional race at age 34.

7. Lost a congressional race at age 36.

8. Lost a senatorial race at age 45.

9. Failed in an effort to become Vice President at age 47.

10. Lost a senatorial race at age 49.

11. Was elected President of the United States at age 52.[22]

All broadcasting careers have small and large ups and downs. Everyone—even the most talented and celebrated broadcast individuals—has suffered some setbacks, losses, and very painful public defeats. The key is to just hang in, and calmly—yet proactively—keep your ball in play, knowing that tomorrow, next week, or next month, with constructive thinking, you can seize and enjoy a victory that will put the past in its proper, grander perspective.

Here is an example. Years ago, I received a call from a news manager regarding a very talented newscaster client of mine. The manager told me that in spite of my client's obvious talent, she didn't fit in with his station's format and presentation, and would be demoted in about two weeks to a lesser anchor role. I immediately called my client, knowing how devastated she would be.

After the initial shock and trauma wore off, sadness (about having to pick up and move yet again), anger, and fear started to set in. During the process, I assured my client that things happen for a reason despite the fact that we do not always immediately see why, and that challenges and perceived negatives can be excellent learning experiences and opportunities to seize other valuable experiences. I told her that the good news in all of this was "that when a very talented person that I represent suffers a setback, or cannot, for some reason, accept what appears to be a great opportunity, something better almost always comes along later." I continued by telling my client that she had to be positive and that I had to be intelligently and creatively proactive in making that better opportunity materialize as quickly as possible. My client was indeed fortunate, because a top station that had been looking for someone just like her still hadn't found the perfect person. Within four weeks, my client was hired for this position, which, from everyone's perspective, would unquestionably enhance her career. In fact, it has, to an extraordinary extent! My client's devastating experience, in retrospect, turned out to be the best thing that could have happened. It allowed me to market her and then to extricate her from her contract.

NEW AGE STRATA-GEM

The issue of whether it is appropriate to delay gratification, and for how long, is a matter of wisely identifying and weighing your values. There are times when it is right to immediately go for the gold and seize the moment. There are other times when keeping the ball in play—until we can produce the right opening or that opening is produced for us—and then going for it will produce a healthier, more satisfying, and more long-lasting result.

Constructive Decision-Making

Constructive Decision-Making and Solutions: The Defensive and Destructive Script of Overcompensation

The two most important problem-solving scripts that I learned while in law school were these: When faced with a problem, first try to understand the situation, and then identify the crux of the problem—or, as we used to say, "spot the (real) issue." (For example, this is a case of negligence, or this is a case of breach of contract, etc.) By performing these steps, we are then better able to find the best course of action, resolution, or proactive, enhancing solution.

One of the reasons some people make constructive career decisions and thrive while others make destructive ones and never fulfill their potential is that the former individuals are open to identifying and correcting their mistakes and non-strengths, whereas defensive individuals try to ignore, rationalize away, and cover up their perceived deficiencies. One of the most prevalent self-defeating—rather than self-enhancing—behavioral patterns that I have come across is that of "overcompensation." To illustrate the dynamics of this defense mechanism, let me depict two scenarios, which, for the most part, raise similar issues:

1. Allegedly, a local station morning-show host, who had been a network news correspondent before assuming his hosting duties, had the

following experience and reaction. One day, after he finished his show and was walking back to his office, he ran into a news anchor at his station, who sarcastically chided him, "So, how are those cooking segments going?"

Allegedly, the host became extremely upset and defensive at hearing the remark. He perceived that the intended implication was that he had forsaken his journalistic ideals. The host's on-air performance changed immediately thereafter. From that point on, his demeanor on the (light and fun) morning show became serious and sullen, and he became confrontational with his guests.*

For this and other reasons, viewership for the show slipped, and he became more of a liability than an asset. Eventually, he was replaced.

2. Allegedly, a beautiful blond woman with a wonderfully warm, effervescent, and engaging presence was offered the chance to become a host on a nationally syndicated entertainment program. At the time she was making a transition from being a fashion model and commercial actress to becoming a TV broadcaster. Because she no longer wanted to be perceived as a "lightweight," and because she wanted to be taken seriously and to be viewed as intelligent, she chose to decline the extraordinary offer. Instead, she decided to find a hard-news anchor position in a local market. After many months of being out of work and looking, she finally secured an anchor job in a small market. In trying to fulfill her quest to be taken seriously, she was so cold, stern, and icy on the air that she turned off the viewers—as well as the management of her station. She lasted about nine months before she and her station had a mutual parting of the ways.

In the scenarios outlined above, both individuals reacted by defensively overcompensating for a *felt inadequacy* that they had harbored within

---

* This morning show host had already established that he was a very good journalist during his network news correspondent days. Evidently he didn't really believe it, as he allowed himself to feel put-down and diminished by someone who was not important in the grand scheme of things.

themselves. They also proceeded to seriously derail their careers with their destructive strategies and decisions.

If these individuals had their choices to make over again, and they truly aspired to be constructive decision-makers, they could step back from the situation in which they were involved and examine their behavior from the perspective of the big picture. This could help them answer the all-important questions:

1. Why did the morning show host feel that he needed to constantly remind everyone of what a good journalist he was, despite the fact that his behavior, in many instances, was inappropriate and job-threatening?

2. What did the host, in his heart of hearts, truly want to accomplish with his decision?

3. What was the most self-enhancing way to correct and improve his situation in order to make it a win/win—or at least the most positive one possible?

4. Why did the female host choose not to take a national position for which she was incredibly well suited, and then perform in an inappropriate manner in the job that she did take?

5. What did she, in her heart of hearts, truly want to accomplish with her decisions?

6. What was the most self-enhancing way to take advantage of the national entertainment program host offer, so as to make it a win/win situation for her?

In the illustrations outlined above, the individuals needed to proactively and objectively explore what alternative scripts of behavior might have had the most constructive means of achieving their heartfelt values and desires. For example, the morning host could have requested that he do some hard-news reporting assignments in addition to his hosting duties. If this could have been done, he could then have derived the pleasure and satisfaction of being a (reporting) journalist again, and he also could have shown his detractors that he is a well-balanced newsperson as he hosted and also reported. This situation might well have provided a means for the host to feel more comfortable with having fun and being warm on a morning show that required a lighter and softer touch for ratings success.

Similarly, the female host could have requested that she cover some harder-edged entertainment stories on her network show, such as how the economic downturn is affecting film, TV, and music, along with other more serious (non-fluffy) stories. Local stations that aired her program might well have welcomed the opportunity to have her do some in-depth stories of her choosing, just to have a national host on their station. There might also have been venues, such as cable television, where she could have done some in-depth interviews, which would have showcased her intelligence as well as her interviewing and writing skills. The constructive behavior in this instance would have been for her to make the most of her high-profile national host position by seeking out supplementary avenues to fulfill her goals, while allowing others (her own program, local stations, cable networks) to reap the benefits of having her appear on their programs. This would have been a win/win/win strategy to design and act upon.

In the above scenarios, the individuals reacted so defensively by adopting the destructive script of overcompensation that they never gave themselves the opportunity to explore what their real strengths were and what constructive, self-enhancing solutions could have been created and implemented to counteract any deficiencies—real or imagined.

Overcompensation is a self-defeating script of behavior that I encounter numerous times each day.

The above individuals also needed to explore, analyze, and determine, as objectively as possible, the real agendas of those who made the derogatory or disrespectful comments to and about them. They also needed to openly explore their own reactions to the comments in order to discern why they felt the urge to react so strongly and defensively. Only then could they begin to determine, in any balanced way, what an appropriate response to those detractors might have been—or if any response, in the big picture, would have been appropriate or necessary at all. Had these two individuals openly examined the true big picture of their detractors and their relationships with them, they might have come to see that the real issue was not about what others said or did. Rather, it was all about how these two felt about themselves and how they inappropriately attempted to cover up their perceived flaws and insecurities.

Constructive Strategies and Solutions

As discussed, I believe that the key to making the most of your broadcasting career is this: When faced with a decision, do not react. Instead, calmly step back and look at the issue, problem, or challenge in the richer, broader scope of the big picture of your most dearly held values, and the impact, if any, that your decision will have on your broadcasting career in the short and long term.

My rule of thumb has been:

> When I react, without thinking clearly,
> All too often, I pay dearly.
> So, no matter how intense the pressure, or how loud the noise,
> I'll step back and see things clearly, and never lose my poise.

Once you identify what your true and most cherished values and goals are, openly and objectively figure out a creative and constructive way to attain them. Individuals who achieve cherished and sustained successes in broadcasting often identify or create healthy and constructive means of reaching enhancing decisions and finding win/win solutions.

As an illustration of this process, I would like to refer back to my client Julianna, who was faced with the decision as to whether she would forgo her much-awaited and extensively planned vacation with her husband so that she could fill in as anchor for the individual whose position she desired to secure. Let's examine her decision-making processes in more detail.

Once Julianna identified that a decision needed to be made and she clearly stated to herself what the issues before her were, she engaged in the following constructive thought processes to help her reach a decision that we both believe ultimately led to her attaining the anchor position that she coveted.

1. First, when Julianna's news director asked her to postpone her vacation just five days before her scheduled departure, she listened, but didn't react. When she did respond, she was wise to not only carefully explain her predicament to him, but to also say that she wanted to be a team player and that she would do everything possible to try to help him and the station out.

This was truly constructive thinking and decision-making. Julianna chose her responses carefully and effectively. She made sure that her news manager was aware of all the plans—both hers and her husband's—that had already been made regarding their vacation, so in case she couldn't or wouldn't change her vacation, he might better understand why. And if she did rearrange her trip, he would hopefully better appreciate all that she had done.

She consciously expressed her sentiments about wanting to be a team player, and reiterated that she would do everything she could to try to work things out, as she knew that in the past, other anchors hadn't been team players and that the news manager had resented it. I often recommend the script of, "You catch more flies with honey than with vinegar." In this case, in spite of the fact that my client felt that a great deal of pressure was being exerted on her to postpone her vacation, she didn't react negatively. Instead, she used a warm, constructive response that she knew her news manager would respect and respond to positively. She thus seized the opportunity to bring him philosophically and emotionally closer to her.

Finally, she told her manager that she would need some time to see what she could do about rearranging her vacation. This period of time would give her the opportunity to think things through, with the aim that she would ultimately make her very best decision under the circumstances.

2. The next thing that Julianna did was to step away from the situation, first by herself and then with me. She looked at her decision in the context of the big picture of her broadcasting career, her relationship with her husband and what his wants and needs were, and the state of her overall mental and physical health. Upon viewing the big picture, she assessed that doing all that she could to secure the main anchor position, at a strong station, in a city that she desired to make her long-term home, was a top priority. And although she was both disappointed that she couldn't take her vacation and irked that her news manager had waited until the last minute to make his request, she determined that

she was not so mentally or physically tired that her health would be at risk if she were to delay her vacation for a month or so. And after consulting with her (understanding and supportive) husband, she learned that he would be okay with postponing their time off. He loved his wife, encouraged her professionally, and knew and appreciated the great value that getting the weeknight anchor position had for her.

After examining the big picture, Julianna realized that this was a time to delay the gratification of taking her vacation now. She would be disciplined and sacrifice her vacation—for the time being—in hopes of getting a bigger payoff later.

3. Julianna also objectively and correctly assessed her competition (Cindy) for the weeknight anchor position. She acknowledged that Cindy was in fact talented, and if she were given the opportunity to fill in for the two weeks, she might well become a much more serious threat to secure the weeknight job when it became available.

4. My client also took the time to assess the various agendas of the individuals who were involved in her decision. Although she knew that her husband was looking forward to their vacation and had taken pains to clear his very demanding professional schedule, she also knew that he truly appreciated what was at stake for her and that he would be supportive if the vacation was postponed. Julianna sensed that her news manager was behind her, and that if he wanted her to postpone her vacation and fill in, he must have had a good reason.[**] She also knew that Cindy wanted nothing more than to fill in for the two weeks and leapfrog Julianna in order to land the weeknight job.

5. Julianna knew that she had gotten off to a good start at the station by immediately being pegged as the #2 anchor there. By temporarily forgoing her vacation and not giving Cindy the opportunity to fill in,

---

[**] We later found out that the news manager knew that the weeknight anchor would be leaving the station in about a month. By having Julianna fill in for those two weeks, he could be sure that the new general manager (his boss) would watch Julianna in the main anchor role. He hoped that the GM would subsequently approve her as the main anchor's permanent replacement.

she would, in all likelihood, at a minimum, maintain that position. This could greatly increase her chances of being named the #1 female anchor if and when the position became available.

6. Julianna realized that in order to attain her dreams, from time to time she would have to be flexible and adopt a soft-hands approach. In this instance, she was disappointed and a bit angry that her plans had to be changed, but she also knew that she needed to have a positive—or at least an accepting—mind-set if she indeed did change her plans. She didn't want any of her feelings of disappointment or anger to show on the air, because if they were evident, then rearranging her vacation to fill in would turn out to be counterproductive. In essence, if she performed poorly, she could set herself back. We both agreed that "if you are going to do something positive (i.e., sacrifice your vacation), the intended recipients—in this case, Julianna's new management and her audience—need to enjoy it. Otherwise, the excellent effort that you make can mean nothing, or can even work against you."

7. Julianna recognized that winning the battle of being able to take her vacation as scheduled—because she was able to get her news manager to (somewhat reluctantly) understand her predicament—would be no victory at all if she lost the war, meaning that Cindy had done such a good job of filling in that Cindy was given the weeknight position.

   Julianna carefully examined the (relative and sometimes illusory) concept of short-term winning by weighing her values and goals in the insightful context of the big picture.

8. Julianna continued to look at her decision through the grander perspective of the big picture in order to see if there were any alternative ways of approaching the situation that she hadn't yet thought of or explored. She asked if there was any constructive way to take her vacation as planned and still keep herself in the best position possible to later secure the main anchor job. Was there a win/win solution here? We came up with one possible alternative. I would call her news manager and ask that his station consider not only committing to Julianna becoming the main weeknight anchor upon the incumbent's departure,

but also negotiating a new, more lucrative agreement reflecting this promotion *before* Julianna's vacation. The news manager responded that had the previous general manager still been running the station, our proposal might well have been accepted; but with a new general manager in place, he was not ready to make any commitments of that magnitude.

With this information in hand, Julianna and I agreed that there was no satisfactory alternative available.

9. Julianna then applied a strategy that had produced positive results for her in the past. That script was: "Like a fullback in football, when you see a hole (an opening), run like heck for the daylight and keep running until you score (the touchdown)." The translation: "If you have an opportunity to proactively seize your goal, do it!" Julianna was appropriately confident about her anchoring skills. As a result, she felt strongly that if she filled in for the two weeks, she would significantly enhance her chances of getting the weeknight position permanently.

10. After going through this extensive study of the situation, as we know, Julianna decided to postpone her vacation.

11. She then engaged in some creative decision-making. She and I decided that along with Julianna telling the news manager that she would change her plans, I would ask the station to reimburse any expenses that she and her husband incurred by changing their reservations, and I would also ask the station to commit to two specific weeks, plus some other holidays off, for her later that year. The news manager happily agreed to all of our requests. I also reiterated to him that Julianna was truly a team player, and that I hoped that her team spirit would be taken into account when her station managers were deciding who should become their next weeknight anchor. He said that her professionalism would serve her well.

Julianna's talents and professionalism did, in fact, serve her well. Three weeks later, she was named the weeknight anchor of her station. Great decision-making, Julianna!

NEW AGE STRATA-GEM

When faced with problems and issues to solve, step back and see the situation in the enlightening context of the big picture. Then proactively and creatively design a constructive *Choreography* for achieving the best possible short-term and long-term outcomes.

Stay Constructive and Make the Very Most of the Cards You Are Dealt

It is an invaluable success-evoking asset to perceive unexpected events, challenges, and/or obstacles as golden opportunities to make something highly beneficial happen. We all know the cliché: When life hands you lemons, make lemonade. Let me give you two illustrations of this process, showing what being constructive is and how it can positively affect what appears to be a disastrous turn of events.

"Bill" is an exceedingly talented anchor and reporter who, like many other of my clients, moved from market to market, learning, growing, enhancing his skills and experiences, and increasing his salary. One of the downsides to living this nomadic lifestyle is that it can be upsetting and unsettling to spouses and children who have to pull up roots and leave friends and cherished relationships whenever another market move needs to be made.

After enduring a number of moves, Bill was given the position of main weeknight anchor at a top-30 television station. According to Bill, this was the first time in his career and in his marriage that everyone in his family was happy. Bill loved his job, and his family very much enjoyed where they were living. All was blissful—until Bill's news manager was fired and "Ted" replaced him. Soon after Ted took over, he called to tell me that he was "sorry," but at the end of the week, Bill would be taken off his weeknight evening anchor shift and demoted to anchoring the weekday morning newscasts. To make matters worse, in two months, when Bill's contract cycle ended, his pay would be cut by 50 percent. The final blow was that at some undetermined point in the future, Bill would be relieved of his anchoring duties altogether.

For Bill, this would be a huge career blow, an economic blow, a confidence blow, and a very public humiliation. So before calling Bill, I needed to gather my big picture thoughts about how we could both make this turn of events as constructive a situation as possible.

I then called Bill to tell him the seemingly horrible news. As expected, he was devastated both for himself and for his family. I tried to console him by explaining that in my years of experience, I have gleaned that things do happen for a reason, but we do not always immediately see what that reason is. The crucial thing for him to do was to remain constructive during this most trying and demoralizing time.

After a moment or two of thought, Bill replied, "But what does being constructive mean in my case?" Having been anticipatory and prepared, (two extremely effective success-evoking *Strategies*), I had given considerable thought to this issue before I called Bill. As a result, I was quick and confident in my response: "Bill, the three things that you can do now are:

1. Remain professional, take the high road, and act as if nothing's happened. No pity parties here. Remember, no one can hurt you, unless you let them!

2. Anchor the next three weeknight newscasts with passion and purpose! In fact, be the very best that you can be—show [station management] that they are making a huge mistake.

3. Come Monday, you will be anchoring the morning newscasts. Let's look at the positive component of this new assignment. The [morning] newscasts will allow you to show much more of your warm personality, your great sense of humor, your ability to ad-lib, and your ability to conduct great interviews. I look at this as an *amazing opportunity* to let potential employers see sides of you that my weeknight anchoring demo tape could never show, because the evening newscasts that you've been anchoring and we've been using are so serious and tightly scripted!

Bill, being assigned to anchor mornings is a brand-spanking-new, fresh canvas for you to paint on. Do your best to decompress over the weekend. Take your family out to a great dinner. My treat! And then come in Monday morning, show 'em your stuff, and make each morning a masterpiece painting. Go get 'em, Rembrandt!'"

As best as he could, Bill understood that anchoring mornings would give him an opportunity to show much more of his likable personality. He agreed to do his best, although he was profoundly hurt and growing angrier by the minute with the apparent snap decision made by his new manager.

Starting the following Monday, Bill did show his stuff. Many station managers were surprised by how Bill "lit it up" in the mornings. Within two weeks, Ted called to say that he was seriously rethinking his decision to take Bill off mornings. "Terrific!" I thought. "Bill has won over his harshest critic. Go Bill!"

Then about a week later, the general manager of a top-five-market station happened to be visiting the city in which Bill was working and watched Bill anchor all week. He said that in all the years that I had been sending Bill's demo tapes to him, he had never seen the charismatic and warm personality that I told him Bill had. (Bill could never show it in the stiff and content-filled evening newscasts, which had, up until that time, comprised his demo tape.)

The GM continued by telling me that he was convinced that Bill would make a great anchor for his weeknight 5 p.m. newscast and asked if Bill was contractually available. I told the GM that Bill's change of anchor assignments triggered an escape clause in his contract. Therefore, he could accept an offer if the deal made sense.

The offer that the general manager tendered the next day was almost too good to be true. Bill accepted it—because it was a great career step for him; because his wife's family lived in the city that they were moving to, so she was happy; and because the offer was from a station, in a city, that he could envision himself working at and living in, respectively, for the rest of his career. So his children wouldn't have to be uprooted again.

The moral of this happy-ending story is that life can throw you curves, and as a result the most well-conceived *Choreographies* will have to be altered. The keys to securing a positive and successful outcome are:

1. Committing yourself, even when you are disheartened, to being as constructive as possible under any and all circumstances;

2. Things in life often happen for a reason. Go constructively with the flow and stay calm; this way, you can make your most career-enhancing moves without your decisions being clouded by potentially destructive emotions.

SECTION IV

Career Choreography™

THERE IS A LOGICAL, SUCCESS-EVOKING
CHOREOGRAPHY
FOR ACCOMPLISHING ALL CAREER GOALS.
THE KEY IS TO CONSTRUCT AND
IMPLEMENT THE MOST EFFECTIVE SET
OF STEPS AND STRATEGIES *IN ORDER TO*
ATTAIN YOUR GOALS.

As we have discussed, my primary means of developing careers is through *Career Choreography*™. I define this process as that certain, well-conceived, logical set of strategic steps that, when effectively implemented, will materially increase your chances to accomplish a career goal. In this section, we will examine various forms and aspects of *Career Choreography*™ through the use of diverse examples and some high-profile cases.

In connection with the upcoming *Choreography* case studies, please be aware that all of the steps that we will discuss were thoughtfully calculated and consciously taken so as to put the percentages heavily in the *Choreographer's* favor that he or she will achieve the desired career goals.

Think of this as the 5 C's of *Choreography*:

1. Thoughtfully Consider and creatively Calculate your steps, and

2. Consciously Construct your *Choreography* and implement your steps,

3. So that you do your very best to Control your goal-attainment destiny.

By way of illustration, let's study two broadcasting *Career Choreographies*™— those of Nancy O'Dell and Matt Lauer. Most television newscasters begin their careers in very small cities or markets, where they are paid very little and very little in the way of experience and polish is expected of them. It is at these jobs that young on-air individuals can make their beginners' mistakes and learn, develop, and grow. Ideally such positions provide opportunities to write, gather information, shoot, edit, produce, and develop the skills of effectively reporting both taped (pre-recorded) pieces and "live" pieces. All of these skills form an invaluable foundation for future jobs in larger and more challenging markets.

Many of the steps and strategies that Nancy and Matt implemented have been discussed earlier in this book. Now it's time to see them in action. Please do your best to absorb them. Be a sponge!

The *Soft Choreography* and the Soft-Concurrent *Choreography*

The *Soft Choreography* is a set of steps that will lay the foundation for you to choose, at a later time, in what direction you want your career to go. In essence, this type of *Choreography* is appropriate for individuals who desire to get the requisite training and experience to pursue *two or more* potential career options, and at some point in the future, when they identify where their real passions lie, they can then make an informed career choice and already have the requisite career training. Essentially, what these steps enable you to be is *pluripotent*; that is, someone with many potentials.

For example, a number of individuals whom I know started out as business-affairs attorneys for major theatrical agencies. Many of them weren't sure whether they ultimately wanted to be a career entertainment attorney or, after spending a few years being trained in entertainment-agency contract law, to pursue being a theatrical agent. Having a thorough entertainment-law background equipped them to do both.

In my case, I eventually chose the agent route. Others stayed as business-affairs attorneys at their agencies or joined private law firms. This initial path of studying and practicing entertainment law yielded different results for different people, with one thing in common: Through choosing to implement a *Soft Choreography*, we were able to keep our career options open until we were able and ready to identify which career course most personally suited our unique skill sets, values, and passions.

Interestingly, one of my associates took his *Soft Choreography* an additional couple of steps. After working as a business-affairs attorney for three years, he became a motion-picture agent. However, he was not certain that being a film agent was his ultimate calling. He wondered, "Maybe being a major motion-picture producer is." As a result, he thoroughly learned the motion-picture business through representing feature-film writers, producers, and directors.

Once again, through a series of calculated *Soft Choreography* steps, he thoroughly learned his business and made the requisite contacts. About five years later, with a wonderful future awaiting him in connection with whichever of the two courses he chose, he decided to become a film producer. Because he thoroughly knew his business, and had a gift for identifying commercial and compelling film properties, he grew to enjoy huge success in the film-production world. You have, in all likelihood, watched and enjoyed a number of the blockbuster films that he has produced.

The Nancy O'Dell
Soft-Concurrent Choreography

I found Nancy O'Dell, who has hosted *Access Hollywood* and currently hosts *Entertainment Tonight*, when she was a morning anchor and investigative reporter in Charleston, South Carolina.* From the moment that I first saw Nancy's work, and thereafter met her, I knew that she had the communication skills, the intellectual and emotional intelligence, the drive, and the look to enjoy an extraordinary on-air career. She had "it."

Upon speaking with Nancy, I gleaned that one day she would love to host a national entertainment program, such as *Entertainment Tonight*—which at the time was the only major entertainment show of its kind. She was interested in hosting a national news show, such as *Today*, as well. As a result, we structured a *Soft-Concurrent Choreography* so that Nancy could eventually host national shows in *either* entertainment or news. Our *Choreography* would call for her to lay a solid foundation in both entertainment and hard news, so as to leave both options wide open for the future.

There is an important distinction to be made here between the *Soft Choreography* of the business-affairs attorneys mentioned earlier and Nancy's *Soft-Concurrent Choreography*. In the case of the attorneys, there was one *Choreography* used to train and prepare them to be business-affairs attorneys, talent agents, or private-practice attorneys. That single *Choreography*, which consisted of entertainment legal training and related experiences, allowed these individuals to choose—and at some later point successfully pursue—any of the aforementioned careers.

---

* I secured for Nancy her position at *Access Hollywood*, but not her position at *Entertainment Tonight*.

In Nancy's case, she pursued *Choreographies* in both hard news and entertainment news, at the same time, in order to leave her options wide open to pursue—at some future point—a career in either hard news or entertainment news.

Same result—but two different forms of the same flexible *Choreography*. Okay, let's continue with Nancy's story.

When I began to send out demo tapes of Nancy's Charleston work, we received interest from various local news stations across the country, as well as from the E! Entertainment Network—which wanted Nancy to host one of its entertainment-news shows. Receiving interest from a prestigious—but relatively new—national cable network such as E! was very alluring, and for some, would have been intoxicating.

As we did with all potential employment opportunities, Nancy and I discussed the pros and cons of working for E! at such an early stage in her career. My counsel was for her to forgo the E! opportunity, because I firmly felt that it was the wrong step in her particular *Choreography*. I believed that no matter whether Nancy aspired to host a national entertainment show or anchor a news program, she needed to work for at least one more local station, in a top news market, in order to continue to develop and hone her live reporting and interviewing skills. I also believed that there were two major drawbacks with the show that E! was proposing that Nancy host. First, it was "taped," so there would be no "live" reporting, hosting, or interviewing experiences from which Nancy could continue to grow. Second, if she hosted an entertainment show for E!, she would have lost the major-market local news experience that a national news program such as the *Today* show would require. Therefore, it was way too early in Nancy's budding career for her to put all her career eggs in the taped-entertainment television basket.

Nancy agreed with my *Career Choreography*™ perspective. She practiced appropriate discipline and delayed the immediate gratification of accepting the position at E! Instead, she went to the NBC-owned station in Miami, Florida (a wonderful news market), where she distinguished herself as both an evening anchor and a live reporter.

As time passed, Nancy's career path became more clearly defined: She was moving psychologically and emotionally toward hosting a national entertainment show. Therefore, the next steps in her *Choreography* were to get her some entertainment/pop-culture reporting assignments at WTVJ with which to market her, and then move her out of news and into the entertainment arena. Soon thereafter, we found the right entertainment opportunity. Nancy joined FOX as a national entertainment reporter—a move that we both felt would bring her a step closer to a career *Gold Ring Dream*. About a year or so later, NBC and FOX teamed up to start *Access Hollywood*, which would be a national, five-days-a-week entertainment-news show. As soon as the *Access* announcement was made, Nancy and I both knew that the absolute right next step in her *Choreography* was for her to become the weekend host of *Access*. (My client Giselle Fernandez, who was part of the show from its inception, had already been named as its weekday host, along with my client Larry Mendte.)

Having successfully worked for both NBC and FOX, Nancy seemed like a natural to be hired as the *Access Hollywood* weekend host. And amazingly, we were soon told that a prerequisite for seeking an on-air position at *Access* was having a major-market live-news or sports-anchoring and reporting background! Nancy's decision to decline the job at E! and instead go to Miami as a local news anchor/reporter allowed her to become an irresistibly compelling candidate for *Access*. And once NBC and FOX got *Access* off the drawing board, Nancy was hired as its weekend host. Two years later, Giselle left her weekday *Access* hosting position. Because Nancy had effectively and consistently executed the next step in her *Choreography*, which was to work tirelessly to be the most compelling and visible member of *Access* possible, she was the logical and natural choice to succeed Giselle as the weekday host. And she did.

Today, Nancy enjoys tremendous success and fulfillment as cohost of the legendary show *ET*—which is her true *Gold Ring Dream*. The reason why Nancy's career continues to blossom in such wonderful ways is because she is such a comfortable, engaging, and compelling communicator. The reason why she has twice been in the position to secure her dream positions of hosting national entertainment shows, which showcase her gifts and talents so well, is because she was intelligent enough to see that there were logical and constructive sets of steps that would put the percentages heavily in her favor and lead her to live her dream. And she effectively implemented those steps.

A More In-Depth Examination of the Nancy O'Dell *Soft-Concurrent Choreography*

Below is a review of Nancy's *Choreography* so that you can study, emulate, and take the very logical, constructive, and self-enhancing steps that she took to achieve her dream positions of hosting *Access Hollywood* and *ET*.

1. *Identify big picture Goals*: Nancy identified her two diverse big picture goals—hosting either a national entertainment show or a national morning news program.

2. *Construct the Choreography*: We constructed a *Soft-Concurrent Choreography* that enabled Nancy to develop a broad-based foundation, so that she would one day have the *option* of pursuing either of her goals.

3. *Explore Opportunities*: We explored the positions that might be right for Nancy, so that we could make an informed decision as to the most enhancing and foundation-building job for her at that point in her career.

4. *Use Appropriate Discipline and Delayed Gratification*: Upon securing an alluring offer from the E! Entertainment Network, Nancy had to decide whether this was the most constructive and appropriate career step for her to take so as to maximize her chances of attaining either of her big picture goals. Because the E! offer didn't include "live" anchoring, interviewing, and reporting, she recognized that accepting this offer, at this particular time in her career, wouldn't be a constructive career step; in fact, it might well be counterproductive. As a result, she decided that the appropriate career step, in this instance, was to be disciplined and to delay gratification; therefore, she declined the offer to host a national entertainment show.

5. *Identify What Skills Need to Be Developed and Honed*: This step required that Nancy make an honest and objective assessment as to what skills she needed to develop and/or hone, so that she would become a strong candidate to host any of the national programs that would fulfill her dreams.

6. *Choose a Position That Will Help You to Develop the Required Skills and Have the Necessary Experiences So That You Put the Percentages Heavily in Your Favor That You Will Achieve Your Big Picture Goals and* Gold Ring Dreams: In this case, Nancy chose an anchoring and reporting position in Miami, a great hard-news and entertainment-news market. As a result, she would have the opportunity to hone her live anchoring and reporting skills on a daily basis. Also, by working for NBC, she became part of a company that produced a number of programs that she might one day host, such as the *Today* show and *Weekend Today*.

7. *Take the Time to Continue to Monitor Your Values and Goals—The Importance of "Recognition"*: As Nancy continued to anchor and report in Miami, she recognized that although she loved doing *both* hard and entertainment news, her focus during this time in her career was veering toward entertainment news. This recognition was important, as it helped us to select and construct a more defined *Choreography*.

8. *Accept Positions That Will Move You Closer to Your Ultimate Goal*: By accepting the FOX entertainment-reporter position, Nancy not only moved herself into the entertainment arena on a national stage, but by working for FOX, she once again aligned herself with an employer that produced a number of national shows that she might one day want to host.

9. *When a Dream Job Appears—and You Are Ready for It—Go for It!*: When we received word that NBC and FOX were creating a national entertainment show and were looking for a female weekend anchor, Nancy and I jumped on it.

10. *When You Have Taken a Constructive and Self-Enhancing Step, Understand Why It Was Positive, and Cerebrally and Emotionally Celebrate It*: When we applied for the *Access Hollywood* hosting job, we learned that a prerequisite for being a candidate for that position was having major market, live, hard-news experience. At that point, I made sure that Nancy recognized that she had made a very constructive career step by forgoing the E! offer and instead opting to pursue hard news in Miami. One big reason for acknowledging and celebrating steps well

conceived and effectively implemented is that the positive reinforcement leads to enhancing and empowering psychological and emotional feelings. These feelings, in turn, will likely motivate you to choose to be disciplined and to delay gratification in the future, because you have previously experienced the sweet rewards that being disciplined in the appropriate circumstances can bring.

11. *If You Are Fortunate Enough to Be Offered a Career-Enhancing Position—Take It!*: This step was a no-brainer for Nancy. I understand and often deal with people's fear of failure and fear of success. But whatever your fears, do not be self-sabotaging! Take the constructive step of accepting a career-enhancing job when it is offered.

12. *Be the Best Employee You Are Capable of Being*: Nancy next made the self-enhancing career step of being one of the best and hardest-working *Access Hollywood* employees possible. This encouraged the executives at *Access* to want to assign Nancy to more high-profile interviews, as she did her best to become their go-to host.

13. *Do Your Best to Continue to Grow Once You Are in Your Position*: Once Nancy established herself on *Access*, she did her best to host prestigious and enhancing outside projects, such as network specials, so that she could raise her national visibility and thereby become more valuable to *Access*.

14. *Put the Percentages in Your Favor, So That If a Coveted Position Becomes Available, You Are the Natural, Logical, and Compelling Choice to Get It*: By taking so many constructive steps during her first year at *Access*, Nancy put herself in the perfect position to succeed Giselle Fernandez as the *Access* weeknight host.

15. *When You Attain a Career-Enhancing/Making Position, Stay Focused, Remain Hungry, and Keep Growing*: Upon ascending to the position as the main host of *Access*, Nancy did everything possible to continue to grow and be *Access's* go-to person. As a result, when Nancy's co-anchor, Pat O'Brien, left *Access*, she was rewarded with a very lucrative and enhancing new, long-term agreement to be the senior host of *Access*.

The *Soft-Choreography* Summation

The steps that constitute a *Soft Choreography* are designed to:

1. Equip you with training, experience, knowledge, and honed instincts.

2. Give you the flexibility to choose which *of a number of career options* is most personally suitable for and attractive to you.

How sweet is that?

The *Hard Choreography*

The *Hard Choreography* is to be utilized by individuals who know exactly what they want. In essence, you take "dead aim" at the *Gold Ring Dream* that you want to achieve and then devise the steps that will give you the experience, the training, the knowledge, and the honed instincts, etc., to attain your goal. For instance, if you know that your goal is to be a network correspondent, a prime-time or national morning show host, or a weeknight anchor or reporter in a specific market, you can then devise a uniquely personal and effective *Hard Choreography* that will put the percentages heavily in your favor that you will secure what you want. Whereas the *Soft Choreography* is flexible and designed to allow you to leave your career options open, the *Hard Choreography* is singularly focused on achieving a specific goal or set of goals.

For example, individuals who want to be dancers, gymnasts, ice skaters, or the most accomplished painters, writers, or sculptors often are "singularly focused" on achieving greatness in their identified arena—to the exclusion of allowing themselves to take advantage of other varied, non-related activities. They know what they want. They can see it, and they hunger for it. For these individuals in particular, the right personally appropriate *Hard Choreography* may well help them to achieve their *Gold Ring Dreams*.

However, it is always important to keep at the forefront of your mind that during the course of implementing any *Hard Choreography*, you can, at any point, change your mind about or modify your originally conceived steps in order to make them more effective. Therefore, even with a *Hard Choreography*, there is always room for flexibility and change. The reason that we refer to this form of *Choreography* as "hard," is because the goal or end that you aspire to attain has been set in stone—but not necessarily the means, which is your *Choreography*.

The Matt Lauer
Hard Choreography

Prior to my representing Matt, my perception of his career was that he was beating out all of my clients for jobs that were incorrect jobs for *him*. My thought process was that a great deal of Matt's early work was on tape—which can be shot over and over again until it is perfect. But the problem with perfect is that it's often plastic—or not real. And one of the things that makes Matt so exceptional is that he is great "live," because he is exceedingly bright, real, spontaneous, funny, quick-witted, and an intuitive, respectful listener. So the taped and tightly scripted positions that he had been taking didn't play to or showcase his strengths.

But then, one fortunate day (certainly for me), I saw Matt conduct an outstanding live interview on *9 Broadcast Plaza* for WWOR-TV, and I immediately called him about my becoming his representative. The next day I flew to New York and we met. At our lunch, I asked Matt, "What would make your heart sing?" After joking that he would like to be employed for longer than thirteen weeks, he shared his real, heartfelt answer: "I'd like to host the *Today* show or be Larry King." To my mind, these were attainable—although lofty—*Gold Ring Dreams*, because they essentially entailed live interviewing, which was one of Matt's great strengths.

As I spoke a bit more with Matt, I realized that his true *Gold Ring Dream* position was to host *Today*, which he had grown up watching. Okay, we had our one, clearly defined *Gold Ring Dream*.

The next step was to construct the most effective *Hard Choreography* possible. Part and parcel of doing this was to examine some of the skills and experiences that hosting a show such as *Today* required. In my mind, I listed the following:

A hard-news background;

2. The ability to synthesize and analyze information and/or breaking news quickly;

3. Extensive live interviewing in both hard-news and lighter-news (i.e., "pop culture") contexts;

4. The "gravitas" and credibility to host *Today* when a major hard-news story is breaking;

5. The ability to be comfortable and to have fun with doing light interviews and segments; and

6. The ability to think quickly and effectively on one's feet.

The aim of this list was to identify what skills Matt needed to develop and polish so that he would be ready for the *Today* show host job if and when an opening there occurred. Unquestionably, our next steps were to develop his hard-news skills and credentials, and then to identify which jobs would most efficaciously help him to develop those skills and the required news experience and persona. I then told Matt that the optimal opportunity would be for him to one day anchor a news program such as WNBC's *Live at Five*, where he would anchor the news and conduct daily hard- and light-news interviews.

The next step was to market Matt to various news stations. After some time, Matt was fortunate enough to be offered the Monday through Friday anchor position on WNBC's morning news show. This venue was perfect for Matt, because it allowed him to showcase his wonderful personality and quick wit, as well as to develop his hard-news skills and persona.

Within weeks thereafter, WNBC launched a weekend morning news show. Because Matt was such an out-of-the-gate hit on weekday mornings, WNBC management asked Matt if he would, "for the time being," work seven days a week, hosting the weekday and weekend morning newscasts.

Matt and I both agreed that the next step was for him to accept this position, as the weekends were even lighter and softer than the weekdays and would therefore play to and showcase Matt's strengths even more. In essence, mornings on WNBC would be "all Matt, all the time." It would be great exposure for someone who aspired to be a network morning show host.

Eventually, Matt was (mercifully) relieved of anchoring the weekends, so that he could focus on his weekday morning duties. However, about a year or so later, another WNBC position came his way. There was an opening to co-anchor the *Live at Five* newscast with the legendary Sue Simmons. As I had counseled Matt years earlier, this was the perfect developmental position for him, as this newscast combined daily interviewing with anchoring the news of the day.

The problem was that WNBC was enjoying such great success with Matt anchoring weekday mornings that they were totally against taking him off that show. So WNBC's solution was for Matt to work a grueling split shift: anchor the 5 a.m. to 7 a.m. newscast each morning, and then come back each afternoon to anchor the 5 p.m. to 6 p.m. newscast—and be thoroughly prepared for both shows!

Matt and I both knew that the absolute right next step in developing his hard-news credentials and image was to anchor *Live at Five*. However, Matt also realized that he didn't want to leave his weekday morning anchoring position because that was where he wanted to end up nationally. So, the only truly constructive step to take was to accept WNBC's offer and anchor both the morning and the afternoon newscasts.

As time passed, Matt became more and more successful. We both agreed that the next step was for me to convince the NBC News management that they should give Matt a chance to fill in for Bryant Gumbel as a host of *Today* when Bryant was off. As some members of NBC management, at that time, perceived Matt as a handsome host without the requisite hard-news "chops" or experience, they denied my initial fill-in requests. So I decided to spend some very concentrated time with Don Browne, the exceedingly evolved, insightful, and well-respected executive vice president of NBC News, at his weekend home in Miami in order to persuade him to have NBC News rethink its perception of Matt. Fortunately (for everyone), by the end of the weekend, NBC News did change its position, and Matt was given the chance to fill in as host of *Today*. His debut was a home run. Soon thereafter, he became the de facto fill-in host for Bryant. And as Matt continued to fill in, his popularity on *Today* grew exponentially—so much so that he soon thereafter was offered the newsreader job on *Today*. Obviously, being a regular on *Today* was the clear and logical next career step for Matt. However, there was one hitch: Matt was still under contract to WNBC and they needed him too. The exhausting solution: Matt would anchor the early mornings at WNBC, run over to the *Today* show and be the newsreader for two hours there, and later anchor *Live at Five*. Because Matt knew that he needed to become part of the *Today* show family if he was going to put the percentages heavily in his favor that he would fulfill his *Today* show dream, he worked all three jobs.

Then NBC management came to Matt one day and told him that they were going to launch *Access Hollywood* and would like him to host it with Giselle Fernandez. They said that *Access* would be on five nights a week throughout the country, Matt would receive tremendous exposure, and he would earn two to three times what he was making as the newsreader on *Today*. The glaring problem was that Matt would have to leave *Today* (*Access* was taped in Los Angeles, *Today* was produced live in New York), and he would lose all the news credibility that he had gained. A *Choreography* crossroads?

Not really. Matt, who is one of the very brightest and emotionally intelligent individuals I have ever met, was able to be disciplined, as he delayed the immediate gratification of hosting his own national show and possibly tripling his salary. He also stayed true to his original game plan and his *Gold Ring Dream* of hosting a national morning news show. As a result, he graciously declined NBC's offer.

As time went on, Matt's popularity as Bryant's fill-in anchor skyrocketed. And although I have no proof of this, I believe that NBC researched whether Bryant or Matt, in the long term, would be the best host for *Today*. My gut tells me that the research confirmed that even though Bryant was one of the very best interviewers in the business, and *Today* was number one in the ratings, the show would improve with the warmer and more likable Matt as its host. Which is why I received a phone call from a top NBC News executive inquiring as to whether Matt would be prepared to enter into secret negotiations for Bryant's position. The thought behind the call was that if the executive could successfully negotiate a deal for Matt to succeed Bryant, that executive would somehow find a way to not successfully negotiate a new deal with Bryant— knowing that he had Matt waiting in the wings, all signed up and ready to take Bryant's job.

The conundrum was that Bryant was Matt's best friend, and Matt has extraordinarily high character and strong loyalty. To Matt's great credit, he would have no part in undermining his friend, Bryant, even if it meant that Matt had to forgo securing his *Gold Ring Dream* job—being the host of *Today*. What would have been a huge *Choreography* collusion turned out to be a non-issue. Matt instructed me to say, "Thanks, but no thanks!" Matt wouldn't enter into any discussions—much less negotiations—regarding *Today* until Bryant himself chose to leave.

A few months later, Bryant did choose to leave, and Matt ascended to his *Gold Ring Dream* position—the host of *Today*. And one of the reasons why Bryant's passing of the baton to Matt went so positively and seamlessly—when compared with Deborah Norville's replacing Jane Pauley, which was not at all well *Choreographed*—was that *Today* viewers correctly perceived that the gracious and talented Bryant wanted the best for Matt, and vice versa. Audiences are very perceptive!

This *Choreography* couldn't have worked out better for Matt, who is an extraordinary person, friend, and communicator.

A More In-Depth Examination of the Matt Lauer *Hard Choreography*

1. *Even Though You Have Suffered Heartbreaking Disappointments and Defeats, or You Feel That You Are in a Life Slump, Don't Lose Sight of or Give Up on Your Most Cherished Goals and Dreams*: Even though Matt had suffered defeats along the way, when I met with him, he was still able to identify his *Gold Ring Dream* of hosting the *Today* show and believe that he could one day attain it. In essence: "You must believe it, so that you can achieve it."

2. *Identify Your* Gold Ring Dream: Matt identified hosting *Today* as his *Gold Ring Dream*.

3. *Identify the Skills and Experiences That You Need in Order to Put Yourself in the Strongest Position to Attain Your Goal(s)*: We recognized that Matt needed to develop his live hard-news skills and persona.

4. *Construct a Choreography That Will Help You to Attain the Skills and Experiences You Need So That You Put the Percentages Heavily in Your Favor That You Will Achieve Your Goal(s)*: Matt and I did this. He then secured a position at a local news station that called for him to anchor and conduct daily, live newsmaker interviews. This was the optimal next step.

5. *Embrace Opportunities That Will Enable You to Grow and Will Equip You with the Experiences That You Need—Even If They Require More on Your Part*: Matt did this when he was called upon by WNBC to anchor both the weekday and the weekend morning newscasts.

6. *Seize Opportunities That Will Allow You to Showcase Your Talents*: Knowing that the WNBC weekend morning newscasts would showcase his interviewing skills, as well as his engaging personality, Matt worked seven days a week so that he could also anchor WNBC's weekend morning newscasts.

7. *Be a Great Employee So That Your Employer Will Want to Reward You*: Throughout the time that I have known Matt, he has not only been exceptionally diligent and hardworking, but he has always been warm and gracious to everyone he works for, everyone he works with, and everyone he meets. Employers and others want to do good things for Matt because he is great at what he does, and people really like him. As a result, when WNBC's *Live at Five* newscast needed a new male anchor, WNBC management was thrilled to offer the position to Matt.

8. *Don't Hesitate to Work Extra-Hard When the Opportunity Can Bring You Extra-Great Rewards*: Matt was asked to do this in three separate instances by WNBC. First, he was asked to anchor the morning newscasts on both weekends and weekdays; second, he was called upon to anchor both the weekday morning newscasts and the *Live at Five* early-evening news hour; and third, he was asked to anchor WNBC's early-morning weekday newscasts from 5 a.m. to 7 a.m., be the newsreader on *Today* (from 7 a.m. to 9 a.m.), and, later, anchor *Live at Five*. This

Words

was a grueling schedule! However, Matt willingly accepted all of these assignments because he knew that they would prepare him for and bring him closer to his *Gold Ring Dream*.

9. *Go For Your* Gold Ring Dream—*Don't Settle for The Brass Ring or the Quick Fix*: When Matt was offered the opportunity to host *Access Hollywood*, it was a chance to host a prestigious, high-profile show that would potentially triple his salary. And what could have made his decision even tougher was that at the time it didn't appear that Bryant Gumbel would ever leave the host position on *Today*. As a result, there was no hint that there was any growth potential for Matt to be promoted from being the *Today* newsreader to its host. However, Matt didn't settle for the brass ring, nor did he opt for the immediate gratification of a huge raise in salary or the ego intoxication of hosting a big national entertainment show. He instead chose to be disciplined and to delay his gratification by staying the *Choreography* course as the *Today* newsreader and Bryant's fill-in host. Matt was resolute in his quest to achieve his *Gold Ring Dream*, and he did!

10. *Don't Hesitate to Work Hard When It Is Appropriate, But Also Know When to Say "No, Thank You."* As we have discussed, many of the steps that Matt took involved agreeing to accept assignments that often encroached on his personal time and were exhausting. However, he consciously chose to accept them because, in part, he wanted to be a good employee and a team player. These were very constructive steps! However, we are all subject to expectations (of parents, spouses, friends), as well as requests or assignments made by our employers, that can be counterproductive and even destructive as we endeavor to attain our most valued goals. In Matt's case, leaving the *Today* show and the hard-news arena for the fluffy and light *Access Hollywood* would have been a *toxic* step if he still aspired to one day fulfill his *Gold Ring Dream* of hosting *Today*. So, even though the highest executives at NBC exerted some pressure on Matt to leave *Today* to host *Access*, and even though he was very, very appreciative of all of the opportunities that NBC had given to him, he graciously (and correctly) said, "No, thank you."

Always keep in mind that there are instances in everyone's life and career when the answer must be, "Sorry, I'd love to help you, but I can't." In Matt's case, he declined NBC's offer because: (1) he had worked very hard to put himself in the perfect position to eventually host a national morning news program; (2) if he took the job at *Access*, his hard-news credibility and persona—which had been an ongoing issue for some network news executives—would have been greatly diminished, so in effect he would have been saying good-bye to ever fulfilling his *Gold Ring Dream* of hosting *Today*; and (3) he and I both knew that the odds were that he would be more successful in the live-interview format of *Today* than in the "taped anchor" format of *Access*. Unquestionably, *Today* showcases Matt's skills and gifts much, much more. For Matt, saying, "No, thank you," in this instance and sticking to his *Career Choreography* guns was the right, appropriate, and constructive step to take.

11. *Character Counts—Big Time*: When an NBC news executive gave Matt the opportunity to negotiate an agreement to replace Bryant Gumbel before the executive entered into negotiations with Bryant, Matt unequivocally declined. He took this step because he would do nothing to hurt (his best friend) Bryant. This was not the way that Matt chose to do business or to conduct his life.

    a. I believe that two things came out of Matt's character-laden decision. First, if and when Matt ever did replace Bryant, both he and Bryant would know that it was because Bryant himself decided to leave *Today*, so the transition would be a comfortable and supportive one—which it ultimately was. But more importantly, because Matt did the right thing by his standards, by acting with strong character, he felt good about how he conducted himself. Acting with character and with concern for others breeds empowering feelings of high self-esteem and self-worth. And these feelings, in turn, lead to making more self-enhancing decisions because you feel that you deserve the sweet fruits and rewards of steps wisely crafted and effectively implemented, and that you are worth doing good things for. Trust me, I have seen more people than you can imagine make self-destructive decisions and take self-sabotaging steps because they suffer from feelings of low self-esteem and self-worth. As a result, they do not feel like they deserve anything good in their lives—and they act out these negative feelings with self-destructive and self-sabotaging behavior.

b. My experiences have also taught me that the individuals who have feelings of high self-esteem and a truly positive self-image are much more likely to incorporate the appropriate use of discipline and to delay gratification in their *Choreographies*, whereas the individuals who feel bad about who they are and how they conduct their lives are much more likely to settle for the often self-destructive quick fix. In essence, they are reluctant to craft and take constructive and self-enhancing steps because they feel that they and their lives are just not worth making the extra effort for. As a direct result, they lack the requisite discipline.

The Samantha Harris
Multi-Platform Choreography

When I first met Samantha Harris, she had just graduated from Northwestern University's Medill School of Journalism. During our first meeting, I was struck by how very comfortable Samantha was in her own skin, her great bright inner and outer light, her intellect and direction, and her overall strong, yet very appealing energy. All of these are very positive qualities and many of the gifts that I look for when deciding whether to represent someone. What I also learned at our meeting was that Samantha's father and mother ran Renaissance fairs during Samantha's childhood, and at those fairs Samantha would sing and dance.

After a few years of keeping in touch, with some cable hosting and reporting experience under her belt, and with a new demo tape, Samantha and I reconnected. I watched her tape, which clearly showed that she had the ownership, charisma, accessibility, and "it" quality that I had sensed at our first meeting years earlier. I then showed Samantha's work to Karen Wang-Lavelle, my highly accomplished associate and the executive vice president (now co-president) of KLA, who wholeheartedly agreed with me regarding Samantha's talent and potential. As a result, Karen and I were all-in and ready to *Choreograph*. When it came to many of the positions to which Samantha ascended, Karen did most of the very effective agenting work.

There were two *Realities* that were clear to me when we constructed our initial Samantha *Choreographies* and embarked on our journey:

1. As the broadcasting business was changing and it was now appropriate for hosts to hold more than one major on-air job, we needed to

co-president

Choreograph Samantha's career on a *multi-platform* basis. This way, she could eventually have and enjoy two or more "big" positions *concurrently*, and each of these positions would materially increase her marketability, career value, brand, and income.

2. Somewhere down the line, Samantha's singing and dancing skills would come into play and be of significant help to us when building her career.

Here are Samantha's *Multi-Platforming* career steps:

Step 1: Samantha became the host of FOX Network's prime-time show *Joe Millionaire 2*.

Steps 2 and 3: Before *Joe Millionaire 2* aired, I pursued for Samantha the available weekend anchor position at *EXTRA*, while Karen secured tremendous interest in Samantha to become one of the hosts of *The View*. To Karen's tremendous credit, she suggested to Samantha that she make a home demo tape specifically for *The View* (a great jump-start *Choreography*), where Samantha would talk about herself, her background, and her views. Samantha did this, and on the basis of this tape she was given the opportunity to fill in on *The View* for two days, which she did beautifully. She fared so well, in fact, that we believed she was going to be offered a hosting position on that show; however, she was soon to be married to her loving, supportive, and very talented husband, Michael, and at the time he needed to be in Los Angeles for his work. So, when Samantha was offered the *EXTRA* weekend anchor position, which was based in L.A., she gladly accepted it and took herself out of the running for *The View* position.

I advised Samantha that *The View*, for her, would be the more career-enhancing opportunity, because it was, at the time, more unscripted and personality-driven than *EXTRA*. Being on *The View* would allow Samantha's great personality to organically come out and shine, and this growth platform would likely take her to her next career-enhancing move and the next. However, I was also very happy about her next move being *EXTRA*, because it worked for Samantha and Michael personally, and Samantha would get to work under and with the vision-ary program executive Lisa Gregorisch-Dempsey, who runs *EXTRA* and who has the gift of being able to bring out the very best in her on-air staff.

Nine months after starting her *EXTRA* job, we learned that due to cost-cutting mandates, the weekend hosting position was going to be eradicated, and we had three months during which to implement and complete the next step(s) in Samantha's *Choreography*. The good news was that during her time at *EXTRA*, Samantha and her work had evolved tremendously—especially her interviewing and storytelling skills.

Step 4: Because of the national exposure that Samantha received on *EXTRA* (and her great talents), Karen secured a full-time position for Saman-tha with E! Entertainment.

Fortuitously, Samantha did a story, as an E! assignment, about the ABC Network prime-time hit show *Dancing with the Stars*. That piece, in which she was able to interact with everyone at *DWTS*, was a mem-orable hit!

Step 5: Karen learned that *Dancing with the Stars* was looking for a new cohost to work with its so-very-talented host, Tom Bergeron. As a result, Karen submitted Samantha for the *DWTS* position. We felt that Samantha was perfect for the job, and that should she secure it, there would be significant benefits to E! in allowing Samantha to be the cohost of *DWTS* while she worked for E!

A few days later Samantha auditioned with Tom Bergeron, nailed it, and secured the job. It was then Karen's and my goal to secure E!'s permission to allow Samantha to do her E! job *along with* cohosting *Dancing with the Stars*. In order to do this, we spoke with a top executive at E! Our goal was to effec-tively explain to him *why it was in the very best interests of E!* to allow them to have Samantha work for E! along with *Dancing with the Stars*. The points that we presented were:

a. Samantha would receive tremendous exposure cohosting the hit ABC prime-time show *DWTS*. This invaluable free exposure would add greatly to her recognizability and value as an E! talent;

b. We would arrange for Samantha and E! to get *DWTS* interviews before others did; and

c. We would do our best to have Samantha introduced and be acknowledged in as many instances as possible as "E! Entertainment's Samantha Harris." As a result, E! would receive a huge amount of free national advertising and promotion. Being the very wise and opportunistic individual that I knew the E! executive to be, he graciously decided to allow Samantha to be the cohost of *Dancing with the Stars*.

Because this win/win agreement was struck, Samantha's exposure, career value, and income increased *exponentially*. And she began her *Multi-Platforming*.

Steps 6 and 7: Because Samantha cohosted *DWTS*, she became part of the ABC Network family. Therefore, ABC was invested in Samantha's success. So we then pursued and secured for Samantha enhancing appearances on ABC's *Good Morning America*, which gave Samantha, *DWTS*, and E! great cross-exposure. It was a win for everyone!

Since *The View* is an ABC show, they hired Samantha as a guest host. Additionally, we pursued the Oscar and pre-Oscar shows on ABC for Samantha, and she had the opportunity to appear in front of 70 million viewers on ABC's pre-Oscar show, as a cohost/interviewer.

Obviously, all of these *Multi-Platforming* opportunities significantly increased Samantha's visibility, brand awareness, and marketability.

Step 8: During Season 6 of *DWTS*, Samantha took only the first three weeks off to have her beautiful baby girl, Josselyn. She then came back, thin and fit, to cohost the last seven weeks of the season. (During this process her friend and cohost Tom Bergeron couldn't have been more supportive or gracious.) The fact that Samantha was able to return so fit and so quickly spawned an idea for her to write a fitness book. This idea was especially appropriate for Samantha, as over the past five years, she had been the subject of numerous fitness articles and had appeared on covers of various fitness magazines.

I have always been a *huge* proponent of individuals writing compelling books as a means of having their audience, as well as new viewers, see a "different" side of them. This different or other side becomes apparent from reading the talent's book and by seeing/hearing the talent being interviewed on TV/radio on various talk and news shows. As we are all voyeurs to varying extents, when viewers are allowed to witness a different, richer, and often much more personal side of a talent, enhanced viewer *traction*, *connection*, and *loyalty* can be the tremendously beneficial by-products of this highly advantageous exposure.

Step 9: Upon the expiration of Samantha's E! contract, Karen secured interest from various potential employers so that Samantha could make a thoroughly informed decision as to whether she should stay with E! or move on to some other career-enhancing venue.

We had known for a long time that the executives at CBS Television Distribution thought Samantha was extremely talented, as Karen had set a meeting for Samantha with these executives about a year earlier. What Karen and I also learned was that the top CBS Television Distribution executives preferred that the hosts of their syndicated entertainment shows be "mini-stars" themselves. This could be accomplished in two ways:

1. Encourage and arrange for their current hosts to get more exposure and recognition in other enhancing venues (*Multi-Platforming*); as a result, these hosts can evolve into mini-stars.

2. Hire individuals who *already* are nationally recognizable (as opposed to building their recognizability). This is analogous to film producers

putting the percentages in their favor that their films will be box-office successes by hiring "bankable stars."

There is a very important point here: In this *New Age of Broadcasting*, when competition for dwindling advertising revenues is fierce, shows are less likely to take risks on unknown hosts. They would rather take advantage of a talent's pre-established audience recognition, likability, and acceptance. It is one of the main reasons stars such as Ryan Seacrest, Mario Lopez, and Tom Bergeron are hosting multiple shows. And Matt Lauer and Oprah can host almost any show they want, should they decide to expand their hosting careers. Why? Because the audience loves them and wants to watch more of them, and program executives are keenly aware of this.

As the executives at CBS Television Distribution already coveted Samantha, and because she was the cohost of the prime-time hit show *Dancing with the Stars*, the CBS Television Distribution execs created a wonderful reporting, hosting, and interviewing position on *The Insider* for her to complement her hosting position on *DWTS*.

So, in Samantha's making the move to *The Insider*, two things happened:

1. She immediately increased her visibility, future marketability, brand, and career value.

2. *DWTS* was materially benefited due to the tremendous cross-exposure that *DWTS* received on *The Insider* and its companion show, *ET*.

Step 10: As a result of her singing and dancing skills, as well as her high recognizability, Samantha was offered the opportunity to play the iconic role of Roxie Hart in the Broadway play *Chicago*. As we discussed, CBS Television Distribution, which is a huge proponent of having its hosts be (or become) "mini-stars," was happy to allow Samantha to take advantage of this great cross-promotional opportunity. And because this very limited Broadway run took place during the summer, when *DWTS* was not in production, the producers of *DWTS* were only too happy to see Samantha and *DWTS* get highly beneficial cross-exposure in a dance-related role.

Sometime thereafter, Samantha left *Dancing with the Stars* and fulfilled a *Gold Ring Dream* when she became featured correspondent and fill-in anchor for *Entertainment Tonight.* You can bet that our *Multi-Platforming* efforts to add value to Samantha's career, brand, and bank account will continue. By the by, as discussed, *ET* is a CBS-owned show. So the next logical step in Samantha's *Multi-Platforming Choreography* is to explore what enhancing opportunities CBS might have for Samantha, as that network now has a considerable investment in Samantha's success, as well as in her increased visibility and recognition.

So let's review a few key points from Samantha's *Multi-Platforming Choreography*:

1. Visibility, recognizability, and success beget other enhancing opportunities.

2. In *The New Age of Broadcasting*, being totally exclusive to one employer and/or one job is outdated and shortsighted—especially in the world of programming.

3. You must look at *Career Choreographies* very *strategically* and see who has alliances with whom and who benefits from your growing and getting increased, beneficial exposure. Do not be afraid to be creative, be imaginative, and aim high ("Aspire higher!").

4. The more visibility and recognizability you have, the more valuable you become to others, and therefore the more significantly your marketability increases.

5. Just as broadcasting is a business for broadcasters, it is also a business for you as a talent. *So perceive and run your career like a business*, and continually and strategically enhance your biggest assets: you, your talents, and your brand!

The Mario Lopez *Choreography*

Here are the steps that my very talented, successful, and highly strategic client Mario Lopez has taken to put himself in the very best position to advance his career, as well as to build his brand and business:

1. Mario became a contestant on *Dancing with the Stars*. Because he was able to make it to the finals and his warm, charismatic personality was able to shine through, Mario again became TV-relevant in a major way.*

2. While doing freelance reporting and anchoring for *EXTRA,* Mario became the host of VH1's show *America's Best Dance Crew*, which added great value to his recognizability quotient and hosting career.

3. Mario soon became *EXTRA*'s weekend anchor.

4. Through focused hard work, Mario attained one of his *Gold Ring Dreams* as he became the main host of *EXTRA.* He worked in a strategic and effective manner to make the show significantly more successful. One way that Mario accomplished this was that he initiated trips throughout the country to meet with local station executives, whose stations air *EXTRA,* in an effort to learn how he and *EXTRA* could best serve the station and its viewership. Essentially, Mario collaborated with Telepictures executives and became a quasi-entrepreneur of *EXTRA,* as he knew that the show's success was his success. These efforts didn't go

---

*As you may remember, Mario starred years earlier in *Saved by the Bell.*

unnoticed by Telepictures executives. As a result of Mario's great hosting talents and his sales efforts, Telepictures used weekend *EXTRA* to
"pilot" ideas for future new shows, some of which Mario hosted.

5. During this time, *EXTRA* went from a conventional studio program
   to an interactive, much fresher show by shooting it at a beautiful
   upscale Los Angeles shopping mall called The Grove. There, Mario is
   surrounded by a live audience, often composed of some very animated
   and attractive individuals, with whom he can interact. This allows the
   show and Mario to be much more organic and real. It gives Mario the
   opportunity to show his great live skills and his accessibility. It makes
   the show a much more fun and relevant experience for all: Mario, the
   audience, and the viewers.

6. Mario wrote a children's book called *Mud Tacos*.

7. He starred as Zack in the Broadway version of *A Chorus Line*, where
   he met his love, Courtney Mazza, who was a *Chorus Line* cast member.
   Thereafter Mario and Courtney had a beautiful child, Gia.

8. As Mario wanted to modify his image from that of an exceedingly talented and successful bachelor to that of a much more well-rounded
   family man, he decided to do a docu-soap titled *Saved by the Baby*. The
   show, which was sold to VH1, portrays Mario as he truly is: a devoted
   and loving son, husband, father, and friend.

9. Mario then wrote a fitness book, *Extra Lean*, and became a member
   of the President's Council on Fitness, Sports, and Nutrition. Next, he
   wrote a book about his experience as a father, titled *Mario and Baby
   Gia*. Mario has also written *Knockout Fitness* and *Extra Lean Family*.

All of these experiences have made Mario a far more compelling candidate
to host a daytime show, such as *Live with Regis & Kelly*, which is another of
his *Gold Ring Dreams*. By getting exposure on so many different shows and
platforms, Mario has become exponentially more viable and valuable to any
and every potential employer. One big reason for this is that with all of the varied platforms on which Mario appears, he can bring a huge and widely diverse
set of viewers with him (diverse viewership streams). Additionally, because

Mario, as the host of *EXTRA*, gets and embraces the fact that in *The New Age* he needs to collaborate in every possible way with his Telepictures employers, Telepictures has graciously reciprocated by being open to allowing Mario to take advantage of many of the career-enhancing opportunities that have come his way. Also, the station managers, whom Mario has gone out of his way to meet and work with, are now far more likely to want to buy and air any future show that Mario hosts or produces because they know him and like him, and they also know that he will give his all to make these show(s) successful.

By carefully and strategically planning and *Multi-Platforming* his career, Mario has become a true *New Age entrepreneur*!

Other *Multi-Platforming* *Choreography* Models and Ideas

In this section, my goal is to present you with some other *Multi-Platforming* avenues, ideas, and options, so that you are better able to create your own *Multi-Platforming Choreographies.*

To start off, let me share with you a *Choreography* of my wonderful, multi-talented client Kimberly Caldwell. When I first began working with Kim, she was a host of the TV Guide Network's shows *Idol Tonight* and *Reality Chat.* A few years earlier she had been a very successful singing contestant on *Star Search* and *American Idol.*

What I loved about Kim's on-air work was that she was truly an "original," in that she was sassy, irreverent, fun, funny, beautiful, accessible, self-effacing, and so very, very smart. She owned it and had "it." Here is her *Choreography* to date:

Step 1: Along with her duties for the TV Guide Network, I helped Kim secure the hosting position for CBS Network's proposed new prime-time show *Jingles*, which was to be produced by Mark Burnett's company.

Step 2: Because Kim was, in part, contractually wedded to CBS, I looked at all venues owned by the CBS Network for other hosting opportunities for her. Then I learned that MTV (which is CBS-owned) was going to produce a music talent show called *Star Maker* and was looking for a host. Fortuitously, this show was also going to be produced by Mark Burnett's company, where the executives loved working with Kim on *Jingles* and thought that she was tremendously talented. I also felt that this was a great venue for Kim, because she was 27, the right age for MTV; she had been a singing contestant on both *Star Search* and *American Idol*; and she wanted to "give something back" to other up-and-coming music talents.

Kim auditioned, and her extraordinary on-air gifts won the day. She secured the hosting position on *Star Maker*.

Step 3: Kim decided to lose a bit of weight, which made her radiant beauty even more evident and marketable. As a result of her new look, visibility, and twenty-something appeal, she was offered and accepted the opportunity to become the face, figure, and spokesperson for YMI Jeans. As a result, all over Los Angeles and other key cities, huge and tremendously flattering billboards and catalogs of Kim modeling YMI Jeans were on display.

Step 4: Kim appeared on carefully selected magazine covers and in engaging articles. She and her very smart and beautiful hairstyle were eye-catching!

Step 5: Through the excellent work of Kim's exceedingly talented manager, Kim entered into a wonderful recording deal with Capitol Records.

Step 6: As a result of this record deal and her exciting lifestyle, Kim entered into a production agreement with Ryan Seacrest Productions to produce a docu-soap about her life and the lives of her colorful family members.

Step 7: She then entered into an agreement for a talk show with E! We expect that this free-flowing format will showcase Kim's winning, authentic personality.

Step 8: We are now developing a late-night show with Kim.

All of these career-enhancing *Multi-Platforming* steps were taken within the two years of our working together. As we discussed, the right, logical career steps can be identified and taken if you understand how to be the most active, creative, and proactive *Choreographer*!

Here are some other *Multi-Platforming Choreography* models to think about and potentially incorporate into your *Choreographies*:

1. *Ryan Seacrest*: Due to his success on *American Idol*, Ryan became a highly recognizable and bankable talent. He parlayed and leveraged E! Network's wanting him to host shows on E! as a means to entice E! to enter into a production deal with his company, RSP Productions. According to those who should know, E! provides RSP with offices at E! and finances eight on-air series through RSP Productions. So, as a direct result of Ryan's on-air talents, he was able to expand his empire so that he now runs and enjoys a thriving production company. This is in addition to his many hosting positions, his extremely lucrative radio deal, and his commercials. About a year or so ago, it was announced that Ryan entered into a new, three-year agreement to host *American Idol* for a reported $45 million! Obviously, the right *Choreographies* can result in exceedingly lucrative payoffs!

2. *Maria Menounos*: Forever and ever, it has been said that news people cannot endorse products or services. First of all, I have never felt fully comfortable with this edict, as newscasts are funded by sponsors, and those news divisions do not perceive themselves or their judgment as tainted or that their newscasts are any less credible by these associations. But in this *New Age of Broadcasting*, please take note that Maria Menounos is a fill-in host of *Today* and occasionally files reports for *Dateline*, yet she is a spokesperson for *Pantene*! A possible big step for Maria, and for news talent generally!

In this *New Age of Broadcasting*, many news operations will do almost anything to get and keep a sponsor.* As a result, who knows what news

---

* For example, according to Michael Malone of *Broadcasting & Cable*, McDonald's contracted with KVVU, Las Vegas's morning newscast, to have McDonald's branded iced coffee cups on the set of KVVU's morning newscast; there were Pepsi containers on the set of WIAT, Birmingham's *Wake-Up Alabama*; there was Verizon FiOS branding on WNBC New York's' sports reports; and KFOR, in Oklahoma City, branded its news helicopter with the name of a local auto dealer (Michael Malone, "Your Ad Here . . . and Here," *Broadcast & Cable*, July 27, 2009, 8). Any journalistic conflicts here? Absolutely! Arguably the same as those of a broadcast journalist endorsing a product or service! But if news departments/news divisions during *The New Age* need to earn supplemental income through patent product and service ties, why should broadcast journalists be precluded from similarly supplementing their income as well?

executives will allow talent to do in the future if it is in those broadcasters' best interests?

On this subject, I know of a news talent who has a station contract allegedly providing that he gets to keep a percentage of the advertising revenues that he personally brings to his station. Assuming that this is true, we can assume that one of the reasons the station retains this news talent's services and pays him extraordinarily well is because he has brought a great deal of advertiser revenue to the station. So the question must be asked: Is there any real difference between this talent endorsing a product or service of a company on-air or in print, and his being able to profit from having the company which produces that product or service pay him indirectly through advertising proceeds? Isn't his objectivity tainted in either case? Yet one is readily accepted by his station's news department, and the other is strictly forbidden as a breach of news ethics.

One *New Age Reality* that stands out is that the once very clear, strong line separating news ethics and the broadcaster's tremendous need for sponsorship dollars is becoming more and more faint.

3. *Tom Bergeron*: Years ago, Tom became the host of ABC Network's prime-time hit *America's Funniest Home Videos*. So it made sense for him to find another major position on a show with a company for which ABC would allow him to work. That would obviously be ABC (or an ABC-owned cable network, or possibly, a syndicated show that is bought by all of the ABC-owned and -operated stations: "a group buy"). When ABC's *Dancing with the Stars* came along, it was a perfect companion show for Tom, and he has been perfect for *DWTS*.

Since the ABC Network has so much invested in Tom, it makes sense for Tom to host specials for ABC as well.

4. *Matt Lauer, Meredith Vieira, Al Roker, and Lester Holt*: In Matt's case, he is living his *Gold Ring Dream* as the host of *Today*. He feels that in order to do his very best work, he wants to devote his full professional time and efforts to *Today*. Of course, Matt is nicely paid, so earning

extra income is not a factor in his decision-making. Yet every once in a while, he hosts a show on one of NBC's cable networks.

Conversely, Meredith Vieira was the cohost of *Today* at the same time that she hosted the syndicated game show *Who Wants to Be a Millionaire?* Who says news talent cannot also host non-news shows because the talent will lose credibility?! I believe that a significant factor in determining whether one will or will not jeopardize his or her hard-news credibility by hosting a non-news program is one's prior background (Meredith's is hard news) and what that person did *first* or is (most) known for. (In Meredith's case, she spent many years as a hard-news journalist for CBS News *before* she hosted *Millionaire*, so she already had established her news "cred.")

Because Al Roker's *Today* duties appear to be less extensive than Matt's, he has the time, and obviously the ambition and energy, to host various NBC shows (including *Celebrity Family Feud*). Al also has his own production company.

Finally, Lester Holt, thought by many to be the hardest-working person in news, has been tremendously wise about the building of his career. Here's why:

a.   First and foremost, Lester is a prince of a human being. People love working with him, so they want to work with him and are happy to offer him many enhancing opportunities.

b.   He never turns down an assignment, unless it has the potential to be career-damaging.

c.   He understands—especially during this *New Age of Broadcasting*—that you creatively and respectfully seek out and do not turn down enhancing career real estate. So he, with great enthusiasm and appreciation:

    i.   hosts *Weekend Today;*

    ii.   anchors *Weekend Nightly News;*

    iii.   reports for *Today*, *Nightly News*, and *Dateline;*

    iv.   hosts *Dateline*; and

    v.   hosts various NBC News–produced cable specials and series.

As a result, Lester has done a brilliant job of *Multi-Platforming* within the NBC News division, and NBC has done an equally brilliant job of growing Lester.

5. *Being a* Multi-Platforming *Local Newscaster*: I see no reason why local newscasters at a CBS, NBC, ABC, or FOX station cannot pursue enhancing hosting or reporting opportunities at their respective network-news and programming divisions, or on appropriate cable shows. This is an excellent means to grow or polish your skills, get valuable national exposure, and to grow your career, brand, business, and income. Additionally, you become more valuable to your current employer by increasing your local recognizability.

6. *Oprah Winfrey*: Obviously, *the* most successful broadcasting *Multi-Platforming Choreographer* is Oprah. She owns, among another entities:

    a.   her mega-hit syndicated show, *Oprah;*

    b.   Harpo Productions, her tremendously successful production company;

    c.   OWN; and

    d.   *O* Magazine.

Oprah also on occasion acts and is involved in and associated with many charitable causes. Because of her unprecedented, ultra-successful *Multi-Platforming*, she can pretty much do anything she wants.

In this section, I have used the *Multi-Platforming* steps of recognizable individuals to give you ideas as to how to *Choreograph* your own *Multi-Platforming* career. In this *New Age of Broadcasting*, there are far fewer rules, and you and your career are and can indeed be what you envision, create, and negotiate. A key question regarding every move that you make must be this: *Does it add positive value to you, your skill set, your visibility, marketability, and ultimately to your career, brand, and business?* If the answer is, "Yes, it does!" then do your very best to craft the most effective *Choreography* possible in order to make the opportunity a *New Age Reality.*

SECTION V

New Age Broadcasting Issues
to Contemplate

Change

"The one thing that remains the same about our business [broadcasting], is that there's always change."[23]

Years ago, a very successful and highly respected news executive made the above offhanded remark to me during one of our negotiations. I have come to see how very right that general manager was. Change is inevitable—especially in *The New Age*, when everyone is struggling to maintain financial viability. In fact, as this book is being completed, ABC and CBS News, as well as CNN, have named new presidents; Katie Couric, Meredith Vieira, and Mary Hart have left their positions as anchor of *CBS Evening News*, cohost of the *Today* show, and cohost of *Entertainment Tonight*, respectively; and the most successful of all talk-show hosts, Oprah Winfrey, has ended her Hall of Fame, syndicated-show run. During the past fifteen years, I have seen scores of local stations change ownership and, in some instances, change network affiliations. I have also seen how ratings of prime-time and other day-part programming go up and down, and with those fluctuations have come increases and decreases in news ratings—and change.

With all of these changes come changes in management. The new management recruits, in turn, make their own changes, as they bring with them new ideas and different perspectives as to how to garner a greater number of demographically desirable viewers. The goal is to do everything possible to increase news and station profitability—or at least to remain viable.

Along with changes in management almost always come changes in on-air talent, executive producers, producers, off-air staff members, news philosophy, news content, news format, graphics, pacing, music, sets, etc. The same can also be said to varying degrees about network and cable news operations, as well as network, syndicated, and cable programs.

A number of years ago, I had a most revealing conversation with Joel Cheatwood, when he was the executive in charge of the Sunbeam Television Corporation stations' news product. As already mentioned, I believe Joel has done more than anyone to revolutionize local news over the past few decades. Our discussion focused on Joel's perception of the positive value of change for his stations. When I asked him why he thought he and his stations (WSVN and WHDH) had become so successful, he replied:

> It's because [Sunbeam] station managers have *complete flexibility*. Other stations have hard, etched-in-stone rules and ways of doing things that take months to change. They (other stations) also have talent contracts that guarantee that their on-camera people *must* anchor and report for *specific* shows. We, on the other hand, have designed *our* operation so that we can *change* things in a couple of hours. *We can creatively and flexibly respond to the always-changing environment.* We can change our tone, our focus; and even create new music. *We can vary which shows our talent anchor and report on.* This [ability to change] makes us able to be both more responsive to the news of the day and to the needs and desires of our viewers. Basically, when a news opportunity presents itself, unlike other stations, we can jump on it and make it our own.[24]

These words of change were from an executive in charge of highly rated stations. On the other end of the spectrum, when a news manager at a low-rated station changed his morning anchor team yet again, I asked him why he had made the particular change that he did. He replied, "We're number three in the market and going nowhere. I gotta change something. So I changed the anchor team [again]. Hell, if it doesn't work, I'll change it again and again until it *does* work, or I'm fired." Just recently, a network news executive shared the following thought with me: "We're always looking [to change and upgrade talent]. We're number three; we need to do something [to increase viewership]."

Here are a few scenarios that I have constructed which, except for some modifications, reflect pre-*New Age*, real-life situations with which I have been involved or that I have seen. The sixth pattern is one that I expect will take place one day.

1. The owner of a #3-rated station decided that this station needed to change its news image, so he hired a new general manager (GM) and news director to put together a hotter, faster-paced, more highly produced news product. They, in turn, hired newscasters from all over the country who could sell this news product with more immediacy and color. These newscasters uprooted themselves (and in many instances, their families), sometimes leaving excellent on-air positions behind, to move to this larger-market station to be part of the new program. A year later, with ratings still abysmally low, it was decided at corporate headquarters that (once again) changes needed to be made. Soon thereafter, the GM and news director of the station left and another management team was brought in. This new team was so totally at odds with their predecessor's vision of news that they even criticized and repudiated it in the local press. Immediately thereafter, the new general manager (again) completely changed the direction and image of the news product, along with hiring an almost totally new on-air staff. Furthermore, notwithstanding the fact that many of the individuals hired by the departed management had no-cut or firm contracts and specific duties (what newscasts they would anchor or which reporting franchises they would be given) written into those contracts, many were not given the assignments they had been promised. Instead, they were told by the new station management that they could either accept the different and lesser positions or they could sit home (possibly damaging their careers) and collect a paycheck. When the demoted individuals complained that prior management brought them to the station with a certain vision and promise in mind, the new management responded, "That was prior management's vision. We're sorry, but we have to execute our own [vision]. It's not personal, *it's business.*"

2. Joe Smith was lured away from a station, where he was anchoring a 4 p.m. Monday through Friday newscast, to another station (a FOX affiliate), where he would anchor the Monday through Friday 6 p.m. and 10 p.m. newscasts. Joe received a four-year contract, which provided for twice the amount of compensation that he had received at his old station. About six months after he arrived at the new station, that station went through an affiliation switch to CBS. The station's consultant advised station management that "considering the station's new CBS program lineup, it would be appropriate to change its on-air news approach. It [the station] should have individuals in its main anchor positions who have established news credentials in the market, not young newcomers." As a result, Joe was demoted from the promised weeknight anchor position to anchoring the morning and noon newscasts. The anchors who were currently anchoring morning and noon (who had been demoted from anchoring the evening newscasts by prior management and who had twenty years of in-market experience between them) returned to their old positions.

3. A group of stations was sold; management was replaced at almost all of the stations. Major on-air changes immediately took place.

4. A longtime #3 station decided to put on an afternoon newscast against *Oprah*, which had received #1 ratings in the market for more than twelve years. The general manager decided that he would hire a woman who looked like Oprah to anchor it and hopefully siphon off *Oprah* viewers. The station hired this person away from a comfortable position in her hometown, for a good deal more money (however, the cost of living in this new city was a great deal higher as well). After a few months, with no increase in the ratings, the station decided that their experiment hadn't worked. They then demoted the Oprah look-alike to weekend anchoring; eventually she had to leave the station and the market (because she had been tarnished by her poor positioning and lack of success at her desperate-for-a-quick-fix station).

5. A #3 station in a large market couldn't make any upward movement in the ratings. The general manager was worried that if he didn't do something quickly he would get axed. (He had already fired two news

directors, so there was no one else he could blame.) He needed something to increase viewership and give him more time. He decided to hire away a legendary anchor in the market and end the anchor's career in a blaze of glory at his station. With a great deal of money, a firm contract, and a lot of publicity, this anchor was hired. Within one year of coming to the station and with no ratings increase in sight, the anchor was unceremoniously told to clean out his desk and go home. He wouldn't be anchoring anymore. The station would pay him for the next two years of his contract to "sit on the beach."* As this anchor had already been making very good money at his former station, he realized the huge mistake that he had made by changing stations. This was not how he wanted to end his illustrious career—in a blaze of embarrassment!

6. [A scenario that will inevitably happen.] "WDED" is one of the five television stations in a Top-20 market. Each of these stations has a full complement of newscasts. The ratings for WDED's newscasts are intolerably low. The ownership decides that the station cannot profitably compete in the news arena and would be better off running soap operas during the day and inexpensive programs in the evening against its competitors' newscasts. Within one week, all newscasts are canceled and the entire news staff is laid off.

The six examples above were constructed more than thirteen years ago. Please be aware that in *The New Age*, talent contract cycles generally are now much shorter in length, which gives the employer *many more* opportunities to terminate talent employment agreements; therefore, employers now oftentimes have less financial liability when they decide that they want to part ways with a talent. Thus change in *The New Age* may well be *more prevalent* and easier to implement than ever before!

These kinds of radical changes take place in the programming arena as well. For instance, one well-known syndicated program hired a male to be its weeknight host, but a few days before the show was to debut, management decided that he was not the right choice. So they paid the talent to sit around the office until they could contractually let him go. As a result, he never had the chance

---

* This is called exercising an employer's "pay-or-play" right. This concept will be covered in the upcoming "Contracts" discussion.

to host the show—as promised—for even one day! Then, after one year, this show, which was billed as an entertainment program, switched executive producers, became a pop-culture show, and replaced its two hosts with two new ones. One year later, the show decided that it needed to be harder-edged—and become a mini-*Dateline*. Its executive producer at the time and its hosts were again replaced. Three months into the fourth year of the show, the show changed its tone once again and hired another executive producer.

I could write volumes about the changes that I have been involved with and those that I have seen, which have been made in pursuit of greater profitability, and thereafter cavalierly explained away as "It's just business," as casually as someone flicks an annoying fly from one's shoulder. However, if you are the talent who is being fired, demoted, or humiliated, this kind of change can be devastating and destructive—professionally, emotionally, and financially. It can indeed be a profoundly life-changing experience.

Herein lies a harsh *Reality*. Stations, due to economic pressures, want as much flexibility as possible to make changes at any time regarding on-air and off-air individuals. Essentially, if you do not deliver viewers, or if you no longer fit in, management will demote you or let you go in a flash. And from management's perspective, it's not personal—it's business.

Of course, from the employee's perspective, what is missing here is a long-term, humane commitment from management and a sincere appreciation of the fact that management seems to give so little consideration to the *Reality* that human beings and their precious careers and dreams are being disposed of willy-nilly with little or no true concern for them.

NEW AGE ISSUE

Individuals who are in broadcast journalism should understand that the people they work for—for the most part—perceive broadcasting as a high-stakes business. Especially in this *New Age*, change is inevitable, and as a result, careers will ebb and flow and often not go as planned.

Murders, Dead Babies, and Fires

Years ago, a client called to say that she estimated that she had covered more than 3,000 depressing, bad-news stories, and that she couldn't take it anymore. She was ready to leave news and work for *Entertainment Tonight*. She was tired of bad and ugly news. She feared that she had become desensitized and was becoming "less human." She said that for a change, she wanted to smile on-air and tell stories that were uplifting and fun.[*]

In this *New Age*, such complaints and laments are even more prevalent. In fact, just recently, a client called to tell me that she no longer wanted to be a local news reporter. She said that the first three stories of her station's previous evening's newscasts were about a murder, a rape, and a six-year-old girl being bound and tortured. My client's new aspirations were to host shows for *National Geographic*, *Animal Planet*, and *The History Channel*, as well as prime-time programs, such as *Dancing with the Stars* or *Wipeout*. Through the years, a number of news executives have essentially confided, "You can be sure that when I go to sleep at night, I don't pray for world peace." This is a *Broadcasting Reality*, because world peace and other good-news stories apparently do not bring enough viewers to the set or keep them there. Conversely, bad news, scandals, war, bloodshed, celebrity gossip, popular figures falling or dying, and bizarre, catastrophic, or horrific video clips do attract and keep viewers. Therefore, news organizations, as well as magazines and talk shows, send their reporters and photographers out to cover these stories and bring back riveting video.

---

[*] As a direct result of my conversation with this client, I wrote the poem that appears at the end of this section.

I recall asking a general manager of a top-rated, big-market station years ago why good news and programs devoted to presenting uplifting stories do not get ratings. He replied that his network had done research on that very subject, and thereafter scrapped the development of a "good news" program, because, for the most part, people believe that their lives are "so screwed up and compromised" that they get a lift out of seeing other people's lives being equally bad or worse than their own. It is sort of the misery-loves-equally-miserable-company theory. Therefore, people like to watch bad news, crime, and stars and icons falling or failing.

Whatever the rationale, an enduring *Broadcasting Reality* is this: If it's negative, if it bleeds, or if it titillates—it leads, it's promoted, it's teased, and it's replayed and repackaged all day! And if there is graphic tape, all the better!

As we discussed, during *Stage Two* of broadcasting history and in *The New Age*, we have become a nation of voyeurs. From my perspective, ever since we watched O. J. Simpson's indelibly memorable, televised Ford Bronco chase, viewers, to varying degrees, have been hooked on televised, voyeuristic events. Essentially, it is like the accident on the other side of the freeway. You hate to see something truly bad happen to someone, but you cannot resist watching what's going on.

Additionally, pop-culture stars, such as Paris Hilton, Lindsay Lohan, and Britney Spears, have learned how to garner millions of dollars of free publicity and remain relevant by doing anything and everything that will keep them news- and TMZ-worthy. The problem for talent is that they must constantly report on these brain-numbing, low-tier goings-on.

Unfortunately, with *New Age* competition for viewers being so intense, and the fight for relevancy and survival being so crucial for broadcasters, covering a steady diet of murders, dead babies, fires, and the Paris Hilton of the moment is not going to go away and will continue to be a *New Age Reality*. Witness the proliferation and apparent success of shows such as *ET*, *EXTRA*, *Access Hollywood*, *Showbiz Tonight*, *TMZ*, *The Insider*, and gossip/pop-culture Internet Web sites, and how all of this pop-culture material is covered in *The New Age* by such reputable news shows as *Today*, *GMA*, *The Early Show*, and all of the cable news networks.

NEW AGE ISSUE

With *The New Age* competition for viewers and advertising revenues as fierce as it is, reporters covering stories on murder, rape, fire, general brutality, and the like, will be a (or *the*) staple of local news. This can become demoralizing and desensitizing for all those who report or work on these stories.

The Broadcast Journalist's Conflict

I became a reporter for the satisfaction and glory,
Of changing the world through a well-researched story.
To make a positive difference was my desire,
To enlighten society, seize the bar, raise it higher.

But now I often feel terribly low,
'Cause I'm given assignments that I know,
Are sellouts and therefore don't call for my best,
And I feel like I'm failing the character test.

I once had dreams, but now nothing is plainer,
I'm no longer a journalist, I'm an info-tainer.
Entertaining and titillating have become the norm;
We don't seek the truth and we rarely inform.
'Cause at the end of the day, we're way too scared,
That our viewers don't care and they're attention-impaired.
So we sell sex and violence, and provocative teases.
We'll air almost anything, as long as it pleases.
Hooking the viewer has become paramount,
'Cause if ratings are low, nothing else counts.

But if I continue to settle, instead of striving,
Morally defaulting, in lieu of thriving,
I will continue to commit the horrendous crime,
Of wasting my career, my potential, my time.

God, as I look back, I had a noble quest.
But reporting degradation and death have left me depressed.
So what I need to do is clear to me;
It's to begin to have fun, and to anchor *ET*!

New Age Intellectual Dimming

Recently I watched a program on PBS discussing the concept of "global dimming," which can occur when multitudinous particles of pollution block the earth's sunlight. That program, titled "Dimming of the Sun," postulated that global dimming was one of the main causes of such catastrophic events as droughts, which have adversely affected millions of people in India and could negatively impact billions in China.

In the preceding section, we discussed how reporting on the exploits of such pop-culture stars such as Paris Hilton, Lindsay Lohan, and Britney Spears can lead broadcast journalists to become very unhappy with their jobs. I would make the argument that news outlets covering this material to the great extent that they do will lead to our country's *Intellectual Dimming*. This *New Age Reality* will be a result of news divisions' giving us—in fact, saturating us with—what we want to see and know, not what we need to see and know in order for us to intelligently and effectively live and govern our lives. I understand that we live in a free country and in a capitalistic society, and that all of this pop-culture pabulum is protected by the First Amendment. However, when I see how much our news outlets focus on pop culture and gossip, and not on important national and international news, I do compare it to individuals eating a steady diet of candy to the exclusion of healthy foods, such as green vegetables. Or someone sitting in front of a TV or video screen all day, day after day, and doing no exercise. Really bad things will inevitably happen!

Today *Intellectual Dimming* is prevalent and is a *New Age Broadcasting Reality*. Much of the pop-culture fare that we crave and that is fed to us by news and programming executives is as intellectually nutritious for us as cotton candy. And as will happen if we eat cotton candy in excess, and to the exclusion of foods that are truly good for us, our diets will quickly become unbalanced and unhealthy!

NEW AGE ISSUE

Today our newscasts and news programs are inundated with pop-culture gossip. Obviously, this is material that viewers want to see and hear, so news entities give viewers a steady diet of it. The result may well be the *Intellectual Dimming* of the viewers and our country.

Subjectivity

"One person's passion is another person's poison."

As you may have gleaned from the discussion devoted to "change," broadcasting can be a very reactive business. When deciding to make changes, management often reacts to ratings and demographic information, research studies, lead-in and lead-out programming requirements, what successful competitors appear to do well, and the opinions of key executives and those of program sponsors. Most of all, managers react to the perceptions and mandates of their bosses, who for the most part are driven by the bottom line.

Though broadcasting in many instances may be a reactive business, it is almost always a subjective one. Here are two illustrations of how different news managers' subjective tastes can radically differ:

1. "Bill" was anchoring for a national cable network. One morning he arrived at work and was told that the network had just been sold. He thereafter learned that as a result of the sale, the upper management at the network, who had hired and been supportive of him, would be immediately replaced. A day later he received a call from a program director who had worked with him years before. This program director said that he was one of two remaining candidates in the running to be

named to the position of president of the network. The caller then said to Bill, "If I get the job, Bill, I will promote you to be our lead evening anchor. You and one or two others will become the go-to people and public face of the network. I cannot believe these guys [Bill's current management] aren't using you better. Anyway, as soon as I get in there, we'll make you a prominent part of the network for years and years to come." This was indeed one of the best calls Bill had ever received. He called his wife to share his excitement.

However, two days later, it was announced that the *other* candidate got the job. Shortly thereafter, the new president of the network, through his new vice president of news, told Bill that unfortunately the network just didn't see Bill as having any future there and that his services would no longer be needed. Bill's style just was not their style. They would pay Bill for the remaining six weeks of his contract, and he could go find another job.

As is almost always the case, news of the firing spread quickly through the network. As soon as Bill entered the newsroom, some of his colleagues—not knowing what to say—avoided him; others awkwardly tried to console him. Emotionally blown away, Bill packed up his things and quickly left to tell his wife and children the devastating news. As he walked to the parking lot, he wondered how one person could see him as the future star of the network and another could so quickly decide that he had no future there at all. The answer: subjectivity!

2. "Stephanie," a weekend anchor, was hired two years ago by the news director of a Top-10-market station. During this time, Stephanie was the main fill-in anchor for both of the weeknight female anchors, and she received excellent marks for this work from her management. One day, the news director called Stephanie's agent and said that in the near future, they would begin negotiations for a new contract for Stephanie, and that within the next six months, she would be promoted to a prominent weeknight anchor position.

However, before negotiations for a new contract could begin, the general manager and the news director were replaced, and all of their plans and changes were put on hold until new managers were hired. About two months later, the new news director called Stephanie's agent and told him that Stephanie didn't have "the heft and weight, or the gravitas" to be a weeknight anchor, as they perceived Stephanie's strengths to be her warmth, her ad-libbing skills, and her perkiness. Instead, they preferred her to assume the station's weekday morning anchor position.

As Stephanie's goal and expectations were to become a weeknight anchor at her station, she told her agent, "It's so very disappointing that the individuals who were going to promote me are no longer here; but, if we can't change their [new management's] decision, then it's time to find a weeknight anchor position for me someplace else. Forget them if they do not want to take advantage of the time I've spent here!"

Six weeks later Stephanie became a weeknight anchor in a larger market.

Regarding subjectivity, I will always vividly remember the evening when a friend invited me to a dinner party attended by her family and their friends, all of whom were from Pittsburgh. My friend told everyone at the table that I represent newscasters and that a number of my clients were television anchors and reporters in their city. As a result, for the next hour I heard: why one person loved anchor X because he was authoritative, but two others found him pompous and unwatchable; why three people loved anchor Y, but my friend's mother found her vapid and cold; and why some people loved the hip way one young anchor dressed, while two others felt that she didn't look or dress like Diane Sawyer. Everyone brought his or her own subjective tastes to the table—literally.

Beauty is in the eye of the beholder, and there is no accounting for taste. These rules apply just as much to broadcast executives and managers, and to those who advise them, as they do to anyone else. Company heads, station managers, owners, general managers, program directors, sales staffers, news directors, consultants, producers—*and even their spouses or significant others*—all have a subjective say as to who is hired (and fired) at a station, and on which newscast or program they should appear. And who is to say that any of them have good taste, a keen eye, or true vision for what can be? How many changes do we see made in broadcasting every day? Plenty!!! Obviously, somebody thought that each person being replaced was right for the position at issue when that person was originally hired. Not only do different individuals have completely different subjective perspectives regarding a broadcasting staff, but managers themselves often change their subjective perspectives. For example, one news director, to the best of my recollection (somewhat jokingly), shared the following illuminating insight with me: "The *worst* anchor in the country is the one that I hired three months ago. The *best* anchor is the one that I'll hire *next* [to replace her]."

Because of the psychological dynamics of subjectivity, not everyone will like or highly value a given person. Not everyone will recognize how smart that person is, how talented, or that he or she is the best at what he or she does. It *is* impossible to please everyone. This is a crucial concept to understand and a clear *Broadcasting Reality* to keep in mind. For your emotional well-being, remember it. And you need to know without doubt that the reasons for the lack of approval or the rejection that a person receives may well have nothing at all to do with the (objective) talent or the abilities of the individual being evaluated, and everything to do with the subjective perspectives and personal experiences of the person doing the evaluating. When you become an on- (or off-) air talent, everyone who comes in contact with you becomes an evaluator. One certainty is this: You will not be everyone's cup of tea.

There is a simple but eloquent prayer that goes like this: "God, give me the serenity to accept the things I can't change, the courage to change the things I can, and the wisdom to know the difference." In life, there are some times— maybe many times—when we just cannot win somebody over. When they just do not get it, or see it, or appreciate it. No matter how much we think that they should. Not everyone got Elvis when he was popular. Not everyone got the Beatles when they were hot. It's a free country, and people can like whomever they choose. As they say, "That's [the dynamics of subjectivity] what makes a horse race." We will be much wiser and happier if we realize up front that not everyone will see our talents and abilities. So, be forewarned that no matter what you do, at some point your emotional health, self-esteem, and feelings of self-worth will take some knocks. Just be aware that everyone who is successful has shared these same emotionally jarring experiences.

Fortunately there is also good news regarding subjectivity. Though one employer may not value you enough, you may be just the answer and the right fit for someone else's subjective taste. The key is to find an employer who will truly appreciate you and your abilities, put you in positions that will enhance you, and intelligently and effectively promote you. I can cite an abundance of previously non-successful broadcasters who experienced many, many bumps in the road and some very tough emotional setbacks until they found an enhancing employer and environment. Katie Couric and Matt Lauer are two such individuals.

NEW AGE ISSUE

With all of the management changes that take place in broadcasting, it is important to remember the *Broadcasting Reality* that taste is a subjective phenomenon. There are times when some people will not see or appreciate your value. Your goal is to work for and with those who do.

Learning to Live with Hitting Singles and Sacrifice Bunts

As we discussed, in the early days of television news, the goal was to serve the public by supplying necessary information. At that time, due to the state of news-gathering equipment, it took a great deal longer to put stories together and to get them on the air. The slower news-gathering process was coupled with the fact that before news became a profit center for stations, there were fewer newscasts for which to report. This state of affairs meant that reporters could take a longer time to research and craft their stories—and in many instances, they were able to derive more satisfaction from their work, while viewers received valuable information. This certainly was the case when stations and networks did more documentaries and long-form news specials.

However, at least six things have changed since those times:

1. News has become a profit center.

2. Innovations in news-gathering equipment now allow reporters to gather and present news much more rapidly.

3. For the most part, stations have many more newscasts than they did years ago.

4. Reporters have to file reports for more newscasts than they did before. So they do more stories and/or have to repackage the same ones, sometimes many times each day.

5. The MTV give-it-to-me-as-fast-as-sexy-and-as-easy-as-possible influence makes news divisions get in and out of stories quickly so as not to lose the perceived attention-impaired viewer.

6. In *The New Age*, resources and competent support staff can be in very short supply, so high-quality work and the feeling of true job satisfaction are rare.

In most cases, local newscasters no longer have the opportunity or the resources to research, write, and report very many meaningful, valuable, and satisfying pieces. I cannot begin to count the number of phone calls that I have received from clients who say that all their station cares about is finding a warm body to throw on the air just to fill a time slot, and then sending that same person out either to do another story or to do a rehash of the first one again. Or they bemoan that their stations "go live" just to "show live"—even if there's no real reason to do so. And even when someone does get a meaningful story, unless the station thinks that the story will increase ratings, one either has too little time to research it or has too little airtime in which to do more than just gloss over it.

I will never forget a conversation that took place with one of my clients years ago. She truly cared about the content of news and about the responsibility that she, as a reporter, believed that she had to the public. She fervently wanted to research, investigate, probe, and enlighten. She had read everything about the history of broadcasting and the lofty ideals of broadcasting's most revered journalists. Month after month, I could hear a waning of her enthusiasm and see a dimming of her radiant inner and outer bright light. Then one day she called to say that she was profoundly sad—even depressed—because she was not making a positive difference by doing meaningful, well-thought-out stories. Instead of her news management saying, "Let's be great!" or even "Let's get it right!" it was more like (to quote the late Marvin Gaye), "Let's get it on!"—on for the noon, on for the four, on for the five and the six, and then repackage it for the eleven.

She finished by saying that she never had the resources, the time, or the encouragement to hit the home run. Instead, she was stuck—due to her station's tight news budget and a news philosophy that catered to the lowest common denominator—having to live with hitting singles and sacrifice bunts, with the sacrifice involving her values, her ideals, and her self-esteem, as well as the viewers' access to thoughtful and in-depth reporting.

I thereafter explained that if we proactively and creatively *Choreographed* things a bit differently, she could indeed hit some triples, home runs, and maybe even a grand slam or two. However, it was painful to agree with my client that especially in *The New Age*, sacrifice bunts and singles are often the sum and substance of local news.

The other day, Dan Le Batard, a very accomplished ESPN Radio sports host/reporter, essentially said, "[Your] happiness is the result of [you] effectively managing your expectations." In this *New Age*, where broadcasters aim to get much more with far fewer staff members and costly expenditures, it is essential for talent to effectively manage their work-product expectations—otherwise they will (continue to) be very disappointed and unfulfilled.

NEW AGE ISSUES

1. Not having adequate resources, preparation time, research assistance, or airtime to do stories that are meaningful, enlightening, and/or rewarding is very often a *Reality* of local news. However, the existence and depth of the problem depend upon each local station's news philosophy and the availability of resources. Feeling empty and that you are anything but a good journalist after reporting on frivolous and gratuitous stories is commonplace.
2. It is essential for the talent's *New Age* psychological, emotional, and spiritual well-being that they effectively manage their work-product expectations.

Plateauing

Employers hire on-air individuals with the idea that they will bring the talent in, get them up to speed, and then recoup the investment in them for years thereafter. That is one reason why talent contracts in large markets have in the past been three to five years long.

Talent, on the other hand, often accept positions because they seek new experiences in a larger market or in a different setting, because they need to learn new skills, or because they see a particular move as a means of achieving some further goals. The problem with this *Reality* is that talent often learn what they want to learn, or experience what they want to experience, and then want to quickly move on to the next position, market, or program. But what frequently stands in the way of talent leaving for a new and more challenging position are the two or three years left on their current employment contract.

I cannot begin to count the many calls that I have received from talent who have expressed their unhappiness, boredom, and frustration because they are no longer learning and growing in their current positions. They feel as if they are plateauing.

There is an inherent conflict here: Talent feel that they have stopped growing, so they must go on to the next position or job. Employers do not believe that they exist as graduate schools for talent. On the contrary, they are running a business, and they are there to take advantage—for a number of years—of the established skills and market familiarity that their on-air staff members develop *over time*.

Plateauing is a prevalent feeling and frustration for young broadcasters who want to keep growing, keep having new journalistic experiences, and keep getting better and higher-profile jobs. They want things to progress on *their* timetable. However, plateauing is also a problem for individuals who have, over the years, truly stopped growing and are bored to tears because they have—thousands of times—been there and done that. In *Broadcasting Realities*, I said that it has always been my gut feeling that there has been a high incidence of alcoholism (in between early- and late-evening newscasts) among established anchors because, for the most part, they now just show up at 5 or 6 p.m. and at 11 p.m. to read copy. They have nothing to do with the creative process and have had few, if any, new and exciting challenges in years. They derive little or no satisfaction from their jobs and have very little real interest in them. In essence, they have become brain-dead and desensitized by year after year having to read stories about murder, crime, and mayhem. But the paycheck and the hours that they actually work are great. So they will not—or cannot—leave their jobs. The only differences that *The New Age* has brought are that the paycheck will be nowhere near as large as in past decades, and there may well be less time between shows for anchors to leave the station and dine.

One solution to the conflict and feeling of plateauing may well be for young newscasters and established veterans to initiate, create, and enterprise their own stories, specials, series, franchises, and other vehicles as a way to keep growing, remain interested, and be and feel part of the process of improving their newscasts' content and increasing their overall appeal. (Because, at the end of the day, we all want to feel like we've made a positive difference.) Otherwise, plateauing and the frustration derived therefrom will remain major problems.

NEW AGE ISSUE

It is important to understand that broadcasting careers almost never rise in a straight ascension. Career advancement will often ebb and flow. The keys to avoid feeling as if your career is plateauing are to proactively and constructively initiate news product-enhancing opportunities and to find and create avenues in which to grow and learn.

Lack of Feedback

"Life is difficult" is the opening sentence of Dr. M. Scott Peck's bestseller, *The Road Less Traveled*. The life of a local newscaster is not only difficult, it can be totally absorbing, especially during the first half of one's career. There are no set hours, and often no set days off. Before you can put down roots in a city, you are off to take a position in another market. It is often the case that broadcasters—until they can strike a balance between their professional and personal lives, put some roots down, and become truly involved in a community—throw themselves totally into and are thoroughly absorbed by their careers. While singular focus is arguably an effective way to maximize one's potential for success, there is also a great danger: One's self-esteem and self-image may well become defined solely by success in the workplace, and they can rise and fall dramatically with day-to-day triumphs and defeats there. Furthermore, the nature and quality—or lack thereof—of the feedback that talent receive at the job can also significantly affect their sense of self-worth.

In almost all cases, talent do not receive much quality feedback regarding their work from their managers. And when they do receive feedback, in many instances it is negative.

Some observations:

First and foremost, most news managers and producers are hired because executives believe that these individuals can create a commercial and profitable product, or improve it. These managers often are hired because they have good or great technical and/or creative news and/or programming skills. However, news directors and executive producers are rarely hired because of their abilities to effectively communicate with or manage people. (If they have these skills, it is a huge bonus.) So always keep in mind the following:

1. Do not be surprised if your news manager isn't focused on making you feel good about your work, your talents, and your future.

2. With the very real, ever-increasing *New Age* pressure on news managers to do a great deal more with less (including being in charge of, or at least being integrally involved in, their employer's Web news content), and to initiate and respond to change in order to effectively compete (and survive) in this new ultra-competitive news and reality-based programming environment, they do not have the time to give very much, if any, in-depth feedback to talent. This is totally understandable with all that news managers today must accomplish. In most cases, their workload is *immense*!

3. There are some news managers who (consciously or unconsciously) embrace the philosophy that it is best to rule through never, or very rarely, giving any positive reinforcement. This way, talent will not become over confident, complacent, or lazy anchor/reporter monsters—especially come contract time.

4. Some managers aren't comfortable articulating their thoughts and feelings about a talent's work, or they have a hard time dealing with difficult issues or conflicts, so they take the path of least resistance—they avoid them.

Regardless of the reason(s), most broadcast journalists in the news and reality-based programming areas rarely receive any regular, tangible, constructive, or quality feedback/critiquing from their managers. This obviously is a problem if you want to effectively meet and/or exceed your management's expectations and if you want to improve and to grow.

NEW AGE ISSUE

It is rare that you will voluntarily receive any regular, high-quality feedback from your employer. Therefore, you must proactively seek out this
information from your exceedingly busy news managers and producers. It
is also important to cultivate worthy, diverse outside sources of feedback.

The Risks of Accepting Positions at Low-Rated Stations and Shows

Years ago, I wrote that low-rated stations tend to be reactive. If something positive doesn't happen fairly quickly after a change or a set of changes is implemented, different changes are soon initiated. In essence, the philosophy of this type of low-rated station is: "We'll keep trying and experimenting, as we have nothing to lose (by changing) until we get it right."

If this was a very real and pervasive problem fifteen years ago, it is exponentially more concerning for talent in *The New Age*. This is the case because low-rated stations, now more than ever before, need to have ratings and financial success, or at least viability; otherwise, they will be forced to file for bankruptcy or go out of business. Therefore, managers at low-rated stations often believe that they have little to lose by consistently making on-air changes. They hope that if they keep throwing different things against the wall, something—anything!—will stick and will resonate with and attract viewers, thereby allowing the station to attain some significant ratings growth. However, newscasters who base their lives and careers upon keeping the positions that they have accepted at these stations have a great deal to lose when management makes changes that involve them. Here are two pre-*New Age* examples.

Story #1: A #3-rated station was looking for two female weeknight anchors. (During the past few years, the station had gone through four female weeknight anchors.) This station was looking for one female to anchor three evening newscasts, including the main early- and late-evening newscasts, and another female to anchor one early-evening newscast and report for the 11 p.m. newscast.

Initially, the station found and hired a female to anchor the three newscasts.

(This choice was made after having three separate meetings with this prospective hire and after cutting two separate audition tapes with her.) Upon the closing of the deal, the female anchor and her husband moved across the country for this wonderful opportunity. Her hiring and a description of the position for which she was hired were announced at the station and in the press. However, before this female hit the air, the station found another female anchor that the station quickly decided was better for the main anchor position. So, before the already announced main female anchor had a chance to anchor her first newscast, her position was changed and diminished. Embarrassed and let down, she wound up anchoring only one newscast. Her replacement anchored three.

Then, within months, the demoted and devalued female anchor was told that she didn't fit into the station's long-term future at all. Therefore, her services were no longer needed, and she could leave. That day! The station would, "of course," pay out the remaining months of her contract.

When the devastated anchor asked why the station hadn't given her any warning of her impending demise and why she hadn't been given one bit of feedback to help her to improve or change her on-air work so as to better meet the station's expectations, the reply allegedly was, "It's nothing we can put our finger on. You've done everything that we've asked. We just feel that you're not part of our future, so we should cut bait here."

When station management was asked how it could bring someone across the country, immediately demote her, and then let her go before even one year of the contract had elapsed—especially since they had seen numerous tapes of her anchoring and had her make two audition tapes prior to hiring her—the management allegedly said, "It's business. Sometimes it [TV news] is a lousy business."

Story #2: A sportscaster who had a "shtick" was sought out by a #3 station because management at the station perceived a need to find someone who would stand out, in order to attract new viewers. Station management felt that a plain "vanilla" (non-controversial) sportscaster would not garner a sufficient amount of market sampling to increase ratings.

After three months, the station received a number of calls and letters saying enough negative things about the new sportscaster that station management pulled him off the air. They said that even though the number of calls and letters was not that great, they could not afford to lose any (of the small number of) viewers that they already had. So they had no choice but to let him go.

When I called that #3 station to say that the #1 station in their market had hired an equally controversial sportscaster years ago and had also received calls and letters after they hired their talent, the response that the #3 station gave me was: "Well, that station's #1. They can afford to give someone time to grow in the market. We can't. We need ratings *now*!"

How many stories do I have of #3 and other low-rated stations quickly bailing out on talent and their lofty plans for them? As the late Jimmy Durante used to say: "I got a million of 'em!"

It's a broadcasting *Reality*—and a profound problem.

NEW AGE ISSUE

Be careful when accepting a position at a #3 or low-rated station. There *is* a reason why these stations always have openings. It is called a desperate need and desire to increase viewership and thereby raise ratings and ad revenues.

Throughout this book I have warned against working for employers whose newscasts or programs are low-rated, because they all too often keep looking for the quick fix and do not stay the course long enough for their talent to succeed. However, there *are* worthwhile opportunities with employers that are not currently rated #1 or #2!

For example, years ago both the ABC and the CBS networks had a great array of news stars on their staffs—especially ABC. On the other hand, the NBC News division was in a building phase and was looking to develop its next generation of front-line talent. Because ABC and CBS had so many established veterans in place, there was little room for younger journalists to grow and receive plum assignments. However, this was not the case at NBC News. That is one of the reasons why Matt Lauer, Jeff Zucker, Katie Couric, Elizabeth Vargas, Brian Williams, Ann Curry, Tim Russert, Al Roker, Chris Hansen, David Bloom, Deborah Roberts, and many others fared so well at NBC. And although not all of these individuals stayed at NBC, all of them were given the chance to grow and to accomplish things that they might not have accomplished at the other networks. In this instance, there were opportunities to be seized at NBC, even though its news division, at that time, was not on top of the ratings heap.

Another reason why NBC, at that time, was a good place to grow your career was that Don Browne had just been made executive vice president. It was Don's goal to bring more women and individuals of color to NBC News. And because Don has tremendous depth of heart, soul, intellect, and humaneness, he was able to identify these same qualities in the new hires that NBC News made. Also, Jeff Zucker, the brilliant young executive producer of *Today*, was just beginning to ascend. The long-running success of *Today* continues to be a testament and clear reflection of Jeff's great vision and talents. All in all, the influence of Don Browne and Jeff Zucker made NBC News a rising star and a very enhancing place to work and grow, even if it was not at the time a ratings winner.

An example of a current rising-star news operation is the CBS-owned and -operated stations that are buoyed by upper-management's excellent taste in both talent and news executives, as well as by CBS's successful prime-time program lineup. The CBS-owned stations, which have been perennially #3 or worse, are far more successful today. For most talent who have recently joined a CBS O&O, the professional payoff has been rewarding and exciting.

NEW AGE ISSUE

Although it is often a very risky proposition to accept a position at a station, program, or network with low ratings, there are times when it can be just the right career-enhancing opportunity for you. Before you make such an important career decision, be sure that you know the history of the company for which you are considering working and who the individuals are who are presently in charge of your division and would be your employers. Two questions you might ask yourself are:

1. Do the individuals who will be at the helm of my division or my company have the requisite vision and a good, strong game plan in mind?

2. Does the company have the resources and the commitment to spend those resources in *The New Age* in order to effectively implement that vision and game plan?

The Pay Disparity in Broadcast Journalism

Years ago, for many broadcast journalists, gathering and reporting news was a calling, and the fruits that were reaped, for the most part, were the satisfaction of researching, writing, crafting, and telling an informative and compelling story that was of benefit to the viewer. Today, high-quality news reporting still may be a calling and a passion for many broadcast journalists, but, as we know, it can also be a very lucrative profession.

It is hard for some to understand and reconcile how networks and syndicated programs can pay some anchors and hosts millions and millions of dollars a year in salaries, while telling others that they will receive no raises or indeed must even accept pay cuts on their comparatively meager salaries. For example, a few years ago, an on-air reporter complained to me: "How can my [CBS-owned] station say that it can't give me a raise on my $90,000 salary, when the same company pays Katie Couric $15 million a year? My station's making money—even during this challenging time. I deserve more! I work just as hard as the anchors. [Station management is] not being fair."

Don Browne, whom we discussed in the last section, in essence once said to me: "[Great] talent is finite. There are very few Michael Jordans who can sell tickets and bring people into the tent. These are the Matt Lauers, the Oprah Winfreys, and the Katie Courics."[25] As Don and I have discussed, whether it is through insightful *Career Choreography*™, serendipity, or a combination of both, these individuals and other megastars of broadcasting have been fortunate to find a positive environment in which to work and an enhancing venue in which to appear. These gifts enable what makes the Matts, the Oprahs, and the Katies special and compelling to shine through and to attract viewers. In addition, Katie had tremendous leverage when CBS News decided to hire her away from NBC, as she was a tremendously successful host of *Today,* and she was already making a huge salary.

I expect that one of the effects of *Stage Three* (the economic downturn) is that almost all salaries have decreased, and that in *The New Age,* the pay disparity between most broadcasters will materially lessen. However, a significant pay disparity may well still exist between individuals who appear on national newscasts and shows versus those in local venues or, on occasion, between individuals working in the same position in the same shop. The key factors in determining salary levels are the perception and acknowledgment of a person's talent, the quantifiable ability to attract viewers, good contract-negotiation timing, and the perceived leverage to secure other (more) lucrative offers. These talents will, in most instances, earn top dollar—whatever that is in *The New Age.*

NEW AGE ISSUE

There will always be pay disparities between major national and local talents, and between individuals in the same newsroom or on the same show. Key factors in determining one's compensation are:

1. who has the acknowledged on-air abilities or "it" factor;
2. who brings viewers to the newscast or program;
3. who has the best timing regarding when they negotiate their employment contract; and
4. who has the most leverage.

The Right of Assignability Versus Controlling Your Own Destiny

Let me share four stories that illustrate the pervasive conflict between a broadcasting employer's desire to assign the employee to positions and programs of the employer's choosing and the employee's need to be assigned to specific positions and to work for specific kinds of programs that she or he perceives to be enhancing.

1. Years ago, I was negotiating a contract with a general manager, "Bill," whom I have known for as long as I have been in broadcasting. He is very successful and exceedingly bright. During the time that I have known him, we have completed many deals together; however, at one point, we, for a period of time, were unable to reach an agreement because we found ourselves at opposite ends of the philosophical spectrum. He was convinced that as long as his station pays an employee the contractually agreed-upon compensation, his management has the unrestricted right to assign and re-assign the employee to any anchor position that it chooses—regardless of whether the employee consents.

   My negotiation with Bill was in connection with my client "Alan," who had been a Monday through Friday, 5 p.m. and 11 p.m. anchor at Bill's station—"Station Z"—for the past ten years. About a year earlier, Station Z had been sold, and along with new management came a new company policy of not contractually guaranteeing which particular newscasts an individual would anchor.

The problem for Alan was that in all of his prior Station Z contracts, it was clearly written that he would anchor only the Monday through Friday, 5 p.m. and 11 p.m. newscasts. Otherwise, he could terminate the agreement at any time. And with new and unfamiliar management having just arrived at Station Z, Alan didn't want to sign a new contract that would allow that station to assign him, for example, to anchor the morning and noon, or the noon and 5 p.m., newscasts without his consent. He felt that he had established a following and a stature in his market, having anchored the 5 p.m. and 11 p.m. newscasts for years, and he didn't want to allow Station Z's management to tarnish his career by demoting him.

What Alan wanted was to control his own destiny. He said to me: "If [new] management decides during the contract to take me off of any newscasts [the 5 p.m. and 11 p.m.], that's their choice; but I do not want them to assign me to newscasts which I feel will be damaging to my career. I must have the right to refuse the reassignment. [If they take me off the 5 p.m. and/or 11 p.m. newscasts,] I want to be paid for up to six months, while I look for another position, and [then] have the right to terminate the agreement when I find it."

The general manager, Bill, felt that as long as his station paid Alan the agreed-upon salary (as the main anchor) and did not reduce it (as a result of changing Alan's duties), Alan shouldn't care which newscasts he was anchoring. As Bill said, "I just don't get it; he's getting paid the same, even if he anchors morning and noon. What a deal!"

I then suggested that the general manager consider the following: "Bill, I've known you for about fifteen years. I remember you as a news director in Baton Rouge. Through the years, you've paid your news-director dues, and then your general-manager dues. What if your company came to you and told you that they were going to demote you to news director of Station Z, but they'd still pay you your agreed-upon contractual salary. How would you feel about the demotion, and the perceived and real damage that the demotion could do to your career?"

Bill thought for a moment and responded, "If they paid me the same amount of money, maybe I wouldn't mind."

"Baloney, Bill! You know you'd mind, and I, your wife, and your ᴎ would mind for you. If you want to continue to grow in this business, you need to develop and to hone your skills as a general manager in a big market. The demotion would preclude you from doing that. And you know as well as I do that once your general manager's contract with Station Z expired, they'd cut your salary to be more in line with what news directors make. Right?"

"Look, Kenny," he said, "I need to do what's best for my television station; and if what's best for Station Z is putting Alan on different newscasts, then I need to have the right to do it."

"Bill, I know what you need, but my client also needs the right to refuse your reassignment, as well as the right to terminate the contract when he's found a suitable new position."

In this instance, both Bill and Alan made compelling arguments regarding the station's right of assignability. It is a profound and complex broadcasting *Issue*.

2. "Marc" joined cable network X as a feature reporter for a once-a-week program. At that time, his verbal job description was that he would do one long-form piece each week on the entertainment industry. However, after three weeks, the program was canceled, and the network news manager (who was very happy with Marc's work) reassigned him to do a daily report for one of the network's five-days-a-week programs.

   Marc was very unhappy about his new assignment, as his reason for leaving local news was to get away from day-of-air reporting, and now he was doing it again. When Marc went to his news manager and requested the right to terminate his contract, the manager refused, saying, "We're still paying you, and you're still doing entertainment reporting. Sorry, but we have the right of assignability."

3. "Rita," who is a successful reality-based program executive producer (and has an excellent track record producing syndicated shows), signed an agreement to develop and to be executive producer for a new talk/magazine show. Upon interviewing for the position, Rita was told that this show would be a cross between *60 Minutes* and *Oprah*. However,

months of low ratings, the head of the company told Rita now needed to become more racy (e.g., more tabloid) in order ratings.

rongly resisted the new direction of the show. She was soon fter told by upper management that she could leave the show terminate her contract), but if she did, she would have to give up about ninety weeks of guaranteed salary. That manager said, "You [Rita] have an agreement with us that says you're the executive producer of our program; but there's nothing in the agreement—nor has there ever been anything in any other executive producer's agreement with our company—that says that we can't change *the tone or content* of the show and assign the executive producer of that show to execute our vision. So, if you want to quit, it will be you who will be breaking the agreement. We'll let you leave, but you must leave now, and we'll stop paying you now. And we do not want you working for another syndicated program for, let's say, one year from today. It's your decision. Stay and executive-produce our show, or leave and find another position—but not in syndication."

4. "Russ" was a hard-news, investigative reporter at a local station in a top-20 market. He interviewed for a reporter position with a syndicated magazine show. At the interview, the executive producer described the program as an early-evening *Dateline* and said that it would be a news show, not an entertainment-oriented or tabloid show.

Weeks later, because of sagging ratings, upper management told the executive producer to make the show more sexy and more blood and guts. In essence: Air anything that will get the viewers to tune in.

Upon being assigned to do stories that he found embarrassing, Russ asked to terminate his contract. The executive producer confided that he, too, was often embarrassed by the kinds of stories that his show was now doing. However, he also advised Russ that "management" would not let any of the reporters out of their contracts, as they (management) could assign them to do whatever kinds of pieces that they want. That's it!

The common element in all of these stories is that broadcasting employers believe—and often stipulate in their contracts—that they have the right to assign you to any position that they choose and can require you to work on any program that they choose, regardless of the program's content, tone, and approach.

Conversely, talent, producers, writers, and other such employees want the right to control their own destinies. Or, put another way, they want the right to accept and to stay in positions that enhance them and their careers. They also want the right to refuse to be assigned to positions or to programs that will diminish or damage their careers and their self-esteem.

I believe that when a prospective employer and a prospective employee agree on what specific position an employee will assume, these individuals have, in fact, had a meeting of the minds as to that component of their agreement—especially if the talent has moved from another market or position and/ or has entered into a contract relying on the fact that he or she would assume a specific position. If the employee is then assigned to a different position without his or her prior consent, there is no longer a meeting of the minds as to that material element of the employment agreement. Therefore, the employee should be able to terminate the agreement anytime thereafter.

NEW AGE ISSUE

For employers: Money buys everything—or at least (total) assignability.

For employees: Careers are precious—and money doesn't buy everything.

Those are the perspectives. There is the conflict.

They are *Broadcasting Realities*.

Striking the Right Balance between Being Forward-Thinking and Being In-the-Moment

For the past 29 years, I have listened to broadcast journalists often impatiently think about and plan for their next job and then their next. And in many ways, that is what the process of *Career Choreography*™ is about. However, I am also often struck by the fact that these highly goal-oriented individuals aren't living in the moment or truly enjoying where they are at present. I view this as a shame, since I believe that it is important—as well as heart-, soul-, and psyche-nourishing—to enjoy the journey as much as, if not more than, the attainment of your coveted ends.

Appreciation of the journey, as well as your arrival, is important for a myriad of reasons. One huge reason is that oftentimes you spend years on your journey and only moments receiving and processing the great news that you've attained your goal. Or what if you do not attain your initial goal and also do not enjoy the journey? In all likelihood, you will not have a very fun or rewarding experience. Therefore, in almost all instances, no matter whether you achieve your initial goal or attain another unrelated one, if you savor the journey, you will have the opportunity to enjoy a great deal more of your work time.

In addition, although I agree that it's important to stay hungry and not rest on your laurels when trying to be the very best that you are capable of, I also believe that it is essential to enjoy and appreciate your accomplishments and successes. This will give you the core confidence and strong self-esteem to withstand the blows that you and your career will inevitably suffer along the way.

So, my best advice is to strike a healthy balance between being forward-thinking and hungry to make your next move(s) and enjoying your journey and your current career experiences.

NEW AGE ISSUE

It is important for broadcast journalists to strike a healthy balance between being forward-thinking and being in and savoring the moment... as these will one day be "the good old days."

The Business of Broadcasting

In the preceding sections, I have discussed the concepts of news executives' often choosing to air brain-numbing pop-culture stories, as well as a tremendous number of desensitizing and bone-chilling stories of crime, mayhem, destruction, and grisly death. Although I have expressed my concerns about the content of these stories and its profound effect on the psyches of broadcast journalists and the intellectual acuity of the viewers, it is clearly and totally understandable why broadcasting executives consistently air this material: While broadcasting may well be a noble calling to inform and intellectually equip the public for some or many broadcast executives, the first and foremost goal for (almost) all executives is to make money and increase profits. In almost all instances, the way to make the most money is by attracting the largest and most demographically desirable audience possible. And the means by which broadcasters accomplish this is by giving the viewers exactly what they (appear to) want—over and over again—so as to keep the broadcasters' hopefully expanding audience coming back for more each day.

Therefore, in many instances it is the *viewers* who dictate what news executives and programmers air—not the other way around. And can anyone really blame news executives and programmers for not trying to raise the content bar regarding what they choose to air if doing so might cause viewers to stop watching their newscasts and programs, which would decrease profits and the worth of their businesses?

My perspective is that it would be great if all newscasts took a bit of a higher road regarding their content, so that as viewers, we would become more knowledgeable and enlightened about how to live our lives in constructive and healthy ways. One means to do this is for executives to strike a *healthy balance* in their newscasts by mixing stories that will serve their viewers with stories that are clearly designed to seize them. It is arguable that by incorporating news that the viewers can truly use and stories that will uplift them, broadcasters will not only keep or increase their ratings and audience share, but also show their viewers that they care about their well-being and respect them. Uplifting and empowering viewers certainly worked for Oprah!

On a related note, I have also discussed here the often seemingly harsh treatment of talent by broadcast executives when they decide that they need to make on- and off-air talent changes in order to improve their on-air product. This, in many ways, is no different than what is done when professional sports teams cut players whom team executives feel they can no longer win with. To put this *Reality* in Darwinian terms: For professional athletes who compete for positions on their team, it is survival of the most talented and team-enhancing. Similarly, for on-air talent, it is survival of the most engaging, credible, and watchable. Essentially, the on-air talent who garner the highest ratings and the best demographics are the ones who most often survive.

What professional sports and news teams have in common is that executives give positions to those players and on-air talent, respectively, who these executives believe will put on the most compelling product to watch, generate the most team success, and make their employer the most money.* In both cases, the executives' first and foremost criterion when deciding who to hire or keep on their team is who will make their team—whether it be in sports or news—*the most money.*

As someone who represents talent, I understand and appreciate what the clear profit-maximizing mandate of the broadcast executive is, as well as the harsh *Reality* of what talent go through when they are trying to secure and/or keep their coveted positions and they *do not* succeed. The experience for talent of being demoted or losing their employment can be truly heartbreaking and devastating for them on many levels. I sincerely acknowledge and truly understand the very hard talent decisions that broadcast executives are called

---

* Where professional sports and the business of news differ is that in sports, if older player A is replaced by younger player B because team executives think that they have a better chance of winning with player B, player A doesn't bring a lawsuit against his employer for age discrimination. However, in the business of news, as we will discuss in an upcoming section, a number of disgruntled newscasters have brought suits for age, race, and gender discrimination when they have been replaced by an individual who is younger, of a different race, or of the other gender. These are *Broadcasting Realities*.

upon to make day by day; however, all one can ask of executives is that they put themselves in the shoes of the talent and treat them with as much compassion, concern, and dignity as possible, as they demote or part ways with them.

As you absorb the information in this book, please note that I am not in any way being critical of broadcasting executives for whom and what they choose to put on their air; because at the beginning, in the middle, and "at the end of *The New Age* day"—literally—broadcasting executives must make *the* most profit-producing decisions that they can, or they, too, will be replaced. This is a very clear *Broadcasting Reality*.

NEW AGE ISSUE

Broadcasting is a business, and almost all content and talent decisions are made in order to increase viewership and profits. This is understandable.

The Issues of Protecting and Preserving the Talent's Image and Brand

Throughout this book, I write that *New Age* thinking, strategies, and *Choreographies* require that on- and off-air talent engage in *Multi-Platforming* so as to increase their visibility, marketability, brand awareness, and income.

In an upcoming section devoted to contract clauses, I discuss the importance of carefully negotiating and crafting your exclusivity provision, as this is the clause that provides and lays the groundwork for what other projects, if any, you can render services for while you are working for your primary and/or current employer(s). An essential prerequisite of being able to successfully negotiate and craft the most advantageous exclusivity provision is being able to convince your employers that they should allow you to render your services on worthwhile "outside" projects during the term of your current employment agreement. In order to be as effective and successful as possible in making your argument, it is important for you to understand some of the very valid reasons why employers in the past have been reluctant or have refused to allow their talent to work and appear on outside projects. Here are four of the main reasons why employers balk at allowing talent to appear on third-party projects:

1. "Vacation is a time for talent to recharge their batteries; not to work and wear them down even more!"

   About fifteen years ago, I lobbied the president of a network-owned station group in an effort to secure his permission for a client of mine to use his (my client's) three weeks of vacation to host a cable series. This executive's very reasonable response was, "Kenny, vacation is just that, vacation; and it should be used as such. Our on-air people work hard during the year. They need to take their vacation to rest up, recharge their batteries, and come back fresh. Our on-air talent need to have their energy. They need to sell it and look well rested on-air. If they work during their vacations, they'll be run-down when they come back to work. That's not why we give them vacations. Besides, we pay our people very well, so they don't need to supplement their income."[26]

I believe that this individual makes a very compelling *Stage Two* argument regarding talent being unable to truly rest and thereby recharge their physical, psychological, and emotional batteries should they work during their allotted vacation time. However, *The New Age* has changed a great many *Realities*. Here is how you can counter the above argument today:

a. *New Age* employers are requesting that on- and off-air talent take pay cuts and unpaid furloughs. As a quid pro quo for accepting less (compensation and security), during your contract negotiations, ask for more vacation time, as well as the right to take unpaid time off. As a result, if you combine your vacation time, "comp" days (for working the sixth and seventh days in any one week and/or overtime), and unpaid time off, you can render services on outside projects and also take time to recharge your batteries.

b. During the *Stage Two* gravy days of broadcasting, many talents were paid better than they are today. Therefore, they did not have a truly compelling argument for doing extra work in order to supplement their incomes. However, in the cost- and salary-cutting *New Age*, there is a real need for on- and off-air talent to supplement their incomes by rendering services on outside projects.

Once again: *New Economic Reality*, new rules, new solutions!

2. "Talent can't render services on competitive shows, stations, or networks."

This is a very compelling and reasonable prohibition, and one that talent will very rarely be able to convince management to modify. However, as we have discussed in the *Career Choreography*™ section on *Multi-Platforming*, it is your job to understand which employers and venues are non-competitive with your current employer(s) and position(s), and to seek them out.

3. "Talent loss of focus."

From time to time, I have heard management argue that they do not want their talent participating in outside projects because the talent will lose focus on their (main) jobs. While this reasoning may have had some validity in the past, it is no longer an argument that has real teeth in *The New Age*. With talent today being asked to work much harder, for (much) less, and being given much less job security, supplementing one's income becomes a very real need. Just as talent must learn to give more and receive less, employers will have to be understanding if talent actually derive some enjoyment and occasionally focus on third-party work, as it's a *New Age* for both the broadcaster and the on- and off-air talent! Besides, I would be willing to bet that talent lose far more focus far more often in *The New Age* because they are worried about how they will pay all their bills, given their reduced compensation (and security).

4. "We need to have control of the talent's image in order to ensure that their image and brand aren't tarnished."

I am in full accord with management that on-air talent, no matter what they are paid, are valuable assets of the employer and its newscasts and/or programs. Therefore, employers have a very legitimate interest in protecting their talent's image and brand by not permitting the talent to render on-air services for an outside project that could tarnish or damage the talent. While I very much agree with management's concerns in this area, there are compelling ways to counter and allay them. Here are some arguments that I have successfully used to enable our clients to accept outside projects when the talent's employer was not in direct control of the third-party or outside production:

a. Secure a position with a show that is already on the air, so that your management can see for themselves the high quality of the production or the content of the show. For example, when Samantha Harris was offered a position on *Dancing With the Stars*, the executives at E! could see the high production quality and family-friendly content of *DWTS*, and therefore understand that being a prominent part of that show could only enhance Samantha.

b. Secure a position with a producer or carrier that has a proven track record of doing first-class work, with top-tier content. This is particularly important if the program for which you propose to do the outside work is not already on the air. By securing an on-air position on a yet-to-be-produced show that will be produced by a very reputable producer and be exhibited by a very reputable carrier, the high quality of the producer's past work product, combined with the program carrier's good reputation, may well convince your employer that you and your image will not be tarnished.

In addition, you may have to supply a program breakdown and/or a set of scripts to your employer so as to allay any content concerns.

c. Arrange for someone whom the employer trusts to have editorial control of or meaningful consultation regarding the content and tone of the show. Recently, I was integrally involved in putting together a syndicated show for a network talent. In order to be comfortable with allowing one of its marquee talent to participate in an outside-produced project, my client's current employer insisted that it have one of its top producers monitor the day-to-day content of the proposed show. This made my client's current employer feel a great deal better about there being sufficient brand and image protection for its employee.

d. If you are the creator or producer of the outside project at issue, do your best to have your employer produce and/or exhibit it. Therefore, your employer will have the desired quality control or input that they want and/or need in order to protect their investment in you.

NEW AGE ISSUES

1. Years ago, during *Stage Two* of broadcasting, the employer had compelling arguments regarding not allowing talent to render on-air services to outside employers. Many of these arguments are no longer as persuasive and can be effectively countered due to *The New Age Economic Realities*.

2. Almost all employers will be concerned about your image and/ or brand being tarnished should you render services on a project over which your employer has no production control. This is a valid employer concern, as your employer has a legitimate interest in protecting you and your image.

The Compromise in Broadcast Journalism and the Value of Emotional Intelligence

nfortunately, I am no longer surprised (but I am still profoundly disappointed) by the large number of individuals who reach decisions which allow them to settle for too little, to take the easy way out, and to be destructive to themselves, as well as to others. In my opinion, one of the foremost reasons why some broadcast journalists rise above the crowd and achieve their most cherished goals is that they are not only intellectually intelligent, but emotionally intelligent as well.

Some attributes that seem to be characteristic of emotionally intelligent individuals are the qualities of zeal and appropriate persistence, along with the ability to exercise *appropriate self-control*. Generally, these individuals know how to motivate themselves and to correctly read and understand the actions and emotions of others.[27] They are inclined to see people, things, and events with the insightful perspective of the big picture, and thereafter act constructively and appropriately with that big picture in mind.

Often broadcast journalists—like most individuals in our society—view their daily career actions and decisions in terms of "me": How does "X" act or event affect *me*? What's best for *me*? How do I increase *my* visibility and thereby enhance *my* career?, etc. I understand the many compelling reasons for talent feeling that they always need to protect themselves and their work product; however, I am of the opinion that the more you can work in concert with, be sensitive to, and be considerate of, the needs and goals of others, the more likely it is that you will achieve your full potential.

Emotionally intelligent people know how and when it is appropriate to protect and enhance themselves. They also understand that for real success to be achieved, everyone and everything involved with their work product must shine. Witness the wonderful chemistry, the excellent production, and the insightful topicality of NBC's *Today* show. Everything works.

A prerequisite for success in broadcasting is emotional intelligence, especially when making and implementing your decisions, be they large or small. Here are some illustrations.

Less-Than-Stellar Colleagues

One issue that all broadcast journalists must understand and be ready to face in *The New Age* is that mediocrity is a *Reality* in broadcasting, as it is in every other field, profession, and industry. Unfortunately, mediocrity seems to be woven into the American fabric.

Much mediocre and destructive behavior can usually be traced back to how individuals were raised, their earlier (non-positive) experiences, and the destructive and counterproductive defensive scripts that they have adopted and acted out over time. Of course, there are a myriad of other reasons why people do not give their maximum effort in all that they do, or why their work may not be of the highest caliber.

One reason for an average or less-than-average work effort may be the end effect of unions. Years ago, unions were a wonderful sword that was used to carve out certain rules and regulations so that workers were treated fairly, even-handedly, and humanely—all worthy goals then and now. However, it is arguable that some individuals* currently use union memberships as a shield; that is, as a means of getting by with a minimum work effort, knowing that their jobs will be protected by their unions.

For example, one day a client called me, nearly apoplectic. He was on his way to cover a huge breaking story for his network-owned station in a top market when his photographer informed him that he (the photographer) unequivocally had to stop for his union-guaranteed lunch break. The one-hour delay caused the reporter and his station irreparable damage in the ultra-competitive climate of covering this story. The reporter's comment to me was, "I know that I just arrived here from Sacramento, but our smaller market [non-union]

---

* But by no means all, or even many.

photographers never would have pulled this. They were our teammates in beating the competition. This guy [his photographer] couldn't care less; he's just collecting his paycheck."

I am not against what unions stand for, nor do I want to imply that many union members do not come to work hard every day, but near-complete job security in the hands of non-proactive, less-than-excited individuals can—and in many instances, does—produce less than top-grade results.

Additionally, with the vast proliferation of news-, business-, sports-, and reality-based channels, newscasts, and programs, the pool of available quality writers—who can write, spell, and know what and where Afghanistan is, as well as why the word "alleged" must be used in certain circumstances—is all but empty. Similarly, competent and experienced producers, directors, and photographers are hard to come by. And that is assuming that management is willing to pay for quality! Which is rarely the case in *The New Age*.

As we have discussed, on the one hand, executives in *The New Age*, because of the large supply of quality talent who need jobs, feel that they have the luxury of hiring only "A players" for key positions. On the other hand, with *The New Age* scarcity of money and resources, management feels compelled to hire on the cheap for many key behind-the-scenes positions. This translates into hiring young and very inexperienced individuals who have to learn on the fly, every day.

The bigger-than-life problem for talent is that it is your face that is on the air, and it is you who are reading the material written on shows produced and/ or directed by these novices—however well intentioned they may be. In fact, just the other day, a client called me to bemoan the *Reality* that the person running her New York City local-market station assignment desk had been promoted from the position of network page just the week before. As a result of that newbie's lack of experience, some reporters missed their slots in the station's evening newscasts by more than an hour—in the country's largest market!

I am endlessly amazed by how many stations and production companies can pay so much money for on-air talent, new sets, research, and so on—and have so much riding on their on-air individuals—yet countless times fail to protect and enhance their talent. So quite often talent winds up being angry with poor or incompetent writing, producing, directing, lighting, editing, or shooting, and angrily criticize the shoddy work—sometimes publicly. The writer or producer at whom the anger and criticism are leveled feels demeaned, embarrassed, and angry at being taken to task by a highly paid prima donna. And you (the talent) become labeled as "difficult," or a "pain" to work with.

On the one hand, you, as a talent, must protect your biggest assets—your on-air performance, your persona, your reputation, and your credibility. On the other hand, you cannot let someone else's low standards or inexperience cause you to react in ways that are counterproductive for you and can diminish your reputation. For example, all too frequently, poor behind-the-scenes work can lead talent to publicly treat inexperienced or inept individuals without respect or sensitivity. This is not only very poor and non-constructive behavior, but it is not going to encourage the criticized and demeaned person to support you thereafter.

The goal here is to act with forethought and emotional intelligence. I believe that you catch more flies with honey than with vinegar. That is, you will probably get the best efforts out of people when you treat them with respect—even if they do not appear to care enough or have the required experience for their positions. Sit down with them and clearly and respectfully explain what you do and do not need and/or want from them. In *The New Age, you may also need to teach!* From time to time, compliment these individuals on the things that they have done well, and articulate why you were pleased. Take an honest interest in their well-being and in their growth. Off-air individuals who respect and like the people with whom they work can be great, enhancing allies and can spread the good word about you throughout the industry. They are often proud to be associated with a high-quality talent who is also a thoughtful and considerate human being.

Conversely, if your relationships with off-air individuals are negative and vitriolic, these individuals can unintentionally or intentionally make you look bad. They can also label you as a bad newsroom citizen. Therefore, having a positive relationship with your coworkers deserves your attention, focus, and strategic best efforts. However, if after trying to work things out with the staff member at issue, you are unsuccessful at improving the situation, then it is absolutely appropriate and necessary to discreetly go to your management, discuss the problem, and devise an appropriate and enhancing solution.

The Squeaky Wheel

With news managers and producers as ratings-driven and as busy as they customarily are, it is no wonder that they do not have the time to be (intimately) familiar with, or to quickly remedy, a bad situation in which you are involved. This *Reality* is coupled with the fact that most individuals in our society deal in reactive crisis management and often never think in terms of being anticipatory, proactive, or preemptive. Therefore, squeaky wheels often do get managers' attention, whereas good-show citizens are often overlooked, since they aren't problems. In my experience, I have found that certain squeaky wheels, in many circumstances, do get the grease. Sometimes, they get (much) more grease than their talents and work merit. Thus, when there is a real problem that you cannot resolve, or you have an appropriate issue to discuss, do not be reticent about approaching management. But be sure that you have all the facts and that you are right—or at least have a firm basis on which to stand. Because if you complain too often or if you are not correct in your facts or your perception, you will quickly lose credibility with management, and you'll be less likely to get what you are looking for in the future.

I also believe that in many instances, squeaky wheels do get more and better assignments because they keep themselves on managers' minds. However, there is a point on the spectrum when the squeaky wheel becomes truly difficult, and then that individual can fall into the highly undesirable "life's too short" category.

The "Life's Too Short" Label

When a talent becomes too much of an internal problem or complains too frequently to management, he or she runs the risk of being branded with the "life's too short" label. This can occur when no matter what the positive benefits are from having a talent at the station or on a show, these benefits do not outweigh the internal poison that the talent has created.

Although being perceived as a problem by management is never a good thing, you may well not get fired because of it—if your ratings are good.

However, if you are deemed expendable in *The New Age*, then watch out! Don Browne, when he was the executive vice president of NBC News, gave me a memorable rule-of-thumb regarding "problem talent." He said that "When the maintenance of a news staff member becomes consistently greater than their talent, it's time to part ways!"

The key is to make emotionally intelligent decisions—that is, to have the insight and the discipline to know the appropriate, constructive, and enhancing behavior to engage in, given the unsatisfactory situation. It is so very important to know which battles are worth fighting and how to make win/win situations of the battles that you do choose to wage.

Your career and reputation are precious—act accordingly, appropriately, and respectfully. Doing this will pay great career and self-esteem dividends.

NEW AGE ISSUES

1. There are many people that you will work with who do not strive to do their best. This can detract from your performance and from the on-air product in which you are involved. Do your best to remedy problems through constructive and enhancing means.
2. There is a time to be a squeaky wheel and a time to lay back and not be a problem. Be as sensitive as possible to what is the most appropriate behavior for you to engage in, given the specific situation.

The New Age Pressures and Their Potential Effects on Truthful, Accurate, Well-Researched, and Humane Reporting

Throughout this book we have discussed how the already intense pressures on broadcasters and talent to increase (or at least, maintain) viewership, ratings, and profits has been ratcheted up in *The New Age*. In everyone's focused quest to accomplish these goals, there can be times when journalistically sound means of accomplishing coveted ends are ignored, compromised, or totally dismissed.

This chapter is devoted to raising your awareness of issues and pitfalls regarding potential compromises in truthful, accurate, balanced, well-researched, and humane reporting. A good portion of our examination was presented in my original book, *Broadcasting Realities*, as this issue is not a new one. However, this problem has, in many instances, been exacerbated by the economic downturn and the lack of any journalistic restrictions on many independent New Media writers.

The Pressure to Secure the "Get" Versus Truthful, Accurate, Well-Researched, and Adequately-Sourced Reporting

There have never before been so many carriers of news. In *The New Age*, you can receive your news from a myriad of sources, among them local stations, broadcast networks, cable networks, computers, smart phones, tablets, radio, newspapers, and magazines. With unparalleled 24/7 access to news comes unprecedented competition to attract and keep news viewers. One clear means to accomplish this is to supply your viewers with *differentiated content*: This is information that is different and better than that supplied by others. As a result, in *The New Age*, news, magazine, and talk-show on- and off-air talent feel an inordinate amount of pressure to unearth a breaking story, to uncover a new angle on an already existing one, to get the material that no one else has either found or aired, or to secure an interview that no one else has been able to obtain.

"The 'get' is newsroom parlance for securing the big interview or news scoop."[28] The "get" can increase ratings and revenues for an employer, bring prestige to a news-gathering organization, and bring the reporter(s) involved much kudos and various coveted awards, greater respect, a more prestigious position with employers, higher-profile assignments, and a more lucrative contract. Additionally, as we will discuss in an upcoming section devoted to the Internet and social media, if broadcasters have the get or some other unique material, they can use it to drive viewers to their Web site, and from the Web to their TV newscasts and programs. So securing the get can result in increased TV and Web viewership, increased ad revenues, and effective TV/Web integration and cross-promotion—all highly coveted *New Age* objectives.

Connie Chung wrote, "A 'get' brings viewers into the tent."[29] As former NBC News president Neal Shapiro put it, "You can't live on big 'gets' alone, but they are the bright neon sign that brings them [viewers] in."[30] These are just some of the reasons why the get is so coveted.

The problem with this *Reality* is that with today's constant pressure to one-up and beat the competition, it becomes easy for the get to take precedence over—or at least make reporters and news-gathering organizations forget for the moment—the principled and thorough means by which they must research a story, gather the facts, check them, and adequately source their material, as well as to consider and disclose the possible motives and biases of their sources. Additionally, because there is such enormous competition today just to secure a sought-after interview or source of information, these interviewees and sources—by virtue of their positions—wield a tremendous amount of power. As a result, reporters may not be as discerning, circumspect, and objective as they might otherwise be with their questioning and reporting. Why? Because they want to curry the favor of these interviewees and sources—or at least not anger them—for fear that they might lose future gets.

Years ago, a highly controversial article titled "Pressgate" appeared in the premier issue of *Brill's Content* magazine. In that article, devoted to discussing the shoddy press coverage of the alleged Clinton/Monica Lewinsky interaction, Steven Brill alleges that independent counsel Kenneth Starr illegally leaked details of grand-jury testimony to special "lapdog-like" reporters, who then reported Starr's information the exact way he wanted them to.[31] Brill claims that Starr gave certain reporters scoops, and these reporters in turn—and in return—wrote stories with little or no adequate and/or additional researching or sourcing of the material.[32] Why? Because these reporters wanted the get, and they implicitly understood the game: Kenneth Starr gave information out to the public in a controlled and choreographed manner, and the reporters would keep getting scoops.

Brill writes that the first three weeks of media coverage of the highly-publicized Clinton/Lewinsky story ". . . careened from one badly sourced scoop to another, in an ever desperate need to fill its multimedia, 24-hour appetite, and as a result the press abandoned its treasured role as a skeptical fourth estate."[33]

In reference to Brill's article, Starr wrote a strong and detailed nineteen-page rebuttal in which he answered Brill's allegations of illegally leaking material.[34] Regardless of whether Brill or Starr was correct, or whether the truth lay somewhere in the middle, Brill cites numerous instances in which top national television and print journalists reported gets to their viewers and readers that, he alleged, were not accurate or balanced, nor based upon eyewitness accounts or firsthand knowledge.[35]

Although Brill, in his article, cites many offenders as an illustration of a major news organization not adhering to established news reporting standards in order to report a perceived get, he discusses NBC News's unconfirmed report regarding President Clinton and Monica Lewinsky being caught in an intimate moment in particular. In this instance, allegedly Tom Brokaw and Claire Shipman broke into pre-Super Bowl programming with the unconfirmed report. A disgusted NBC reporter later called the unsubstantiated report "outrageous," as Brokaw and Shipman reported something without verification "just in case it turns out to be true."[36]

Three months later, when Brokaw was asked why he had aired that kind of a bulletin, he said, "That's a good question. *I guess it was because of ABC's* *report.*[*] Our only rationale could be that it's out there, so let's talk about it. . . . But in retrospect, we shouldn't have done it." [37]

The reason I quote Brokaw is because he explains that NBC News went with the bulletin—the get—as a reaction to the ABC News report. NBC—normally an excellent news-gathering organization—appears to have acted precipitously and incorrectly in this instance. Why? The competition made them do it.

Brill also alleges that many print journalists—as well as other experts in their fields, who might normally be more circumspect in what they report in print—seem to be much less cautious and less principled when answering questions on TV, especially on "news" talk shows (i.e., those aired on NBC, ABC, CBS, MSNBC, CNN, and FOX). Why? Maybe because these pundits and experts receive great career-enhancing exposure on TV, and some may even be rewarded with a lucrative full-time position on these programs if they can supply gets and spicy or provocative speculation to the viewers. As Brill writes, "Talk TV is the speculation game."[38] However, he warns that, "a rumor or poorly sourced or unconfirmed leak aired or printed in one national medium ricochets all over until it becomes part of the national consciousness. In short, once it's out there, it's out there."[39]

Years ago, a number of articles were written discussing CNN's embarrassing retraction of Peter Arnett's report, "Operation Tailwind." This piece alleged that during the war in Vietnam in 1970, the United States had used nerve gas in Laos as part of a mission to kill American defectors there.

When Floyd Abrams, a First Amendment attorney, was asked by CNN to investigate the story, he found that the reporter's allegations were unsupported and that the story should not have aired. When Abrams appeared on *The Charlie Rose Show*, he said,

> "I concluded that there was insufficient material for the broad-cast to have gone on the air; insufficient basis to sustain the broadcast today; that the broadcast was not fair; [and] that

---

* The "report" to which Mr. Brokaw refers, allegedly, is that of an ABC News reporter. Brill alleged that the report appeared to be erroneous; however, Brill wrote that ABC used it as a predicate for other reporting and interviewing, and later embellished it.[(140)]

the broadcast hadn't taken into account sufficiently the views of the people who disagreed with the thesis of the producers... That, [with] everything taken together, my conclusion is that the broadcast was simply insupportable."[40]

Were the direct or perceived pressures felt by the reporters and producers of this story to get CNN's new magazine show, *NewsStand*, off to a rousing start the cause of this alleged lack of journalistic competence? Or was it just the pressure to secure and to air a major get? Who knows? What is clear is that the reputation and image of one of the world's most well-respected and top-notch news-gathering organizations, CNN, suffered for a brief time because of someone's alleged poor judgment.

With pressures as intense as they are for broadcasters and talent to survive and remain viable in *The New Age*, it is arguable that the cutthroat and often standards-relaxed competition to secure the get has been ratcheted-up yet another level.[**] This very valid concern can be distilled from a *Los Angeles Times* article entitled, "Jackson Media Frenzy Faulted: Separating Truth from Rumor and Figuring Out Who Represents the Singer Aren't Easy in an Era of Nonstop News."

In this article, Michael Jackson's veteran public-relations consultant, Ken Sunshine, strongly criticizes the "error-prone" media coverage of Jackson's death, as well as the very poor standards that news divisions utilize when choosing their "motley" group of so-called experts whom they put on-air to enlighten viewers. Here in pertinent part is what Sunshine says:

> "People should be embarrassed when they print, blog, or say things
> on the air that are proven to be untrue...

** An illustration of this alleged relaxation of standards took place when Houston's KPRC-TV allegedly incorrectly Tweeted that dozens of bodies had been found in rural Texas. To quote TVSPY, "Spurred on by Tweets @BreakingNews and @newyorktimes, the story bounced around the Internet last Tuesday afternoon. But in the end, the police, acting on a tip from a psychic, didn't end up finding any bodies."
"The speed at which the eventual non-story traveled around the world gave many pause, as they considered the responsibilities that news outlets have in using their Twitter and Facebook accounts to share developing stories. 'Even in the age of intense competition and instant reporting,' wrote NPR blogger Mark Memmott, 'it's important for news outlets to remember they should stick to what they *know*, not what they *think* on stories like this'" (www.mediabistro.com/TVSPY-media-falsely-accused-in-KPRC's-dead-bodies-report-b1234).

The people that [the media] get to interview: Where are the standards of choosing somebody to go on-camera? The so-called experts, who the hell are these people?"[41]

One *New Age Issue* that is raised by Mr. Sunshine's vocalization of his perception that television news outlets have indiscriminately chosen so-called Jackson insiders to appear on-air, and that these insiders have given false information, is this: Does allowing *others* to give misinformation to the viewer as a means to one-up other news outlets or advance a story relieve that news organization from adhering to established news principles because the false information doesn't come directly from a news-division staff member?

In the interest of balanced reporting, I must ask this question: Are the aforementioned breaches of journalistic ethics and others that have taken place pervasive, or are they only isolated instances? There are individuals who compellingly argue that instances in network and cable news of the intentional disregard or omission of sound journalistic principles are, in the grand scheme, isolated. Years ago, a very wise, well-respected, and experienced network news executive shared his opinion with me that the number of instances in which excellent news-gathering organizations are in the wrong is *minuscule* compared to the number of correct reports that they file each year. This, he says, is analogous to the airline industry and the issue of plane crashes. Although crashes do occur, their number is tiny when compared to the number of successful plane trips.[42]

I would also add that no news gathering institution can be, is, or will ever be, perfect, as it is comprised of human beings—and human beings are not perfect. But when considered in a big picture context, news organizations such as NBC, CNN, ABC, CBS, and FOX have heretofore established relatively great track records for accuracy.

Taking this latter perspective into account, I end this section this way: Although I cannot quantify how prevalent intentional or unintentional breaches of sound journalistic ethics are, there is no question that they are an enduring *Broadcasting Reality*. With the competition for viewers and survival as intense as it is in *The New Age*, there continue to be potential pitfalls for all *New Age* broadcasters and talent.

NEW AGE ISSUE

With the intense *New Age* pressure on talent and broadcasters to secure an interview or piece of information first, there is great potential to bypass sound journalistic standards and principles.

The Value of Being Humane

Two other pressing issues should also be examined: Does the value of being humane—that is, the quality of having compassion and consideration for others—play any role in what the tone of a story or an interview should be and whether or not a news-gathering organization should air a particular story? And if compassion does count, has the competition to air the get made us lose or forget about the role of compassion in broadcast journalism?

On this subject, the story of *USA Today*'s allegedly pushing tennis legend Arthur Ashe to confirm or deny that he was HIV-positive comes to mind. In his book *Days of Grace*, Ashe recounts the conversation he had with *USA Today*'s managing editor of sports, Gene Policinski. Here in pertinent part is the conversation, beginning with Policinski's pivotal question.

> "Are you HIV-positive, or do you have AIDS?"
>
> "Could be," I [Ashe] replied.
>
> I couldn't lie to him.
>
> I also told Policinski flatly that I had no intention, at that time, of confirming or denying the story. I tried to argue with him, to make him see my position.
>
> "Look," I said with some force, "the public has no right to know in this case."
>
> As I saw this situation, the public's right to know really meant the newspaper's right to print. Of course, there would be people interested in, even titillated by, the news that I had AIDS; the question was, did they have a right to know? I absolutely didn't think so. The law was on the side of the

newspaper, but ethically its demand was wrong, as well as unnecessary.

"I am not a public figure anymore," I argued.

"You are a public figure," Policinski insisted. "And anytime a public figure is ill, it's news. If he has a heart attack, as you did in 1979, it's news. We have no special zone of treatment for AIDS. It's a disease, like heart disease. It is news."

Match point had come, and I had lost it....

I reminded him [Policinski] that I hadn't confirmed the story, as far as I was concerned.

The newspaper had put me in the unenviable position of having to lie if I wanted to protect our [my family's] privacy. No one should have to make that choice. I am sorry that I have to make that revelation now.

Was I justified in claiming that I had a right to privacy? Or was *USA Today* justified in asserting its privilege? For the record, the newspaper had acted with some deliberation.

No one could doubt, however, who had forced my hand.[43]

Tennis champion Chris Evert, regarding the press's course of action in "outing" Ashe, said, "It's like the press has given up a *touch of humanity*"[44] (emphasis added).

In the above situation, *USA Today* more than adhered to sound journalistic principles and appeared to have the law on its side. The question is, Did the value of being humane—being compassionate—regarding Ashe's desire for privacy outweigh printing the get?

Let's push the envelope a little further. I am aware of at least two totally separate instances in which individuals reported stories in newspaper gossip columns about two newscasters' personal lives that had the potential to seriously damage the careers of these two individuals. In both of these instances, the reporters had no firsthand knowledge of the information that they reported.

When I questioned these columnists as to the basis for their reports, and after I detailed the very serious personal and professional ramifications that their reports could have for them (the subjects of these reports), both columnists admitted that they had heard the personal gossip from people with whom they in fact had little or no familiarity. The reporters then apologized.

Here are the relevant questions: What is the public's right or need to know potentially harmful personal gossip about someone when that gossip in fact may not be true, regardless of whether or not the person at issue is a public figure? Is improperly sourced gossip what the Framers of the Constitution sought to protect with the First Amendment?

Is it humane to go with a get that has not been solidly researched or sourced *because you can protect yourself by saying "sources say" or "rumors have it,"* when the damage to someone professionally and personally can be devastating?

A related *New Age* issue is the *Reality* that bloggers who write or "report" stories are not governed by sound journalistic principles, such as making certain that a story or piece of information that is released is confirmed by at least two reputable sources. Because no such rules are in place for bloggers and other Internet writers, *anything can be written about anyone at any time.* And, as Brill writes: "Once it [a story or piece of information—true or not] is out there...it's out there for everyone else to use and piggyback onto."[45]

In an insightful *Broadcasting & Cable* article titled "News Orgs Battle Wacko Jacko Claims," written by Marisa Guthrie, the writer discusses the New Media's lack of sound journalistic standards and its dubious reporting regarding the death of Michael Jackson. In the article, former NBC News and CNN anchor and reporter Campbell Brown remarks:

> "This is random people throwing things up against the wall to see what sticks. Who are we kidding? I'm reading blogs just like everyone else. There's all kinds of misinformation out there."[46]

In the same article, Zev Shalev, the former Executive Producer of CBS's *The Early Show*, observes:

> "There are so many falsehoods. Every blog, every tabloid has a different idea of what's happened."[47]

Another pressing *New Age* issue is that with so many New Media writers printing inaccuracies, these falsehoods are circulating in the Internet information world, and they are thereafter stated by others as fact and/or used as the basis of future stories.[48] This is a significant problem.

There is also an abundance of Web sites that accept anonymous contributions from anyone with any axe to grind. These contributions may be totally untrue, vicious, and highly damaging; additionally, statements can be made with no attribution or corroboration necessary. So any unsound, crazy person or angry, vindictive individual can say anything he or she wants to say about anyone—including you!—and stand behind the shield of anonymity!

I love this country and its freedoms. I am in full support of the First Amendment. However, I do not believe that the Framers meant to protect anonymous or totally unsourced information that either the reporter or the Web site operator or owner *knows is false* or *should reasonably know is false*! Therefore I believe that those individuals who own or operate Web sites that carry anonymous, libelous information, if they meet either of the above criteria (regarding knowledge or that they should have reasonably known of the falsehood), should be held liable for damages *along with* the individual or individuals who wrote or contributed the false information at issue.

Let's continue to discuss the quality of being humane in deciding what is aired or printed. This is a story that was told to me years ago.

It was a slow news day. Then, suddenly, word of the Oklahoma City bombing cut through newsrooms like a sharp knife cuts through warm butter. One newsroom member allegedly blurted out, "Oh God—but thank God!"

In essence, what that reporter meant was, "Oh God, too bad for the many people who lost their lives and loved ones, and for those who will be permanently injured. BUT, thank God, we have a HUGE story. A tragedy! Just the kind of story that makes for great news and monster ratings. 'Breaking' national stories are defining moments for individuals and news departments. Stars will be born. Maybe one of those stars will be me!"

That reporter was sent to Oklahoma later that day by her station. Upon her arrival there, she camped out for hours at the home of a family that had lost a loved one in the bombing. She stayed there until she could ambush her prey.

Eventually, she was able to interview the grief-stricken mother of one of the men who had died. Throughout the interview, she allegedly asked question after question, trying to dredge up every bit of pain, hurt, and heartache from the victim's mother. Upon her return to the newsroom, the reporter allegedly was thrilled to report to her news management and colleagues: "I not only got the interview...but I made her [the victim's mother] cry! Wait 'til you see it [the videotape of the interview]. It's great!"

Unfortunately, this type of story is not new for me. Much too often, I have seen tapes or read articles in which broadcast and print reporters—in their efforts to create compelling or titillating television or copy—have trampled upon individuals' moral rights of privacy, their emotional well-being, and sound journalistic principles. Witness the paparazzi's alleged triggering of the high-speed chase and the car accident that ended in the death of Princess Diana. These acts were all done in search of the get, the rating point, increased readership, the Emmy, the recognition, the piece of videotape, or the story that will earn the reporter the next (better) position, or other perceived rewards. All of these are worthwhile ends. The problem lies in the insensitive and/or inhumane means of attaining them.

Jerry Maguire, the character played by Tom Cruise, said, as he was unceremoniously fired and kicked out of his athletic representation firm, "There's such a thing as manners...a way of treating people."[49] In many ways, this section is all about manners—the manner in which broadcasters, talent, Internet reporters, and social-media reporters conduct their professional lives, the manner in which they respect the subjects of their stories and their interviews, and the manner in which they respect their viewers or readers.

In law school, I learned about *the balancing of interests*. For example, in a right-of-privacy case, a judge must balance the interest of the alleged victim's right of privacy against the interest of the public's right to know relevant information. This latter right is given to the public under the First Amendment.

In *The New Age*, every news-gathering and -conveying entity is under tremendous competitive pressure to air or print whatever reliably sourced material it can. The question raised in this section is whether the quality of being humane or compassionate in reporting should play a bigger role than it currently does for news divisions and other reporters. And if it should, are there indeed times when the desire to air or print the get or the harmful, hurtful information will be outweighed by the need to be a humane and compassionate reporter?

NEW AGE ISSUES

1. In today's highly competitive news environment, there exists intense pressure to secure and to air the get—and to be the first to do it. This pressure can conflict with or overshadow the values of truth, accuracy, balance, and compassion in reporting. This is a *Broadcasting Reality*.

2. Is improperly sourced or researched gossip what the Framers of our Constitution truly sought to protect with the First Amendment? Should you be able to protect yourself when saying or presenting false material by simply preceding it with, "Rumors have it" and "Sources say"?

3. Should Web site owners be held liable for false statements or statements made on their sites that a reasonable person should know are false?

The Value of Diversity and Its Impact in *The New Age*

As we have discussed, in *The New Age* there is a paucity of open positions for which out-of-work or job-hunting talent can compete. As a result, the competition to attain any precious available position is fierce. Regarding this *Reality*, there are two issues to examine: Is this competition "fair," and is it equally weighted for all applicants? The answers are, in most instances, "Maybe" and "No."

We know that over the past 35 years, broadcasters have gone to great lengths to provide both ethnic and gender diversity on their newscasts and programs, as well as in their newsrooms and production offices. In recognition of these *Realities*, many issues arise in connection with the practice of ethnic and gender diversity in *The New Age*. However, before we address these issues, let's study some relevant background information.

The Concepts of Racial Discrimination and Affirmative Action

"Minorities"

Professor Man Keung Ho writes that when one is a member of almost any "minority" group, that person shares a unique social and cultural heritage that is usually passed on from generation to generation. That heritage encompasses a member's sense of belonging to the group, and the group's unique way of valuing, feeling, acting, and perceiving the world. [50]

One common history that most ethnic minorities share is that they, in a number of instances, have been discriminated against, held back, and treated as inferior by mainstream society.[51] Ho writes that the term "minority" can mean an out-group whose worth, culture, values, and lifestyles are depreciated, devalued, and stereotyped. "Minority" is often synonymous with blocked access to politically and economically powerful in-groups and the full benefits of the American way of life. Ho says that the prevalent American (majority culture) way of life generally standardizes individuals and is intolerant of cultural and racial differences.[52]

In our discussions, we will respect Professor Ho's perspective on the potentially demeaning or diminishing definition of the word "minority" by not using it unless it is incorporated into a quotation. Instead, we will use the terms "ethnic group" and "individual(s) of color" to be synonymous with what we generally understand the terms "minority" or "minorities" to mean.

The Lack of Ethnic Diversity in TV News

Years ago, there was almost no ethnic diversity in news. Ed Bliss writes:

> The headline appeared in the *New York Times* on December 3, 1972. It called attention to a study conducted by the Office of Communications of the United Church of Christ. According to the study, half of the commercial television stations in the country didn't employ as anchor, reporter or producer, let alone as manager, any black man or woman, American Indian, Oriental or Hispanic. News was being reported largely from the perspective of white males.
>
> Discrimination was not limited to television. A survey made by the *Columbia Journalism Review* and B'nai B'rith in 1968, found that of all employees in the news media, broadcast and print, blacks constituted only 4.2%. If the sign in some of journalism's show windows said, "Minorities Wanted," it also said, "Not Too Many, Not Too Fast."[53]

In a 1998 *RTNDA Communicator* article, Bob Papper and Michael Gerhard discuss the Court of Appeals's finding that the Federal Communications Commission's EEO rules at that time were unconstitutional and thereby overturned the FCC requirements that stations actively recruit "minorities."[54] (Subsequently, the FCC modified its EEO rules. These new rules are discussed below.) Interestingly, when asked about the impact of the FCC EEO regulations being found unconstitutional, Papper and Gerhard reported (in 1998) that almost all white news directors with whom they spoke expected no change in the recent proactive ethnic diversity hiring practices should the aforementioned FCC hiring guidelines disappear. However, *every* non-Caucasian news director whom they interviewed felt just the opposite.[55] For example, Barbara Hamn, then the executive director of news and programming at WTKR in Norfolk, Virginia, said (apparently assuming that most news-station owners and executives were white), "I just think that most people are more comfortable with their own...and that's what they're going to go back to." Hamn continued, "If nobody's holding your feet to the fire, you're not going to go out of your way to find minority candidates. You hear people complaining of how difficult it is to find minority candidates for producer and director positions... and [if FCC guidelines no longer exist] it's going to be easier to just wipe your hands and not worry about it. And that's frightening."[56]

Will Wright, former WWOR-TV news director, echoed Hamn's views when he said, "I don't think we should need a law that tells us who should get served in a restaurant. But it turns out that [we] do."[57]

When discussing some (Caucasian) manager's statements that hiring practices would not change should there no longer be any EEO rules in effect, Phil Alvidrez, who, at the time, was the executive news director at KTVK in Phoenix, said:

> I just don't believe that history gives us any promises or confidences that that's going to happen. And if anything, I see a swing back in a lot of people's attitudes toward race, and that's sad because it takes a lifetime to reverse this kind of thing.[58]

I agree with Hamn's, Wright's, and Alvidrez's perspectives and concerns. Personally, I believe that many managers often do tend to hire people like themselves. Therefore, if most station and network owners and executive managers are white, they will hire whites.* This is one of the overriding reasons why, until a few decades ago, newscasts were "lily white."

Although in some areas there is far more diversity in *The New Age* than there was years ago, one stunning statistic stands out. Today there are *no* individuals of color permanently assigned to anchor ABC's, NBC's, CBS's, CNN's, or FOX's weekday evening newscasts of record. None! So, for all of these network news divisions, when it comes to Monday through Friday evenings, until literally days before this book went to press and I closed a deal for my esteemed client, Lester Holt, to become the host of NBC News' *Dateline,* it has been virtually "all white, all night!" However, with profitability, viability, and relevancy being the predominant values today, I also believe that network, station, and program executives will hire and air anyone who will win for them, regardless of who and what they are. So if diversity attracts and keeps viewers, newscasts may well be diverse. Because profits rule!

Affirmative Action

Affirmative action is a concept and practice designed to give a particular ethnic group or certain ethnic groups an equal chance to succeed, or to put it another way, it is a means by which the playing field can be leveled. In my experience, there are two main ways to practice affirmative action. One is to make sure that

---

* Interestingly, just as this book was going to print, I was given a study, conducted by MediaMatters for America, titled "Gender and Ethnic Diversity in Prime-Time Cable News" (mediamatters.org/reports/diversity_report). This report focuses on the gender and ethnicity of every guest who appeared on four programs on each of the three cable networks, CNN, FOX, and MSNBC, during prime time in May 2008. The data on ethnic representation were not at all encouraging regarding on-air diversity:
"Overall, 84 percent of the prime-time guests on the three cable networks were white. FOX News was the whitest network, with 88 percent white guests. Both CNN and MSNBC came in at 83 percent. According to the study, less than 3 percent of the guests on cable news and only 1 percent on MSNBC were Latino." Additionally, there were some ethnic groups that were excluded entirely.
It is arguable that one can conclude from these findings that when broadcasters aren't policed regarding diversity hiring, or when there doesn't appear to be any financial incentive to have on-air ethnic diversity, their news product will, for the most part, lack meaningful diversity. From my perspective, in *The New Age* there seems to be significant anchor and reporter ethnic diversity in local news. Depending on the network, there is a fair to good amount of ethnic diversity on broadcast network newscasts and much less ethnic diversity in cable news.

every candidate is treated and judged equally in all hiring processes and then let the most qualified person win. The second is for executives to *predetermine* what race they want their talent hire to be, thereby completely excluding candidates of all other races from the competition.

The first practice, ideally, would allow the best candidate, regardless of race, to secure the position. The second practice *guarantees* that a member of a specific ethnic group will get the job. For some, this second practice smacks of reverse discrimination, and it may have some detrimental side effects, both for the individual who is given the job and for those who never had a chance to be considered because of their race. As I discuss later in this section, this practice could have negative legal repercussions for employers as well.

Nobel Peace Prize winner Dr. Martin Luther King, Jr., was a proponent of an affirmative or proactive means to compensate the African American for society's past injustices and defaults. He wrote:

> Among the many vital jobs to be done, the nation must not only radically readjust its attitude toward the Negro in the compelling present, but must incorporate in its planning some *compensatory consideration* for the handicaps he has inherited from the past.[59]

Early on in broadcasting history, the reason members of certain ethnic groups were hired for specific broadcasting positions was to redress the wrongs of which Ed Bliss wrote—of having no or very little ethnic diversity in newsrooms. However, as time has passed, in many (but certainly, not all) instances, there have been many compelling business reasons to practice and encourage ethnic diversity. Now, many managers strive to hire individuals who represent the racial composition of their viewership. This has come about for the following reasons:

1. The Federal Communications Commission has put stringent Equal Employment Opportunity (EEO) regulations in place. These regulations require that TV stations achieve broad outreach in their recruiting for job vacancies as a means to meaningfully increase diversity in the job-applicant pools. Additionally, the FCC mandates that stations

document their diversity outreach efforts in an annual EEO report, which is to be posted on the station's Web site and maintained in the station's public inspection file.[60]

2. Various coalitions and interest groups have effectively put pressure on stations to hire members of their particular race. If the stations do not, I am told, the coalition will complain and lodge protests with the FCC, with the hope that license-renewal pressures will force the station to hire more of their own.

3. Diversity can be a goal for such reasons as that it is mandated as a condition of a sale. For instance, in Comcast's acquisition of NBC Universal, included in Comcast's agreement with the government were several memorandums of understanding. These memorandums require Comcast to take diversity seriously, with agreements in place to add ten new minority-focused channels to its cable lineups, to expand distribution of the minority-targeted networks it already carries, and to convene a diversity council composed of African Americans, Asian Americans, Hispanic Americans, Native Americans, women, the LBGT community, people with disabilities, and veterans.[61]

4a. By having more individuals on their air who reflect the racial composition of their viewership, stations hope to attract viewers of those races to watch their broadcasts.

4b. By reflecting the ethnic diversity of the community that a station serves, its management believes, the station will be more successful. As one well-respected vice president of news said, "My belief is that if you're not a reflection of your community, you're in trouble....You're not going to have any viewers. They're going to say, They [the on-air staff] just do not seem to be like us. They do not reflect our views, so we're gone."

4c. By striving to attain diversity of background and opinion in its newsroom, management believes, its news operation and product will be more broad-based, more balanced, and therefore more effective.

5. The individuals doing the hiring—along with deriving the hoped-for

financial benefits of having their news product ethnically reflect its viewership—believe that having ethnic diversity on the air is the right thing to do.

So for a myriad of reasons, broadcasting executives engage in affirmative action by mandating that they hire a person of a specific race for a particular position, while completely excluding individuals of other races from consideration. Here are four illustrations of this process at work.

Story #1: A number of years ago, I had a white reporter client whom just about everyone at her station respected and liked. As the expiration of her contract approached, she received numerous offers to anchor and report in various places. At one point, the then-current African-American weekend anchor received an attractive job offer at another station, which she accepted. Thereafter, my client began to fill in as the weekend anchor. From everyone's perspective, she did an excellent job. Her management—who desperately wanted to have her stay at the station long-term—told me so. Even her co-anchor went to his news director and recommended that they put my client into the vacated spot.

When I asked her management why they didn't give her the weekend anchor position so that everyone would be happy, the news director replied, "Kenny, you know I must fill that job with a black. The black coalition will be picketing and down my throat within five minutes if I put your [white] client in there!"

I replied, "You know that you're forcing my client to leave your station and her hometown to take a weeknight anchor job in another city. However, if you promote her [to weekend anchor], you'll be able to groom her as your next weeknight anchor. She'll happily stay at your station for the rest of her career! It's the perfect plan."

His response: "Yes, in an ideal world it would be perfect, but not in the real world. I gotta hire a black."

My client thereafter left her station—and her hometown—to become a successful weeknight anchor in another market. Ultimately, the station that my client left hired an African-American female from a smaller market to replace her and be the weekend anchor. About two years later, that African-American anchor left the station for a job in another city.

Story #2: A weekend Latino anchor was lured away from a station ("Station A") to another one ("Station B") in the same market to become its 4, 5, and 10 p.m. weeknight anchor. The current 4, 5, and 10 p.m. weeknight anchor at Station B was African-American. Station B management decided to relieve the African-American anchor of his weeknight position, after many years of service, because of poor research results.

When the hire of the Latino individual was announced, a prominent black interest group vehemently protested the move and asserted so much pressure on Station B's management that Station B reneged on part of its promise and contractual obligation to the Latino anchor; Station B retained the African American as the weeknight 10 p.m. anchor—until he was ready to leave.

From my perspective, this rethinking (or retreating) by Station B occurred as a result of the fact that the market in which Station B is situated has a significantly larger African-American population than Latino, and the interest groups for African Americans are far more active, protective, and influential than those for Latinos. In essence, it was to Station B's benefit to satisfy an employee of one race over an employee of a different race, because one employee's race and special interest group was more important to a station's viewership and license-renewal prospects than those of another.

Story #3: The Latino coalition is very strong in a major market, and Latinos make up nearly half of its population. As a result of intense Latino coalition pressure, stations in this market are under close scrutiny and a great deal of pressure to hire many Latinos for their news programs—and they have. Interestingly, there are many Asian Americans living in this market, but for many years there have been far, far fewer of them on the air than Latinos. In fact, one major station in that market didn't have one Asian American on its air for more than a year. It appears that because there was no Asian-American interest group putting pressure on any of the stations, hiring Asian Americans was not a priority.

Allegedly, a few years ago, the Hispanic coalition was exerting tremendous pressure on one particular network-owned station in this market to hire more on-air Latinos, so much so that the general manager's position was in serious jeopardy. Allegedly, one of the results of this pressure was that the contracts of two very well-respected and experienced white reporters were not renewed, and two far less experienced, smaller-market Latino reporters were hired in their places. This was accepted without incident or notable attention from any parties.

Story #4: An 11 p.m. weeknight anchor position became available at a large-market station. A day or so after the opening was made public, the general manager and news director of the station called the agent for "Tom," the 5 p.m. weeknight anchor, who was white. They said that it was "very likely" that Tom would be assigned to anchor the 11 p.m. newscast once they "went through some formalities."

However, after a series of heated meetings with prominent members of the black coalition, who urged that Michael, the station's African-American weekend anchor, be promoted to anchor the 11 p.m. newscast, the general manager and news director changed their plans and assigned the 11 p.m. newscast to Michael.

Within a year or so, Michael had attained so much acceptance and success that he was promoted to anchor a second evening newscast.

The Issues

It is a *Reality* of broadcasting that there will be some positions that talent will not be offered because they will not even be in consideration for them. In seeking to attain ethnic diversity, many employers feel that they need to engage in exclusionary hiring practices. To state this *Reality* in the most constructive way possible: Employers want to be ethnically sensitive to and reflective of their viewership. Put another way, employers cannot afford to put their license renewal in jeopardy or to alienate significant portions of their viewership by not being ethnically diverse.

This *Broadcasting Reality* has both good and bad points.

I, and a multitude of others, am a huge proponent of ethnic diversity on- and off-air. I believe that ethnic diversity is needed and necessary. The issue lies in the means of achieving this desirable end. Ideally, but especially in *The New Age*, most individuals would like to feel that they have an equal opportunity to secure any and every highly sought-after position for which they are qualified. However, the past practices of stations have shown that until outside pressures were exerted, only whites, for the most part, were hired for on-air positions.

As I mentioned in Story #3, Asian Americans were underrepresented (and in one case were not represented at all on-air at one station) in a major California market because no outside pressure was being put upon the stations to make an Asian-American on-air hire. So the question becomes: If some employers cannot be ethnically responsible on their own, what are the most effective ways to protect individuals of color from white executives' alleged predispositions to hire whites? In the past, coalition and FCC pressure exerted on station owners and executives to practice affirmative action or people-of-color compensation has been the predominant means to accomplish this. Recently, networks have hired individuals whose primary responsibilities are to ensure that news staffs are ethnically diverse. The hiring and promotion of ethnically diverse executives has also been a catalyst for hiring ethnically diverse on-air and off-air staff members.

Another issue in connection with affirmative-action hiring practices is the perception and fear of some executives that once they hire someone of a particular race for a position, it will be extremely difficult to fire** or demote that person or to replace that person with an individual of any other race because such action will almost surely subject the station or network to protests, pressures, and allegations of discriminatory practices.

I have found that depending upon the market and the race of the individual at issue, stations in many cases *do* feel compelled to replace one person of color with a like individual, mainly as a result of coalition pressure and occasionally fear of viewer withdrawal. Not only does this practice preclude individuals of other races from being considered for these positions, but it certainly ties managers' hands with regard to how to most effectively configure and construct

---

** An illustration of this fear came up when I was proposing that an African-American reporter be offered a *very specialized* correspondent position. Everyone concerned agreed that my African-American client—like some other of my non–African-American clients—didn't have the specific (scientific) knowledge ideally needed for this position. In the past I had successfully overcome this obstacle by proposing that the employer at issue sign my (white) clients to a contract that contained an employer's right-of-termination clause after one year if my client was not doing well as a result of lack of expertise and comfort with the subject matter. In this last case, however, the individual doing the hiring for this company declined to hire my (African-American) client. He said, "Kenny, normally I might try your proposal, but with a black [candidate], if [after a year] I fire him because it doesn't go well, I subject us to all sorts of [racially based] problems. It's just not worth it."

their talent lineup. However, there is one other question that should at least be explored: If stations feel that once they put an individual of a particular race in a particular position, they are "forever" locked into a person of that race for that position, will this have a chilling effect upon putting a person of color in the position to begin with?

Another issue is how one's newsroom colleagues feel about a person of color getting or keeping a job based solely or largely upon the criterion of race. For example, in Story #1, I discuss the situation of a very talented and popular white female anchor who had to leave her station because the only anchor position that was open had to be filled by an African American. Everybody at the station knew this. How did this affect the way others perceived, treated, and valued the African-American anchor who ultimately was given the job? And how did the well-known fact that this African-American anchor was offered the job—in lieu of the white female—solely or largely because of her race affect the African-American anchor's own self-esteem, confidence, and growth?

These are real questions that often have no clear answers.

NEW AGE ISSUE

For a number of reasons, it is often important for networks, stations, and producers to engage in exclusionary hiring practices in order to have ethnic diversity on the air. The goal is a desirable one; the means are debatable.

The Issue of Gender Diversity: Affirmative Action in Connection With Who Is Given a Particular On-Air Position and How That Decision Is Reached

In 1998 the case of *Janet S. Peckinpaugh v. Post-Newsweek, et al.* was tried and decided. Below, I have reprinted a paper that I wrote regarding the *Peckinpaugh* case, as I believe that it identifies and discusses some very important concerns and *Realities* for broadcasting employers. (Please note that I had been Ms. Peckinpaugh's agent for more than fourteen years. I was deposed twice before the trial and testified at trial.)

The Dilemma That the Janet S. Peckinpaugh Case Poses for Broadcasting Employers Who Seek Ethnic On-Air Diversity

For the past sixteen years, I have been a proactive representative of, and *Career Choreographer*™ for, some of this country's finest broadcast journalists—many of whom are ethnically diverse. Along with many other individuals involved in broadcasting, I fervently believe that newscasts and reality-based programs must be ethnically diverse, both on the air and off. However, in light of the recent federal court decision in *Janet S. Peckinpaugh v. Post Newsweek Stations Connecticut, et al.*, I am concerned that constantly beleaguered and well-meaning news and reality-based program executives, who strive to attain ethnic diversity on-air through certain exclusionary hiring practices, may well be unknowingly violating anti-discrimination laws and thereby subjecting their companies to potential major damage awards.

As a talent representative, I am called upon almost daily by news and programming executives who say that they have an opening, or a potential opening to fill, *but that they MUST hire an individual of a specific race to fill it*. Often, these executives say that they want to reflect the ethnic make-up of the community that their newscasts and programs serve. They may also share the belief that cultural diversity in the newsroom and on the air best serves their station, the content balance of their newscasts and programs, and their viewers.

These are all worthy goals. The issue is: How to legally attain them. I submit this paper to encourage vigorous discussion on this subject.

Below is a scenario that I have constructed which illustrates a *potentially* dangerous on-air decision-making practice:

In a top market, where there was a very large Hispanic population, but also a substantial Asian population, a station had a 5 p.m. weeknight anchor position open. During conversations with various agents, the news director of that station confided that he needed to find an Hispanic anchor to fill the opening.

After four or five months of being unable to find the "right" Hispanic individual for the position, station management eventually conducted focus-group testing to assist in finding the best (Hispanic) candidate. This test sample was comprised *solely* of Hispanic broadcast journalists.

During this time, there was an Asian weekend anchor at the station who was very highly regarded. When that Asian anchor's representative called the stations' news director to suggest that his client be given the 5 p.m. position, the news director replied that an another time, in another setting, the Asian anchor would be an *excellent* choice for the job; however, in this instance, he *must* hire an Hispanic individual to fill the spot. This was the case notwithstanding the fact that there was already an Hispanic individual anchoring the weekday morning newscasts.

When the representative then asked that the station include his Asian client in the focus-group testing, in order to determine the community response, the station management declined. They said that they must fill the position with an Hispanic individual, as they wanted to ensure that their station's on-air personnel reflected the ethnic composition of their viewing community. Therefore, regardless of the fact that there was a significant Asian population in the station's market, and that there was no Asian weeknight anchor at the station, the Asian anchor was not included in the focus-group testing.

One month after the research was completed, an Hispanic individual was given the position.

Recently, in the case of *Janet S. Peckinpaugh v. Post-Newsweek, et al.,* a federal court jury found, among other things, that the Post-Newsweek company was guilty of gender discrimination. In that case the management of WFSB in Hartford, Connecticut, hired anchor Al Terzi from its competitor, WTNH, in New Haven. When Mr. Terzi was hired, the plaintiff in the case, Janet Peckinpaugh, who had been a ratings winner at both WTNH and WFSB, was anchoring the 5 p.m. and 6 p.m. weeknight newscasts, and was one of the females being considered as a co-anchor with Mr. Terzi. The station conducted viewer research, having all three of its weeknight female anchors take turns sitting next to Mr. Terzi, in order to determine who would be the best choice to anchor the 5 p.m. and 6 p.m. newscasts with him. After receiving the research results, Ms. Peckinpaugh was removed from anchoring the 5 p.m. and 6 p.m. newscasts. These newscasts were then anchored by Mr. Terzi and another female anchor. Ms. Peckinpaugh was reassigned to anchor the Monday-through-Friday noon and 5:30 p.m. newscasts with another female anchor; however, she was eventually taken off the noon and 5:30 p.m. newscasts so that WFSB could have a (traditional) male/female anchor pairing on those newscasts, as well. Thereafter, Ms. Peckinpaugh was offered a lesser contract to anchor WFSB's weekend newscasts with a male anchor.

The jury, in this case, found that WFSB management committed gender discrimination by taking Ms. Peckinpaugh off the noon and 5:30 p.m. newscasts after *pre-determining* that their anchor team *had* to be the traditional male/female pairing. In this instance, WFSB's management allegedly never considered that two females anchoring the noon and 5:30 p.m. newscasts could be their most effective pairing.

As an extension of this theory, I would argue that the

original testing of three females with only one male, Mr. Terzi, also constituted gender discrimination, because station management again allegedly *pre-determined* that the 5 p.m. and 6 p.m. news-team pairings *had* to be male/female. Since each of the females was paired *only* with Mr. Terzi, the focus-group testing precluded a finding that the best anchor team could be comprised of two women. In the Peckinpaugh case, the plaintiff was awarded both compensatory and punitive ($3 million) damages in connection with the finding of gender discrimination.

According to Mike Allen, in his *New York Times* article, "Jury Awards Anchorwoman $8.3 Million in Sex Bias Case" (January 29, 1999, A-17), "[a]fter the verdict, Mr. [Bill] Ryan, the Post-Newsweek station's president, said that the discrimination laws apply to hiring, not to pairing [of broadcast journalists]." Obviously, the *Peckinpaugh* jury found that *these laws* do *extend to which particular individuals broadcasting employers put on the air and to* how *these employers reach and justify their on-air decisions. This finding can apply equally to on-air decisions based upon race.*

Using the *Peckinpaugh* case as a guide, if news and program executives and their consultants *pre-determine* that an individual of a *specific race* must be hired for a particular position, and *preclude* individuals of other races from being *equally* considered for that position, they may well be found guilty of racial discrimination. The smoking-gun evidence will be if stations and/or their consultants perform viewer research and the candidates in that research are only of one specific race (or if the research is skewed in favor of individuals of a specific race).

Therefore, according to *Peckinpaugh*, broadcasting executives should not make an on-air decision or be involved with research based upon the *pre-determined*, etched-in-stone goal of having individuals of only one race as candidates to fill a particular position. The key, under *Peckinpaugh*, is to allow candidates of *all* races to have an equal opportunity to compete for any given position, and to let *neutral* research help determine who fills which on-air roles.

The dilemma in all this is: Broadcasting employers want ethnic diversity on their newscasts and programs. However, certain often-used exclusionary hiring practices that ensure diversity on-air actually place employers at risk of violating discrimination laws. On the other hand, if employers open up on-air decisions to candidates of all races, as the *Peckinpaugh* decision appears to mandate, employers run the risk of having less, or no diversity at all on the air. Therein lies the problem presented by the *Peckinpaugh* decision.[62]

NEW AGE ISSUE

It is commonplace in broadcasting for news- and reality-based programming executives to seek out individuals of a specific race to fill a particular position in order to reflect their viewership as much as possible. Although the goal of having on-air diversity is an admirable and important one, in light of the *Peckinpaugh* decision, the methods by which well-intentioned employers seek to achieve this end may need to be studied and changed.

The Challenge for *New Age* Broadcasters to Use the Internet and Social Media as Both Effective "Swords" and Anticipatory "Shields"

In this section, we will discuss a few of the many important *New Age* questions and challenges that broadcasters must answer and deal with when using the Internet and social media both offensively and defensively.

A. The Issues and Goals of Attaining Maximum Internet Profitability and Integration

As each *New Age* day passes, network-news, local-news, and programming executives continue to focus on how they can attain significant Internet profitability and integration. These efforts are essential for three key reasons:

1. At a time when broadcasters desperately need to identify or create as many meaningful ancillary revenue sources as possible, achieving significant Internet profitability would be an economic boon—especially if true advertising integration can be achieved.

2. Having a top-tier and *strategically* informative Web presence can drive a broadcaster's viewers to watch its TV newscasts/programs, which can increase TV viewership.

3. Having a vital and compelling Internet presence can keep broadcasters (especially those networks that do not have a 24/7 cable news presence) and their news divisions relevant and continually connected to

their viewership, and this 24/7 connection can bolster and enhance the broadcasters' TV news efforts and overall brand awareness.

In this section, we will discuss all of these subjects and issues.

We now live in a world where it is imperative for broadcasters to understand how to make the very most of the Internet and social media. "As of the end of 2010, more people get their news from the Internet than from newspapers—and [during 2010] more ad dollars went to online outlets than to newspapers."[63] These are just two of the findings of a survey conducted by the Pew Project for Excellence in Journalism. Almost half of all Americans in the survey said that "they got at least some of their news on a mobile device or tablet."[64] Another Pew Research Center survey revealed that news consumption in the United States is on the rise again, as a direct result of online and mobile channels; however, it found that online news is *not* replacing traditional news forms.[65] Instead, those who already consume news are *consuming more of it.*[66]

For *The New Age* broadcaster, life has changed dramatically. Unlike fifteen years ago, when viewers sat glued to their TV sets to watch a major TV event, we now have multiple platforms to watch as an event unfolds.[67] In a 2009 *Los Angeles Times* article, Scott Collins wrote that the Michael Jackson memorial service can be viewed as a "landmark" in media integration, as "fans gathered around TV sets, computers, and smart phones, and traded information on Facebook and other social-media services."[68] According to Mr. Collins, the Jackson memorial service was a catalyst for huge waves of online traffic, as many viewers turned to their computers to watch the ceremony. On the day of the memorial, MSNBC.com set a new one-day record for total online video streams; while the results for CNN.com and FOXNews.com were exceeded only on Inauguration Day that past January. At its peak, CNN.com logged 781,000 concurrent live streams; FOXNews.com peaked during the memorial service with 677,000.[69] As a means of illustrating how much the use of the Internet has grown, consider that approximately two years later, during the Japan disaster, CNN.com registered *800 million global page views and 160 million video starts.*[70]

Recent studies have shown that a substantial number of individuals are on their computers, smart phones, and/or tablets while they are watching TV.[71] This "three-screen experience," as it's come to be known, is quickly becoming the norm.[72] Research also shows that *online activity reinforces TV viewing.*[73]

This last assertion that online viewing reinforces TV viewing, if true, is obviously of tremendous importance to and for broadcasters, since in *The New Age*, anything that will enable broadcasters to positively engage viewers and increase viewership is tremendously valuable and must be maximized.

In a *Broadcasting & Cable* interview, ESPN President George Bodenheimer discusses the very positive/complementary impact that digital products, such as smart phone and tablet ESPN apps, have had on ESPN-TV viewership. In one part especially pertinent to our discussion, he says, "The beautiful facts about all things digital [are] that when it comes to sports, they are making the entire pie grow. All of the new [digital] products [e.g., the iPad app] that have been created by ESPN over the last few years have done nothing but supported the growth of the traditional TV business.... As you produce more digital products to serve fans, it helps grow the traditional TV business. We've seen zero cannibalization, and I don't expect to see [any].... ESPN had its highest-rated year in its history last year, and we continue to see record usage numbers across our digital sites."[74] This is very good news for broadcasters!

With *so* many individuals turning to the Web to get their news—often *before* they turn to TV—two pressing *New Age* questions and challenges for broadcasters are:

1. How do broadcasters entice viewers to *consistently* go to *their* Web site? (We will discuss this challenge later in this chapter.)

2. How do broadcasters consistently drive viewers from their Web site to *their* TV station, network, or program?

One means to meet this second challenge is for the broadcasters to whet the viewers' appetites on the Web by letting them know that on the broadcasters' TV newscasts or programs, the viewers can see:

1. an exclusive interview or video;

2. a compelling or unique story or video; and

3. *the* best or most complete coverage of a big event or an important story.

Obviously, broadcasters identifying and implementing other effective means to drive viewers to *their* TV newscasts and/or programs is a major *New*

Age goal, which if attained can bring the broadcasters significant financial rewards.

With *New Age* media integration growing by leaps and bounds, what does all of this Web news viewership mean to broadcast and cable network news divisions? The answer appears to be that it can be highly beneficial in many instances, but it can be a cause for concern in a few others. For example, the ABC and CBS Network News divisions do not currently have 24-hour cable news networks that rival what NBC News has with MSNBC, CNBC, and the Weather Channel, which serve as a tremendously valuable means of supplying viewers with up-to-the-minute news and establishing and keeping a strong connection with their viewers throughout the day. However, some individuals feel that an effective Web news presence for CBS and/or ABC News can be a "field-leveler," especially as more and more individuals get their news from the Web.[75]

A very interesting Web news perspective is offered by Andrew Tyndall, publisher of *The Tyndall Report*. He says that with people getting their news from different platforms, the Web could be a way for broadcasters (such as ABC News and CBS News) to take back the news from competing cable outlets. Tyndall argues that by having an effective 24/7 Web news product, "the advantage of the 24-hour cable-news networks is not a long-term advantage, it is a medium-term one. When everyone gets all their television [news] online, it makes that advantage disappear."[76]

If Mr. Tyndall is correct in his assertion that with an effective Web presence, ABC and/or CBS News viewers will not opt to watch cable news, it appears that cable news viewership may be negatively impacted. However, I believe that, at least for the foreseeable future, when there is a major story or event, viewers will continue to turn to cable TV, *along with the Web*, for live coverage of the story or event if their favorite network news isn't on the air.

With regard to broadcasters' increasing profits through TV/Web integration, there is new evidence showing that while television advertising is much more "emotionally engaging" than online ads, "the combining of the two provides maximum brand equity, especially if the Web content is related to the TV experience."[77] This is according to a new biometric study that was part of FOX Broadcasting's 2011 up-front programming presentation.[78] Therefore, broadcasters and advertisers—working together—can secure maximum profitability through attaining maximum television and Web advertising integration. One means of achieving this is through *seamless content integration*.[79]

The FOX biometric study focused on the differences between how television versus online advertising emotionally engages the viewer.[80] Innerscope, the company that conducted the research, defines *emotional engagement* as "attention to something that emotionally impacts you."[81] The study found that the most effective means to advertise is to have an integrated campaign, in that TV creates and builds brand equity, and this equity can be increased online.[82] The study concludes: "Neither one [television or the Web] is as strong independently. TV is strong independently. Online is not as strong independently, but overall they are enhanced when they work off each other with similar content."[83]

What this all means for broadcasters is that they are charged with creating a compelling, user-friendly, TV content- and advertising-compatible Web presence. They must have Web platform(s) that will bring a substantial number of eyeballs to their Web advertiser-presence and will effectively promote and reinforce product identification and desirability. However, social-media pioneer and former CNN anchor Rick Sanchez points out that broadcasters relying on their Web presence *alone,*

> "[do] not maximize today's potential digital formats. It's becoming increasingly imperative for broadcasters to create healthy media relationships with their viewers and potential viewers for the purposes of branding their product, engaging social-media users, and perhaps more importantly, linking their stories, video, information, and announcements onto portals like Twitter and Facebook. This is particularly important because studies are now showing that more and more Americans are getting more news and information from each other as a shared experience."[84] (We will discuss the dynamics of this "shared experience" in the next section.)

With Web viewership growing, the burning question for *New Age* broadcasters continues to be: How do they effectively generate substantial Internet revenues? One answer is to find a means to convince advertisers, as many cable networks did so successfully in *Stage Two* (by creating and airing unique niche programming), that their Web content attracts an audience that advertisers want to reach and that they can most effectively reach this audience by advertising on the Web.

CNN has very recently adopted this strategy by "offering all of its substantial (advertising) clients an 'ROI [return on investment] toolkit.' [This toolkit] provided research on cross-platform reach and frequency, and delivery of influential consumers, to illustrate how associating with CNN content boosts brand awareness and interest to purchase a client's product."[85]

The goal for broadcasters appears to be that they must identify what makes them and their product unique/special/better—similar to CNN using its tremendous worldwide credibility and upscale viewership—in order to entice advertisers to support their Web presence.

It is also of the utmost importance for *New Age* broadcasters to create differentiated and better content than their competitors, as well as an online brand, tailored to consistently attract and engage a large online audience. Once this has been accomplished, broadcasters can compellingly market to (potential) advertisers *their* Web site's great advantages, which include immediate content delivery, access to unique content, and a highly desirable demographic. Since attaining significant Web profitability for broadcasters in the near future is all-important, there are three compelling *New Age* questions that must be asked and correctly answered:

1. Are the current network strategies and personnel the ones that will enable broadcasters to attain true Internet profitability?

2. Do new/different Internet sales strategies need to be implemented and Web-savvy advertising minds enlisted in order to take revenue-hungry and relevance-seeking broadcasters to the promised land of Internet profitability?

3. If the answer to this second question is "yes," and fresh new sales and advertising perspectives, thinking, and strategies are needed, where

---

* Obviously, the tremendous difference between the cable executives' pitch of years ago to advertisers and that of *New Age* Web-site executives is that when advertisers put their money into cable ads, it siphoned away ad dollars from TV, whereas when advertisers use their ad dollars to support a TV station, show, or network, *and* its Web presence, it is a complementary process—not a competitive one.

will the individuals come from who can supply the right answers and strategies?"

NEW AGE ISSUES

1. Two of the primary foci of broadcasters are to attain optimal Internet profitability and multimedia integration.
2. It is possible that when network news divisions that do not have a 24/7 cable-news arm develop effective 24/7 Web news sites, they may negate the need for their viewers to turn to the 24/7 cable news networks for their off-hours news needs. This change has the potential to one day decrease cable news viewership. However, from my perspective, for the foreseeable future viewers will turn to TV, along with the Web, to see live coverage of a big story or major breaking news.
3. It is essential that all broadcasters have an effective strategy for seamlessly integrating TV and Web advertising.
4. It is also essential that broadcasters figure out how to make the Internet a meaningful, profit-producing entity. The answer lies in convincing advertisers that unique and timely newscasts, programs, and content presented on the Web attract a highly valuable target viewership. This is the sales pitch that *Stage Two* cable network executives effectively made to advertisers when they were able to successfully lure advertisers and ad dollars away from the broadcast networks.

** Ben Grossman, in his article "Don't Be Afraid to Hire a Rock Star," says that employers should consider hiring "some non-traditional people for traditional positions....Be gutsy," he says, "and hire smart people, especially from non-traditional ranks" (Ben Grossman, "Don't Be Afraid to Hire a Rock Star," *Broadcasting & Cable*, August 3, 2009, 6). Although Mr. Grossman was not directing his comments to the field of TV/Internet integration, his theory may well apply here.

B. Some Important Internet and Social-Media Issues For Broadcasters To Consider

"The Internet age is not what it was at its inception."[86] Unquestionably, over the past few years, there has been tremendous growth and there have been many advancements in the Internet and social-media arenas. Below are some of *The New Age* issues broadcasters now face.

Two of these issues are how broadcasters perceive and whether they do or do not take full advantage of the Internet as a means to meaningfully grow their business. My good friend Joel Cheatwood, who has been gracious enough to give the readers of this book his highly enlightened digital perceptions, warns that in *The New Age*:

> One of the biggest mistakes made by media companies/stations [regarding] their digital strategy is that they treat devices [such as the] computer, iPad, iPhone, etc. as pure extensions of [their] television platform. They [broadcasters] repurpose television content (clips) and believe that [this] will suffice. It doesn't. The digital audience's needs are different and [this difference] requires a strategy that [provides] unique content for these [digital] platforms. [Broadcasters need to] take the time [to learn about and get] to know the digital audience. [If they do, broadcasters] will find out that it is NOT a carbon copy of the television audience and therefore shouldn't be treated as such. (emphasis added)
>
> [Broadcasters] have to look at the digital extensions as an opportunity to expand [their] core brand beyond just television. [Additionally, broadcasters] probably won't see a significant uptick in television viewers as a result of [the broadcaster's] efforts on the Web, but [they] will train the audience to understand that [their] brand extends beyond television, and as lifestyles continue to change—and have

already changed with younger viewers—[the proactive broad-casters] will be positioned to benefit.

As technology continues to change, clearly the potential for content on Web sites and other digital extensions goes well beyond the specific devices [that currently exist]. [For example], by next year, the overwhelming majority of new televisions will be Internet-capable and ready.[87]

We can distill the following from Joel's astute observations:

1. It is imperative that *New Age* broadcasters do not treat television and digital audiences, needs, and content the same, as they are NOT the same;

2. Broadcasters must get to know who their digital audience is and identify how to best serve its needs; and

3. Broadcasters must look at their digital extensions as an opportunity to expand their core brand beyond TV.

My longtime friend and client, Rick Sanchez, is credited with being the first national news anchor to combine network news with the power and global reach of social networking platforms such as Twitter, MySpace, and Facebook. (He fused Twitter and CNN on his CNN show, *Rick's List*).[88] By doing this, he took TV, which is essentially a linear, or one-way communication medium,[89] and made it a compelling and highly informative dialogue between him and the viewers. As Rick says in his book, *Conventional Idiocy*, the social media gives the viewers the opportunity to "engage with us [the news divisions] and with each other."[90] Truly effective *New Age* news dissemination is now a "national conversation" and a "shared experience."[91] As Rick puts it, it is no longer "me talking; it [is] 'we' talking."[92]

Rick believes that where pre-*New Age* broadcasters used their Web pages to disseminate their product online, *New Age* digital platforms mandate that broadcasters have two-way conversations with their viewers if the broadcasters want to remain truly viable and connected to them. Therefore, it is essential that broadcasters effectively make the very best use of platforms such as Twitter and Facebook. According to Rick, it is absolutely imperative for *New Age* broadcasters to understand the difference between establishing and maintaining a Web page and carrying out an effective social-media strategy. "The former invites viewers into the [broadcaster's] home or domain. The latter takes the [broadcaster] into the viewers'—those who communicate through social media—home or domain."[93] Rick concludes that "Twitter, Facebook, and MySpace have changed the way we communicate [with] each other. Now they are changing what [and how] we [*New Age* broadcasters and viewers] together communicate to the world."[94]

What we can glean from Joel and Rick is that: It is exceedingly important for *New Age* broadcasters to have a thorough understanding of social media, who uses social media, how to most effectively integrate social media into their TV news product, and what the content needs and expectations are of the social-media users/viewers.

NEW AGE ISSUES AND IDEAS

1. A big mistake made by (some) broadcasters regarding their digital strategy is that they treat devices such as the computer, iPhone, iPad, etc. as pure extensions of their television platform. They aren't. The digital audience's needs are different than those of TV, so broadcasters' strategies, content, and presentation in connection with *The New Age* media must be different, as well.
2. Broadcasters need to take the time to learn about the digital audience and understand what their (unique) needs are.
3. Broadcasters have to look at digital extensions as a golden opportunity to expand their core brand beyond television.
4. As technology continues to change, clearly the potential for content on Web sites and other digital extensions goes well beyond the specific devices that we now use.

5. In *The New Age*, it is vital for broadcasters to understand the difference between establishing and maintaining a Web presence
   and carrying out an effective social-media strategy.
6. It is also essential for broadcasters to use a multi-platform approach for branding and disseminating their product that takes into
   account the fact that increasing numbers of consumers get their
   news today from each other via social media.[95]
7. In *The New Age*, it is essential for broadcasters to remain viable
   and connected to their viewers by effectively integrating social
   media into their TV news product. This way, during this interactive age, broadcasters will be able to initiate and maintain relevant
   and responsive two-way conversations with their viewers. (This
   requirement is discussed further in the next section.)

C. The Issues and Goals of Broadcasters Using Facebook and Twitter as Anticipatory "Shields"

Almost all of the broadcasting-related social-media articles that I have read and discussions that I have had have focused on how to reach and engage viewers in the most effective manner, so as to keep and increase TV and Internet viewership; how to stay relevant; and how to maximize profits. Essentially, the issue is how broadcasters can "play offense" and proactively use the social media to their advantage. However, an exceedingly insightful article by Michael Malone in *Broadcasting & Cable* points out that many broadcasters may not yet have developed an adequate set of anticipatory *defensive* social-media strategies.[96]

Malone details how meteorologist Geoff Fox, after 26 years of service to WTNH, was terminated by his station. Fox, whom I have had the pleasure to know and represent for many years, was by many accounts quite popular in the Hartford/New Haven market and since 2003 had been an active blogger.[97] According to Malone, once the public learned that Fox was let go from WTNH, the way that station handled the viewers' response to Fox's termination became "a case study for the burgeoning social-media world, as nothing short of a firestorm erupted on Facebook—[with] viewers rallying behind Fox and blasting WTNH for dismissing the popular weatherman."[98]

The significant problem that arose for WTNH was that thousands of viewers expressed their displeasure about Fox's termination through the "Keep Geoff Fox on Channel 8" Facebook page, as well as by contacting WTNH and commenting on the station's Facebook page and/or requesting an explanation.[99] However, the station stayed silent and failed to respond to the upset online viewers—which significantly exacerbated the problem for WTNH.[100]

Malone's article presents the issue this way: "While many local TV execs are quick to tout their social-media efforts on Facebook and Twitter, the Geoff Fox incident showed that some may not have considered the downside of social media, as much as the upside."[101]

On this subject, Fox said, "When you're inviting your audience to participate in social media, certain implications are made that you're going to listen to viewers....This was a textbook case of how not to use social media."[102]

When WTNH and other broadcasters fail to respond or respond inappropriately to viewer online comments and concerns, the viewer can feel that management "couldn't care less" about them or their concerns. At a time when broadcasters are doing all they can to engage viewers and increase viewership, not having the correct anticipatory defensive social-media strategies can be a devastating mistake.

Two clear lessons are to be learned from the WTNH management's apparent choice not to respond to viewer complaints and comments:

1. In this world of social media, viewers have legitimate expectations that communication with broadcasters is a two-way street. Therefore, broadcasters are expected to thoughtfully and appropriately respond to viewer comments and questions—especially on strong emotion-evoking and important issues—or else broadcasters risk alienating and/or losing viewers.

2. Broadcasters must have an effective anticipatory social-media strategy ready to implement *before* they make decisions or moves that they know or should reasonably intuit will evoke viewer comment, concern, questions, or unhappiness.

On the subject of having anticipatory defensive social-media strategies, social-media marketing executive Gillian Verga advises: "It helps to have a robust social-media strategy well in advance of a potential crisis. You do not want to wait until the crisis and then try to establish your Facebook presence."[103]

NEW AGE ISSUES

1. Broadcasters must develop appropriate anticipatory defensive social-media strategies as a constructive and enhancing means by which to proactively address and respond to their viewers' comments, concerns, and protests.
2. Ignoring viewers may well open up broadcasters to significant and potentially relationship-ending criticism.
3. The social media are two-way-street forms of communication. Broadcasters can used them as a sword, but they must also be able to use them effectively as a shield. But this cannot be achieved without acknowledging that *The New Age* media is fast becoming a *two-way* form of communication, and that when using social media, broadcasters are inviting themselves into the viewer's/user's domain.[104]

Opportunities for Talent and Production-Executive Program Ownership in *The New Age*

Program ownership and the opportunity for talent and production executives to receive program royalties is most certainly a contract issue, which could well be discussed in the next section. However, because these are very important *New Age* issues and concepts that raise many ancillary questions, we will discuss these very intriguing subjects here.

Let's begin by setting forth two clear *Broadcasting Realities*:

1. Every talent, producer, and production-executive employment contract that I have seen has a "Results and Proceeds" clause. What this provision is designed to ensure is that anything that the talent (on-air person, producer, or production executive) produces, develops, writes, or creates during the term of their employment contract is owned by the employer. Essentially, everything that the employee creates or develops—whether or not it is work-related—is deemed a "work made for hire," which means that the employee has no ownership in or monetary rights to the material that the employee has created or developed.

2. In *The New Age*, the old rules of talent employment contracts have changed or should change, since employers are almost always paying less, offering less secure contracts, and exacting more. Consequently, talent (on-air individuals, producers, and production executives) should ask for concessions that they hadn't thought to request or could

not secure before. Essentially, *The New Age* has changed the rules for both the employer and the employee.

Okay, using the above two *Realities* as our base, let's discuss some longtime issues and some potential *New Age* solutions:

1. First and foremost, in *The New Age*, talent—on- or off-air—should absolutely be able to own any material that they develop that is not directly derived from their work or work product. This clause should be negotiated into all talent employment contracts. For example, if someone works for a cable news network as a reporter, producer, or executive, and that person develops a game show, a comedy series, a drama, writes a song, writes a screenplay, or authors a book that is not directly related to their work or work product, the talent should own it.

2. However, if applicable, the appropriate division of the employer's company should get a "first look" at the material (such as a publishing division of the employer if the material at issue is a potential book) and have the first opportunity to make an offer. However, no first look or other similar contract stipulation should preclude the talent from selling the material to the highest or most appropriate bidder.

3. If a producer or production executive creates a program that is in the wheelhouse of the employer (say, a talent or production executive at *ET*, *Access Hollywood*, or *EXTRA* develops an entertainment or pop-culture game show), and the employer either produces the show or sells it, the talent should, in many instances, receive an appropriate share of the proceeds from the disposition of the show. My reasoning: If the person who develops the salable show is an on-air talent, the employer is paying that talent for their *on-air services, not* their *off-air creative services*! If a producer or production executive creates the show, although it is a much closer case, the answer should lie with what the underlying clauses of the individual's employment contract provide: If the contract calls for the talent to produce for or run, say, *The Insider* or *Deal or No Deal*, that person is *not* being paid to create or develop *new* shows. He or she is being compensated to run *existing* shows.

The very wisest course of action here is for talent and production executives to *pre-negotiate* the compensation that they will receive should a program that they create or develop be aired by their employer, or sold or licensed to a third party by the employer. Any such show compensation and royalties should be *in addition to* the salary that the talent receive for performing their basic, day-to-day job duties.

4. What about the production executive who has launched very successful new shows under her watch? For example, until recently, an exceedingly bright and talented executive had been employed at a major television production studio. During her tenure at least three major talk/magazine shows were launched. As I have never represented this executive, I have absolutely no idea what she did or did not have in her employment contract, but I am willing to bet that if her employment contract provided for a small percentage of the gross revenues that her employer receives for the licensing of those three shows to various stations and station groups, the percentage would have substantially exceeded her annual salary.

   I would also argue that Jim Bell, the incredibly talented *Today* show executive producer, who helped launch two more hours of *Today* (from 9 a.m. to 11 a.m.) while successfully navigating the transition from Katie Couric to Meredith Vieira, is a superstar. And he should be paid like one—perhaps through some ratings-bonus compensation formula.

Three years ago, during a weekly television department staff meeting that I attended at a major theatrical agency, we discussed the subject of how the program-production and sales landscapes have changed during the economic downturn. At that meeting, one agent wisely observed, "Now is the time to find the right partners."[105] (Which is how we will survive and thrive in *The New Age.*) I wholeheartedly agree!

If in this *New Age,* struggling employers want their most gifted on- and off-air talent to be "their partners" by accepting less money and less security, the talent must be *their partners* across the board! The concept and spirit of this *partnership* should be kept in mind when all on- and off-air talent negotiate and craft their employment contracts.

NEW AGE ISSUES

1. On- and off-air talent should be able to own and/or receive royalties on the shows and books they create that are subsequently licensed or sold, as long as:
    a. these properties are not directly derivative of their day-to-day work;
    b. their contract duties clause does not specifically provide for them to create such properties; and
    c. part or all of their annual compensation is not consideration for creating such properties.
2. In *The New Age*, employers want their talent to be *partners* in accepting less compensation and security, thereby enabling the employers to survive and/or remain profitable during uncertain economic times. Therefore, it is only fair that talent should also be the employer's *partners* when it comes to income-producing areas and ventures.

SECTION VI

The Content and Psychology of Television Employment Contracts

The Psychology of Contracts

An Overview

One of the keys to enjoying a successful career in broadcasting is to negotiate and secure contracts that reflect and effect your most important values and goals. Therefore, before you enter into any contract, it is of the utmost importance for you to identify and list your priorities. Then, depending upon the stage of your career and what you need and want to accomplish, you will want a number of contract clauses to be written into your contracts in very specific ways.

For almost all major TV news and programming positions, an employment contract between the talent and the employer will be drawn up and signed. In 99 percent of these instances, the employer—or an outside law firm—will write that contract. It will contain numerous clauses that will protect the employer's monetary investment in the employee, minimize the employer's downside monetary risk as much as possible, and give the employer maximum flexibility in connection with the employee's duties, days off, schedule, and job security, while at the same time limiting and circumscribing, as tightly as possible, the employee's rights and options in all areas.

For example, years ago, one of my clients was offered an agreement with a station that provided for a firm four-year commitment by the talent, while the station could terminate the agreement at any time with sixty days' notice. When I asked the news director what his rationale was for such a one-sided contract, he responded, "The station is taking a big risk in bringing new people to the station, and it needs to protect itself if things do not work out." I replied, "What about the person who is uprooting her family to accept your position? Doesn't she deserve at least a couple of years to prove herself? And what if things at the station aren't to her liking? Why should she be stuck there for four years? Also, how can you rationally argue that your station's interests are more important than this person's career and family stability? Shouldn't there be equal rights in this contract?" (Of course I knew what his answer would be.)

"Maybe," the news director replied. "But it won't happen here [at this station]. And besides, Kenny, I don't even have a contract; at least your client gets some protection. I can be blown out tomorrow."

Another example. An anchor at Station "Y" had been successfully anchoring there for more than ten years. She was offered a new five-year contract that called for her to commit to five years, firm, to the station, but the station had the right to terminate the agreement—without cause—after 18 months and 36 months, successively. In this case the station knew exactly whom they were hiring and they loved her work—yet she still didn't merit equal rights under her new contract.

"Why?" she asked management.

Management responded, "'Cause we don't give no-cut contracts."

"But why not?" she asked.

The reply: "'Cause we don't."

Throughout my career, I have asked employers how they could justify their unfair contracts, since in most cases, there is no logical rationale or humane justification for them. These employers often reply, "Hey, that's the way it is" or "That's the way it's always been." Okay! That makes sense—right?!

A more exact answer would be, "It's because we [the employers] can get away with it." However, in *The New Age* talent has far more opportunity and justification to secure more equitable contract provisions in some very important areas.

One more true story: Years ago, an anchor at a small-to-middle-sized market station entered into a five-year agreement with her station. Her salary was approximately $37,000 for the first year, $39,000 for the second, $43,000 for the third, $48,000 for the fourth, and $53,000 for the fifth. The station could terminate her employment at regular intervals, but she was tied to the station for the full five years. This anchor, whom I didn't represent until years later, was a true superstar talent, with a horrible—but all too common—one-sided employment contract. During the second year of that contract, a broadcast network offered her a position to anchor/host its weekday (Monday through Friday) morning show for a salary between $400,000 and $500,000 a year. Her station wouldn't let her accept the position and threatened to sue the network for inducing a breach of contract if the network had any more conversations with her. The network, which didn't want others stealing its people, quickly withdrew its offer to this anchor. The conclusion was: The anchor had to stay at the station for three-and-a-half more years under her original contract. And with timing as critical as it usually is, she was never again offered a position of that magnitude at a network.

To quote a 1970s hit song: "It's sad to belong to someone else when the right one comes along."

The moral of the story: Because this anchor didn't have any termination rights or an out-clause for a network or for a top market position, she couldn't accept this career-making offer. Contrary to what some lawyers and others say, contracts are *not* made or written to be broken—they are made to be enforced. And because employers do not want *their* employees to be hired away by other employers while under *their* contracts, they will almost always back away from offering a position if a newscaster is under contract to someone else. They do so not because they feel it is morally or ethically wrong to court talent, but because they don't want to be hit with a tampering suit, and because if they steal from others and get away with it, others can, in turn, do the same to them. It is the implied law of the broadcasting jungle and a *Broadcasting Reality*.

The important point to remember here is that at the end of the day, talent often live or die because of their contracts. So it is of profound importance to understand contracts and the provisions within them. When it comes to contracts, once again, Chester Karrass said it best: "You don't get what you deserve, you get what you negotiate!"

Okay, let's get started.

The "Duties" Clause and Talent-Toxic Words to Identify and Negotiate

The "duties" clause in a broadcasting employment contract sets forth the duties that a talent "will," "can," or "may" be assigned to render for the employer during the employment term. The words "will" and "shall" provide for affirmative obligations that a talent and an employer assume when they enter into their agreement. For example, "Artist *shall* anchor at least two of employer's 4 p.m. or later weekday newscasts, and shall report, write, edit, etc." So, except for when the "pay-or-play" clause (which we will soon discuss) or some other negotiated contingency clause is instituted by the employer, the talent is guaranteed certain specific assignments. However, if the talent-toxic words "can" and "may" are substituted for "will" and "shall," the employer basically has no obligations to guarantee talent any duties, and the talent has no rights in this area and (maybe) no recourse.

So, if you are talent, you want words of *specificity*, such as "will" and "shall," in your duties clause. If you are the employer, you want words of *flexibility*, such as "can" and "may."

Another of the potentially most damaging words in an employment contract is the word "or." It looks pretty innocuous, but it can be a killer if it appears in your duties clause. Why? Because it can negate *everything* that appears before it in the contract—no matter what you have negotiated or have been given. Here is an example:

> Artist will anchor all of the station's evening newscasts, be a "special sweeps reporter," host specials, *or* be assigned to any other duties at management's discretion.

At first blush it appears that you have secured some wonderful guaranteed duties—but then the dreaded word "or" appears, which means that management has the choice of assigning you to *all* of those specific duties, to *none* of them, or to other, undesirable duties such as overnight reporter, photographer, editor, producer, and floor sweeper. In this instance, if you have the word "or" in your duties clause, as described above, you have secured absolutely *nothing*! You and what you do are totally at management's *New Age* mercy and discretion.

Okay, now let's substitute the word "and" for "or" and see the incredibly enhancing difference:

> Artist will anchor all of the station's evening newscasts, be
> a "special sweeps reporter," host specials, *and* be assigned to
> other duties at management's discretion.

Because the word "and" is written into your duties clause instead of "or" (assuming that the "pay-or-play" clause in your employment contract is not invoked and you therefore render services for your employer), you are now guaranteed to perform the specific duties that originally motivated you to enter into your agreement with your employer. Always remember, the word "and" is *inclusive*, as it *includes* in your package of duties everything that comes before and after it, whereas the word "or" is *exclusive*, as it allows management to *exclude and negate* everything that comes before and after it.

You must also take care to avoid being fooled by the tricky "and/or." If there is an "or," even with an "and," the duties that precede it can be negated.

As with "and/or," the word "initial" in the duties clause basically voids everything listed in that clause. The following clause, for example, could destroy your career progress:

> Your *initial* duties are to host *The Early Show*; at any time you
> can be assigned to any other anchoring, hosting, reporting,
> producing, or any other like duties.

If the list of your duties is preceded by the very limiting word "initial," what you have is an apparent promise that for at least one day, one week, one month, you will host *The Early Show*. But at any time during the contract, you can be demoted to a reporter or producer. By the by, in reality you do not even have the contractual guarantee to host one day of *The Early Show*, as every contract has a "pay-or-play" clause, which provides that the employer's *only* obligation to you is to pay you. Therefore, there is no real guarantee or obligation to put you on air...*ever*! A bit later in this chapter we will discuss the various remedies for the potentially career-decimating, but very rarely used, "pay-or-play" clause.

Another thing to look for in your duties clause is the dreaded *slash* ("/"). It is most frequently used in the following way:

> Artist's duties shall be as an anchor/reporter.

The problem with the slash is that there is no clear understanding as to whether it means "and" or "or." As a talent, you want it to mean "and," so that your duties include anchoring *and* reporting. You do *not* want it to be interpreted as "or," so that there is no obligation on management's part to use you as an anchor. The best way to protect yourself here is to secure the deletion of the "/" and have an "and" written in to replace it, which will make clear to everyone your rights and management's obligations.

Finally, you had best delete any language in the duties clause regarding "in station's/employer's/management's discretion." Especially in *The New Age*, your goal in the duties clause is to *identify* and circumscribe, with as much specificity as possible, what your duties are (and are not), so that you know what your employer can require you to do. The words "in management's discretion" fly in the face of such specificity and pretty much allow management—current and future—to assign you to do anything *they* want!

Exclusivity

The exclusivity provision in your contract is of critical importance, as it can well determine whether and how you can grow your career and *Multi-Platform* it.

First, the exclusivity provision in your contract spells out what else, if anything, you can do and who else, if anyone, you can work for (*along with* the employer with whom you have your current employment contract), as well as what conditions, if any, must be met before permission to work for others is granted.

Employers almost always want total or very restrictive exclusivity. This means that you can do nothing else, or very little else, except work for your employer. You are thus not contractually free to accept other positions that could provide added exposure—possibly national visibility—which can materially enhance your career, marketability, and brand. Also, being able to anchor, host, report, or produce for programs that are not produced by your primary employer can substantially increase your income.

Here are some examples of the importance of your exclusivity provision:

> You are a weekend anchor and reporter in a local market, such as Phoenix, and pursuant to your contract, you will earn $90,000 this year. Along comes an opportunity for you to host a show on the National Geographic Channel. The executives at Nat Geo will "block shoot" the show over a seven-day period. They will pay you $8,000 per show for your hosting services and guarantee you a minimum of ten shows as a first order.

Here is what you stand to gain if you are contractually allowed to enter into the Nat Geo agreement, or if your Phoenix station management grants you permission to do so:

1. You will host a national show, which gives you national exposure. Who knows who will see you and what might evolve from this experience and exposure?

2. You will get invaluable experience and "tape" from the hosting opportunity.

3. You will increase your annual income by about 90 percent for seven days of work.

4. You may well become more recognizable nationally and in Phoenix.

5. You will add significant value to your career.

6. You will have fun doing something different and using different muscle groups. It will break up the monotony of your day job.

Now, here are two real-life scenarios to ponder:

> During this *New Age of Broadcasting*, your management wants
> to keep your salary "flat." Instead of fighting for a minuscule
> raise, in many instances, it is exceedingly smart to say, "Fine.
> But I would like the right to host/report/produce a cable
> show during my vacation time and/or to host/report/pro-
> duce on a network show that is the same as the station's affilia-
> tion." (For example, if you are at an ABC-owned or -affiliated
> station, you can render services for any entity owned by ABC
> Network or Disney.) As we will discuss later, should your
> employer ask you to take a pay cut or unpaid leave, loosening
> up your exclusivity provision can be the very smartest, most
> career-enhancing move you can make. It doesn't cost your
> employer anything, and it can materially enhance your life,
> career, marketability, and bank account.

Let's review what we obtained for Samantha Harris when we were able to
convince the E! executives that it was in E! Network's very best interests to
open up its airtight exclusivity and allow Samantha to cohost *Dancing with
the Stars*:

1. It made Samantha a major network prime-time host and personality.

2. This added tremendous value to her career, visibility, marketability, and
   brand.

3. It resulted in E! and Samantha receiving a great deal of valuable additional exposure on the ABC Network, in magazines, on radio, and
   so on.

4. It markedly increased her value to E!

5. Her annual income increased *exponentially* (more than fourfold).

6. It gave her the visibility and star quality that led CBS Television

Distribution to create a lucrative and career-enhancing position for her on *The Insider*.

Look at what having creatively negotiated exclusivity provisions in their various employment contracts has allowed Ryan Seacrest, Mario Lopez, and others to accomplish! They are *Multi-Platforming* geniuses!

In some ways, this *New Age*—when many of the old, etched-in-stone rules are changing; when salaries are going down; when security is being diminished—is *the ideal time to redefine your relationship with your employer*. If the individuals for whom you work want you to take less, have less security, take unpaid leave, *then you need to negotiate*. Counter with something that costs them and their companies *no money*! *Secure a far more beneficial exclusivity provision that allows you, your career, and your income to grow exponentially by being able to Multi-Platform*!

Ideally, if your initial employment contract is with a local news station, try to secure the following:

> *You are exclusive in all local news and you won't appear on any other station in your market.*
>
> This allows you to work on/for all cable shows; network shows that your station is owned by or affiliated with; and all nationally syndicated shows, as long as the show at issue appears on your station in your market and doesn't require services that conflict with your services to your station.

Ideally, if your initial contract is for a show on a cable network, try to secure the following:

> *You are exclusive in cable, and free to enter into any other agreements as long as the subject of the show is not the same or substantially similar in content.*
>
> This allows you to anchor/host/produce for all network, syndicated, and local programs, as long as they are not basically the same show.

Ideally, if your initial contract is for a show on a network, try to secure the following:

> *You are exclusive in network television but can host/anchor/ report/produce for all syndicated, cable, and local shows, as long as the local show is with a station that is owned by or affiliated with the network with which you have your initial contract.*

If you are unable to secure the ideal, the next step is for you to carve out the logical, most career-enhancing potential opportunities and have those *pre-approved*. One option is: *Artist can host and/or report on a national cable program, as long as said duties don't conflict with artist's duties to employer.*

Obviously, if you are going to carve out specific types of shows in any contract, you must carefully think through what you will want to do, what opportunities may present themselves, and what will be enhancing growth opportunities *during the course of a long-term contract*. So this exercise takes time, careful consideration, and knowledge of potential opportunities. Therefore, it is imperative for you to understand what is and is not directly competitive with what you currently do and for whom you do it. The key here is to negotiate and agree upon exclusivity provisions that allow you to perform services for specific shows or—a far better alternative—to carve out your right to perform services on specific kinds of shows or on specific "carriers" which an employer can be convinced are not competitive with that employer.

If your local news management will agree only that they will consider outside opportunities as they arise, and when advised of the opportunity, they agree to "not unreasonably" withhold their approval, always remember: What is "reasonable" is a very subjective criterion. And what may seem reasonable at one time, or to your current employer, may not seem reasonable at another time, or to another executive. What you want to avoid is being at the mercy of the magnanimous good mood of your employer when a career-making opportunity presents itself. So the more *Multi-Platforming* specificity that you can provide for in your contracts, the better. For example, you can also try to have management pre-approve that a show on your station's network or a cable show that doesn't tarnish your credibility be deemed "reasonable."

Always remember: If it is not in writing, one day when memories become short, there will be a (potential) dispute—and *you will* probably lose!

What you want to strive to include in all of your exclusivity provisions is your right to:

1. Write books, as long as they do not intimately discuss subjects that involve your employment or tarnish your news credibility;

2. Act, as long as your acting doesn't tarnish your news credibility;

3. Enter into radio contracts;

4. Have a production company, as long as you present all projects to your employer first (give them a "first look") before you are able to freely market the project(s) in issue; and

5. Make personal appearances. Some news operations frown upon or do not allow on-air talent to make paid personal appearances because it compromises a talent's objectivity. However, if I am not mistaken, aren't paid ads that sustain news divisions just that, *paid*? If they do not tarnish the news division's objectivity as to if and how they will cover certain stories, in this *New Economic Reality*, restrictions on paid appearances should be examined at a minimum and permitted on a case-by-case basis. The norm should be that what is good for the goose is equally good for the gander. If news divisions are sustained by sponsors, talent should be able to make paid speeches!

The key here is that the exclusivity provision is not just some unimportant or etched-in-stone "boilerplate clause." It is clearly just the opposite! It is precious!!! How it is written and what you are or are not allowed to do along with your initial-contract job responsibilities are of the *utmost importance* to your career, brand, and potential income growth. Every word of your exclusivity clause must be reviewed and written in light of the possibilities for you to grow your career.

Always remember this: You are a very important asset of your employer, but you and your career are far more valuable assets of *yours*. And *time waits for no person*. If you keep entering into multi-year contracts that do not provide for your *Multi-Platforming*, you are, by omission, allowing employers to prohibit your growth. In many cases, allowing you to host a national (or a second) show will cost your employer *nothing*! In fact, your national exposure may materially benefit your employer. Not negotiating your exclusivity provision so that you have the *right* to work on additional shows may cost you, your career development, and your bank account *dearly*!

Term

The "term" is the length of the contract. However, keep in mind that a contract will include a number of provisions by which the employer can end the contract before it runs its full term. For example, an employer can usually terminate the agreement "for cause." Cause for termination is usually triggered if the employee is insubordinate, refuses an assignment, refuses to show up to work as scheduled, breaches the contract in some way, cannot perform services for a stipulated amount of time ("incapacity"), commits a "morals infraction," etc. In most contracts, the employer can also terminate the agreement without cause—that is, for any reason at all—at certain intervals in the contract (e.g., every 13 or 26 weeks, or each year).

The thing to remember is that if you do not plan to stay at a station or in a market for a long time, you will want to negotiate as short a contract as possible. If the employer can terminate you without cause on a regular basis, get as short a contract as possible, because in that situation, you have no real security anyway. If you take a position for a comparatively low salary, secure a short contract, so that with growing success in the position, you will be able to negotiate a new, more lucrative contract sooner. Conversely, if you plan to stay in the market for a long time, if you are able to secure a lucrative, no-cut deal for yourself, and if long-term security is of great value to you, then a long-term, secure deal may be most appropriate. During better economic times, I learned that in success you will almost always make more money by signing a series of shorter agreements than by signing a long agreement and getting (very small) percentage raises each year, or no raises at all.* However, because most

---

* Note that there are many variables that one must take into account before passing up a good long-term, secure deal that provides for an enhancing position in a desirable market.

executives plan to stick to the economic models that they instituted during the economic downturn, signing short contracts in hopes of entering into more lucrative ones sooner is no longer a sure thing.

It is also important to do your best to secure various termination provisions for yourself, so that you can end the term of a contract when a career-enhancing opportunity comes your way. These provisions will be discussed below.

As with every other provision of your employment contract, when you negotiate its term, be clear as to *why* you are entering into the agreement. For example, years ago, one of my clients became an anchor in Los Angeles strictly because she wanted to host a national entertainment show and almost all of the producers of these shows are based in L.A. So when her prospective employer gave her a choice of a two-year deal at $200,000 and $210,000, or a three-year deal at $215,000, $225,000, and $235,000, she wisely chose the two-year deal, because her goal was to get exposure and leave; not to grow as a local news-caster. Obviously, the two-year deal gave her this option more quickly, even though she would have earned a bit more money with the three-year agreement. In her value system, if she chose the longer deal because it was more lucrative, she would have been "penny-wise but potential growth foolish."

Regarding the term of a contract, keep in mind that an employer will be reluctant to let an on-air employee terminate a contract during its early stages, as it takes time for an employer to recoup the investment in the talent. Allowing someone whom the viewers like and have grown attached to terminate a contract early can diminish or damage the on-air product and result in a loss of ratings and revenues for the employer. It is important for talent to understand and to appreciate that stations and programmers have a real and legitimate interest in keeping continuity of talent on the air.

Cycles

These are intervals during the term of a contract when the employer can terminate the agreement without cause—for any reason—or for no reason at all.

Ideally, during the term of a contract you would like the contract to be firm—that is, without cycles. However, most *New Age* employment contracts will include cycles—possibly many of them. The talent's goal is to have as few of them as possible and thereby enjoy as much security as possible.

As a compromise, you would like to have maximum security at the beginning of a contract, so that you have enough time to reach your comfort level and show your employer that you are a valuable member of the broadcast team.

There are many reasons why you want to obtain the most secure contract possible. For example, when new managers are hired, they often make it a priority to learn who can and cannot be terminated in the near future. It is a *Broadcasting Reality* that a news manager is more likely to terminate the person with the cycle coming up and stick with the person who has a good amount of guaranteed time left on their contract. This is because as a rule, managers do not like to take people off the air whom they will have to pay for an extended period of time. It is cost-ineffective. Therefore, those broadcast journalists who have firm (no-cut) contracts often have a better chance of keeping their positions during news purges, as the news manager either learns to live with them or begins to appreciate them. Another reason is that talent with firm contracts can wind up outlasting news managers who were not the talent's biggest supporters. And as we discussed above, it generally takes an anchor or host between twelve and eighteen months in a new venue before that individual reaches their full comfort level; therefore, having as much time in a position to become as comfortable as possible is always optimal.

For a myriad of valid reasons, then, try to negotiate a contract with as much security as possible.

Vacation

In *The New Age*, it is tremendously important that you appropriately value and effectively negotiate the vacation provision in your employment contract(s). This is a *Reality*, because if you are able to loosen up the exclusivity provision in your contract, you can perform services on other shows during your vacation. So if you are not given a raise or you receive a small raise or a pay cut, try to secure more vacation, *even if you take it unpaid*. Then you will have the time necessary to perform services for a second (or a third) employer, which means you will receive compensation for the shows that you render services for during your off time and also add significant value to your career. One means of explaining to your employer why you should be granted additional vacation time is: "I need the time off so I can secure and render services on non-competitive programs and make up for the diminished salary I'm (now) earning. And, who knows, maybe the exposure that I receive on the other (supplemental) show that I will host/report for will increase my visibility, and you will benefit as well." Remember: Oftentimes, you will not be able to *Multi-Platform* by appearing on or producing other programs if you do not have the necessary vacation time to do it. So, in this *New Economic Reality* you must very carefully and insightfully negotiate your exclusivity and vacation provisions, so that you have the *contractual right* and the time off to *Multi-Platform*.

What to Do When Employers Ask You to Amend Your Employment Contract So That They Can Secure Givebacks from You That Are Beneficial to Them

When clients call to tell me that their news manager or program executive has come to them asking if they will take an "unpaid furlough" for seven or ten days, or take a pay cut because economic times are (still) challenging/bad, I am more than a bit irked. Why? Because I cannot remember when management handed out bonuses during the gravy days! There's a reason I can't remember it. It's because they never did! Employees under employment agreements have never been treated as partners with their employers during the good times! And, in fact, *every time* a client, years ago, said to me, "I want you to go to management, because our show has received record ratings (and consequently, the employer has enjoyed materially increased revenues), and see if you can get me some sort of a bonus or other perk for our success," management inevitably responded, "Kenny, your client has a contract. We don't come to you when the ratings [and therefore, our revenues] go down and ask for money back. Right?"

Years ago, in most cases I would have had to agree with the manager's logic. But now, in this *New Economic Reality*, the rules (which worked for years for employers) have changed. Employers are now coming in droves to employees asking that talent agree to amend their employment contracts and take unpaid time off, thereby diminishing the talent's negotiated and agreed-upon annual compensation; or requesting that the employee take a pay cut—*and they are offering nothing in return*!

Well, I shouldn't say "nothing." To a person, everyone who has sought my counsel on this subject has expressed the sentiment/concern/fear "that if they don't acquiesce to management's requests, they will pay for it, either when their contract expires or when their next contract cycle comes up and management can terminate the contract." So what is presented as an "ask" or request can be more like a velvet fist! As a result, in almost all cases, the talent acquiesces.

This section is not intended to belittle or impugn broadcasters or management. Far from it. I totally understand and appreciate the very real economic pressures that weigh so heavily on their shoulders. But I also believe that if the wants and needs have changed for both management and talent, and management is asking talent to give up something, then talent should be able to get something *in return*! If management is going to ask talent to amend contracts that they have negotiated, then talent should get some "consideration" for doing so—especially if the requests that talent put forth do not cost management *any money*.

We are all familiar with the cliché, "With challenges and setbacks come new options and opportunities." So I say, "Okay, Management, we feel your economic pain and acknowledge your need and desire to save money. We all want television news and programming to survive. However, if you are asking talent to give up certain hard-earned, previously negotiated things, we merely ask that you, too, be flexible and let talent secure what they need as well."

So when your management comes to you asking that you take an unpaid furlough or a pay cut, here are some things that I would do in response:

1. Request that the remainder of your contract be made no-cut, or firm. This way you give up some compensation, but you gain some security.

2. If your contract is nearing its end or is totally secure, ask for it to be extended for a year, or two, or three, and for it to become no-cut. Here again, you give up some compensation for more security.

3. Rewrite your exclusivity provision so that you can host, anchor, report, or produce for other shows that will add to the value of your career

and marketability and increase (and thereby supplement) your income. This will provide the means for you to *Multi-Platform*!

4. Secure more paid vacation, as well as the right to take a few more unpaid vacation weeks per year should you need them. This will allow you to take advantage of enhancing *Multi-Platforming* opportunities that come your way.

5. Limit to at most once a year the number of times that management can ask you to take an unpaid furlough.

6. Secure any other contract changes that would benefit you. Remember: *Employers' asking you to modify your contract is a renegotiation of your contract.* Just as it "takes two to tango," a negotiation or renegotiation takes two parties, and it should reflect the thoughts, goals, needs, and aspirations of *both parties*!!!

If management is going to use this *New Economic Reality* to "change some things" to their benefit, so should you!

Once again, a contract modification is a renegotiation—and a renegotiation should not benefit just one party. It is time for the proletariat to rise up! All kidding (sort of) aside, this is a golden opportunity for both sides to give a little, adapt, and find a means for *both* of you to reset and make *The New Age* a win/win time.

The Program-Cancellation Clause

In many instances syndicated programs such as *Entertainment Tonight*, *Access Hollywood*, *EXTRA*, and *Inside Edition*—and to a lesser extent network and cable programs—provide in their employment contracts that if the specific program that you have been hired to render services for is canceled, your employment contract can be terminated by your employer, usually with no more than two weeks' notice. (Please note that this provision is different from, and in addition to, the employer's right to terminate the contract *without cause* at the end of a cycle.) The thinking behind this clause is that once a show for which you have been hired to render services no longer exists, the employer wants to immediately eliminate the obligation to continue paying you.

Be aware that often the existence of this clause in an employment contract is not raised by the prospective employer during the negotiation process, since it frequently appears in the contract as a provision of the standard "boilerplate" terms and conditions. Therefore it is imperative that you and/or your representative inquire ahead of time as to whether the contract that you are negotiating contains such a clause. If it does, try to delete it. Please note that although in most instances deletion of the program-cancellation clause is very difficult to achieve, with sufficient leverage, some degree of negotiation and improvement may be possible.

Compensation

Compensation is the money that you earn under a contract. In almost all instances, the goal is to secure as much money up front as possible. I suggest this because contracts usually have cycles, so there is absolutely no guarantee that you will see the big increases that are provided for in the later years of your contract.

I have heard people say that they would rather not be paid too much money, because stations will be more likely to fire them if their salary is high. Be aware that for the most part, stations have money to spend on people who are "A players." They have no money to spend on people who aren't. So get as much as you can within reason at the beginning of a contract, and then be an "A player."

I have also been told that with a higher salary come more and higher profile responsibilities. I believe this. If employers are paying talent a lot of money—especially if a current manager and regime negotiated the contract at issue—they will want to prove to their bosses that the salary is justified, and therefore they will often put their highest-paid people in high-visibility and important situations.

One thing that I have learned over the years is that when a manager says, "I can only pay you 'X' for this contract, but when you become a success, you can 'kill me,' 'get me back,' or 'get even' in the next contract negotiation [years later]," DO NOT BUY IT!!!! First of all, that manager will most likely not be there when your next contract comes up, and the new manager will not care about honoring what his or her predecessor promised. Second, with the passage of time, things can change and memories can become short. My experience is that no one pays you more money in a subsequent contract to make up for what you did not secure in an earlier one. Especially in *The New Age*, a good rule is this: Get it—or forget it.

The Ratings-Point-Increase Bonus

During *The New Age*, when broadcasting employer revenues and profits are dwindling and talent salaries are being cut, one means to supplement your annual salary is to negotiate a ratings-point bonus as part of your employment contract. Essentially, what this means is that if the program or show that you are anchoring, hosting, or executive-producing shows a year-to-year ratings increase, you share in your employer's success by being awarded some sort of bonus. Once again, you should be *partners* with your employer during the economically challenging times, as well as in financial success.

The conceptual allure of this type of clause is that it doesn't cost your employer any extra money, unless the employer receives a financial benefit as well. However, in *The New Age*, some employers may counter that even though ratings on the show that you work for have gone up, due to the still weak economy, the employer has received little or no additional monies. You can then counter with the two criteria that would justify your receiving a bonus:

1. The newscast or program that you render services for has shown year-to-year ratings growth; and

2. The employer has received increased revenues or other valuable consideration in connection with that newscast or program.

If, at the conclusion of negotiations regarding this provision, you are unable to secure additional compensation for ratings increases on the show(s) you anchor or host, you can then ask for a non-monetary reward such as increased vacation time or more contractual security.

Clothing Allowances

Many stations no longer give clothing allowances because of administrative problems, tax issues, and the fact that talent has occasionally abused the privilege by buying clothes that are more appropriate for personal use. Imagine that! From my perspective, notwithstanding all of these issues, with some effective station involvement, I would think that it is in the employer's best interests to pay talent a $100,000 salary plus a $5,000 clothing allowance, rather than a salary of $105,000; the employer receives the value and the guarantee that some amount of money will be allocated to appropriate talent dress, which would enhance the talent, as well as the employer's newscasts or programs.

Be aware that employers who give clothing allowances, for the most part, are afraid that the talent will not pay taxes on this allowance and that the employer will ultimately be held liable. Consequently, employers are now taking taxes out of the clothing allowances "up front" (when the allowance is given to the talent). So what may initially seem like a good amount of money for a clothing allowance may not be as meaningful after taxes. When negotiating a contract, try to provide for your clothing allowance to be "grossed up," so that after taxation you have received the necessary amount of clothing allowance.

Employee's Right of Termination

It is important to try to secure a right-of-termination clause, with as little notice as possible to your employer, so that you can extricate yourself from your contract when you are no longer being assigned to the duties that you were promised.

A number of stations will grant this clause, because should you be demoted, an employer quite often will not want an unhappy employee on-site and also will not want to pay a salary to the demoted talent, who is now receiving an inappropriately high compensation for the lesser and newly assigned position (especially in *The New Age*). Even if you do not have this clause in your contract, you can probably negotiate your way out of your contract—but it will be on the employer's terms and timetable, which may not necessarily be good for you. Needless to say, if you can negotiate an unconditional termination provision into your employment contract, when a negative change in your duties takes place, you will be in a clearer, cleaner, and better position to leave when a career-enhancing position is presented to you.

Depending upon your job goals and where you aspire to work next, you may want to negotiate a right-of-termination provision (an out-clause) for yourself if you were to receive a bona fide offer for a position at a station in a desired larger market, on a nationally syndicated or cable program, or at a network. Generally it is easier to secure this type of clause if you are working in smaller and mid-sized markets. You are much less likely to be able to negotiate this clause once you are in a top-10 or even a top-15 market, or if you are a main weeknight anchor in a top-20 market.

When negotiating this clause, try to secure a notice of termination to your employer of 30 or 60 days, but no longer than 90 days. The out-clause should also be *unconditional*, meaning that your current employer should not have the right to monetarily match the third-party offer for which you can contractually leave, and thereby retain your services for the length of the matched deal.

In essence, if you have an out clause, you should be able to use it—with no ifs, ands, or preclusions.

The Pay-or-Play Clause

This clause, which is in almost all broadcasting contracts, provides that an employer can fulfill its obligation to you just by paying you your guaranteed minimum salary—but you, in turn, have no right to perform any on-air or other services for the employer. In essence, employers can pay you off, but they do not have to use your services or air your work.

In almost all instances, your career will not be enhanced if you have an extended period of time when you are not on the air. Therefore, once again your best bet is to negotiate for a termination clause in your contract providing that if your contractually stated duties negatively change, you can terminate your employment agreement with appropriate notice.

Moving Expenses

Many employers are now giving lump-sum moving-expense checks with taxes taken out. Before agreeing to a moving allowance, make sure that you can move (with airfares, as well as temporary housing and packing fees included) to your new job on the *net* amount of money (the gross amount after taxes are taken out) that you will receive from your employer. You should also ask your employer to pay the broker fees incurred in selling, buying, or renting a house or an apartment; however, you should realize that in *The New Age*, this kind of compensation is extremely difficult to secure.

Right of First Refusal

At the conclusion of many broadcasting contracts, there is a right-of-first-refusal or a right-of-last-refusal clause, which means that for a specified time before and after a contract expires, the employer for whom you currently work can match an offer that you receive from certain defined other employers and keep you in place—even if you do not want to stay.

If you have a right-of-first-refusal clause in your contract, the first question to ask is whether the employer's right to match an offer extends to all TV employers, to just the specific market that you are in, to the specific kind of show that you are doing (news, talk, magazine, etc.), and/or the means by which the show is carried or distributed (network, syndicated, and/or cable). The employee's aim is to make an employer's right of first refusal as narrow as possible. For example, if you work in Phoenix, the employer's right of first refusal should be applicable to that market only. So if a Phoenix-based employer wants to hire you away from your station, your station would have the right to match the offer and thereby retain your services. However, if you want to go home to Chicago and work there, the right of first refusal should not extend to that market, and you should be free to work there after the expiration of your current Phoenix station contract.

Ideally, you would like to include in the right-of-first-refusal provision that your current employer must match not only the offering station's monetary terms, but also the position that you are being offered. If you accomplish this, then if the station across the street offers you a weeknight anchor job, your current employer is not allowed to match the offer and thereby retain your services (and make the defensive move of precluding you from going across the street to work) by offering to match the other station's monetary offer, along with a lesser or different position, such as weekend or noon anchoring.

Additionally, if a prospective employer offers you a firm agreement (meaning that there are no right-of-termination clauses, or "cycles," for that employer), it is to your advantage to have a contract with your *current* employer that obligates them to match not only another station's monetary offer, but also the "no-cycle" or "firm" component of the third-party offer. The reason for this is that if you do not have this provision in your current contract, your current employer may be obligated to match only the monetary component of the prospective employer's offer. Therefore, once your new agreement with your current employer begins, your current employer can arbitrarily terminate your new contract—e.g., six months or one year into it—depending upon what your current employer's "cycle" clause provides for, which could result in a problematic scenario. On the one hand, you have been precluded from accepting a long-term, firm ("guaranteed") deal with a new employer, and on the other hand, six months or a year later, you can be terminated by your current employer when you may not have any other attractive positions to consider.

Therefore, a good rule to follow is that the more specific the deal points are that your current employer has to match in order to retain your services, the more advantageous it is for you.

The other "matching" component to pay attention to is the length of the first or last refusal. For talent, the shorter, the better; for the employer, the longer, the better. For example, if the right of first refusal is 60 days, this means that if the talent wants to accept an offer within 60 days after the expiration of their contract, the talent has the obligation to bring that offer to their current employer, and that employer has the right to match it and thereby retain the talent's services under the terms of the matched deal.

If you do not want to give your current employer the opportunity to match the deal, and the right of first refusal is 60 days, you can wait sixty-one days to accept another employer's offer—thereby letting the right of first refusal expire.

If you do this, you no longer have the obligation to bring the offer to your current employer, and your employer no longer has the right to match the offer.

A problem arises, however, if you agree to an unreasonably long right-of-first-refusal time period—for example, six months or one year. This period may well be too long for a station to wait for you, and too long for you to sit out with no income. In such a situation, you may have no choice but to present the third-party offer to your employer and hope that your employer will not match it. In many instances, employers are compassionate. If you effectively explain that a third-party offer provides you an opportunity that your current employer cannot or will not extend to you, in all likelihood your employer will decline to match the third-party offer, leaving you contractually free to accept the new position.

One last point: Be sure that your contract provides that the right of first refusal is operative only at the natural expiration of the contract. If the contract is terminated beforehand, without cause or through no fault of your own, the right of first refusal should not apply. This way, if your employer terminates the contract because he or she no longer values you enough, that same employer should not be able to keep you from going to a competitor by matching the competitor's offer. In essence, what you want to protect against is your current employer making the defensive move of keeping you away from someone, rather than making the offensive move of keeping you because you are truly valued.

The Covenant Not to Compete

The covenant-not-to-compete clause is found in fewer and fewer *New Age* broadcasting personal-services contracts. It provides that for a defined period of time (maybe six months or one year), upon the expiration or termination of an employee's contract, the talent cannot appear on-air (and in some cases, work off-air) for a competitor. For example, this competitor can be any station in the employee's local market if the contract in issue is in local news. Essentially, a covenant-not-to-compete clause allows the employer to preclude the employee from rendering on-air services to anyone that the employer designates as the "coverage area" for any period of time the employer wants, usually one year or less, depending upon how the employer chooses to write the clause. Some covenant-not-to-compete provisions (hereafter "covenants") go so far as to preclude employees, for a defined period of time, from rendering *any* services for a competitor (writing, producing, etc.), and they may preclude individuals from working in other media, such as radio. They may even preclude them *from simply seeking future employment for the designated amount of time.* For example, a person who was let go from a station without "cause" but who would like to stay in his or her current market would not only potentially be prohibited from working in broadcasting in that market for a one-year period, but also be prohibited from even *seeking* employment there until after the one-year covenant has elapsed.

Does it seem *fair* and *equitable* for a general-assignment reporter who was let go from a station (after one year of employment there), because that station didn't care for the reporter's work or needed to cut costs, to be precluded from working and seeking employment in the market of her or his choice for one year? *Absolutely not!*

As far as I am concerned, depending upon how a covenant-not-to-compete is drafted, it can be one of the most *unfair, inequitable, inhumane,* and *draconian* clauses in any broadcasting personal-services contract.

The test that courts have often used in the past for the legality and enforceability of such covenants is whether they are *fair* or *overbroad,* both in their *reach* (whether they are overly restrictive and thereby preclude too much) and in their *duration* (whether they last too long). Twelve years ago I wrote: "My inclination is that many, many broadcasting *covenants* will be struck down by courts as *overbroad* both in reach and in duration." Over the years, many covenant-not-to-compete clauses have in fact been abolished in different states by the legislatures or by the courts. The problem with talent challenging the covenant's legality is that talent almost never want to incur the great expense of bringing a suit against a company with deep pockets, and neither do they want to spend the time necessary to fight a suit through to its conclusion. Additionally, they are *scared to death* to incur the silent wrath of the broadcasting community by suing one of their own.

The last reason is a *big* one. On-air individuals feel (often rightfully) that if they publicly fight a broadcasting employer—even if they are *absolutely correct* in their position—other employers will brand them as a "malcontent" or a "troublemaker" and be reluctant to hire them for fear that they may one day cause *them* problems, too. Therefore, the talent, out of practicality and fear, bite the bullet and do not challenge clauses, such as covenants not to compete, which preclude them from earning a living in their field for as much as one year, in a city in which they would like to make or keep their home. This is a sad *Broadcasting Reality*.

From the employer's perspective, they have made a legitimate and substantial investment monetarily, promotionally, and in on-air time in the broadcast journalists whom they hire. They argue that they will be *materially damaged* if, as soon as their contract with an employee expires, that employee goes to work for a competitor. *Employers* feel that this would be unfair and inequitable to *them*.

I believe that there *is* merit in their argument, up to a point. But just as a punishment is (ideally) supposed to fit the crime, so too should the breadth and scope of a covenant-not-to-compete clause be adjustable to *appropriately* fit the situation and the station's *real* investment in the *particular* talent. *One covenant does not fit all*!

For example, should a general-assignment *reporter* who earns $45,000 annually and is let go after one year of service due to cost-cutting measures be subject to *the same* one-year covenant-not-to-compete clause as a main weeknight anchor who is promoted, earns $300,000 annually, has just completed a five-year contract, and is offered a new five-year contract by his or her station, beginning at $400,000 annually? Does the station have the *same* monetary investment in the reporter as the anchor? Does the station have the *same* promotion and on-air investment in both individuals? Is the station *damaged* to the same extent if the reporter, as opposed to the anchor, is immediately employed by a competitor?

I would argue that there are *material* differences here, but rarely, if ever, are these differences taken into account and reflected in the way covenants are drafted!

Let's continue. What if the *reporter* mentioned above began his career in a market by working for five years for Station A? He then leaves Station A, sits out a one-year covenant not to compete to join Station B (in the same market), which then fires him one year later, because they no longer like his style of reporting. In this case, Station B (which fired the reporter) didn't pay his moving expenses when he first came to the market; nor did it *introduce him* to the market. I would argue that Station B had invested *very little* in the reporter, and that its one-year covenant not to compete is *unfair* and should be held to be patently *illegal* by a court.

Let's consider three other scenarios:

1. Susan is a single mom anchoring the weekend newscasts at Station X. Her station decides not to offer her a new contract at the expiration of her current one. In order to maintain custody of her son, Billy, Susan must continue living in her market and must maintain her current salary level. The general manager at Station X says that he must enforce its covenant not to compete and therefore not allow her to seek or accept on-air employment in the market for one year. The general manager says that he feels "bad," but he cannot set a precedent regarding the elimination or negotiation of the covenant. He explains that Susan has been a wonderful employee, but that her style of delivering news doesn't have the intensity and immediacy that his new news director wants for his anchors and reporters. Consequently Susan, whose current employer has *no* intention of retaining Susan's services, is *precluded* from earning a living anchoring or reporting for any TV or radio employer for one year in the one city where she needs to live in order to retain custody of her son. And while she is allowed to secure a position as a writer or producer in her market, neither position will enhance her on-air career nor allow her to earn near the salary that is required for her to keep Billy.

2. Ted is a husband and father of three. He is a noon anchor at Station Y, earning $75,000 per year. At the end of his contract, Station Y demotes him to a reporter and occasional fill-in anchor, and stands firm that his salary needs to be cut to $60,000. Ted also has received serious interest regarding a 5 p.m. weeknight (Monday through Friday) anchor position, starting at $100,000 per year at a station in the same market. Ted has a six-month covenant-not-to-compete clause during which he cannot *accept* employment in his market. The prospective employer, with the 5 p.m. anchor opening, tells Ted that the position may not be available in six months and that Ted will take a substantial risk if he sits out for six months in hopes that the position will still be available for him to accept when his covenant not to

compete expires. Ted reluctantly decides that he cannot play Russian roulette with his family's income, so he accepts the position at his current station for $60,000.

3.   Ann is a weeknight anchor at Station A, earning $210,000 per year. Her station offers her a new three-year contract beginning at the lower salary of $190,000 per year. She is very popular, and both of her newscasts are rated #1 in the market. Ten days before the expiration of her contract, Station B offers Ann a five-year, no-cut deal, starting at $250,000 per year. Ann's current employer, Station A, says that it will enforce her one-year covenant-not-to-compete. Station B cannot wait a year for Ann, so they revoke their offer.

For most people, Ted's and Susan's cases would probably be more compelling illustrations of why covenant-not-to-compete clauses need to be more appropriately limited and written. However, in a capitalist society, should Ann be precluded from attaining the true market value of her services during her prime earning years once her contract has expired? Does this not smack of restraint of trade?

My perspective is that in a case when someone is demoted or asked to take a pay cut, *no* covenant or a minimal covenant of no more than 30 days—*for which the employee is paid*—is appropriate. The covenant not to compete clause should be used as a *shield* by a station to protect its legitimate investment and *continued interest* in the fair and gainful employment of an employee—not as a *sword* to preclude a competitor's hiring someone whom the current employer no longer values enough, or at all, thereby professionally and financially damaging that employee.

In the case of Ann, there is somewhat more of a meritorious argument for a covenant not to compete—*to be paid for by the station*—for a maximum of 90 days. (It is also arguable that Ann, unlike Ted and Susan, has the clout and the leverage to negotiate the covenant not to compete down to a reasonable length of time.) *However, my best solution to this problem is to follow the practice of the network-owned stations in markets such as Los Angeles, where stations have rights of first refusal but no covenants not to compete.* Therefore, if Ann's current station wants to keep her, it would have to match Station B's offer and pay the market price for her services. I would argue that in the case of Ted, his current employer would have to match the money *and* the position in order to keep him.

In a situation such as Susan's, where someone is not renewed (or is terminated "without cause") by an employer, that employer should *not* be accorded *any* form of covenant not to compete or right of first refusal. Once again, the right of first refusal should be used as an *equitable shield*, not an *onerous sword*—so that a station can make a *defensive* hire. I would also limit the scope of any right of first refusal to the market at issue.

"Negotiate" Versus "Discuss"

It is of the utmost importance that you know what you can and cannot do during the term of your contract.

A number of contracts say that during the term of your contract, you cannot *discuss* future employment with a prospective employer; some provide that you cannot *negotiate* with any third party; and some say that you have to negotiate exclusively with your employer until the end of your contract with them.

These provisions reflect employers' positions that they do not want their employees discussing or negotiating future employment with other employers while still working for them. Their perspective is understandable. The employers believe that they deserve the best opportunity to try to re-sign their own employees while they are still under contract to them.

The converse is this: How can talent know what is available to them, and on what terms, if they cannot discuss employment with prospective employers until their contracts have expired and they risk being out of work?

My recommendation to talent is to make sure that you are not precluded from *discussing* future employment with other potential employers during the term. It is okay to grant some period during which you are obligated to negotiate exclusively with your employer. But for the last 90 days of your contract, ideally, you should be able to seek and negotiate offers with all prospective employers, so that during the last 30 days of your contract, you can make an informed decision regarding what your options are. Your employer is still protected by the right of first refusal at the expiration of your contract. This way, you have the best opportunity for ascertaining and/or receiving the fair-market value of your services.

The Incapacity Clause

Almost every broadcasting contract contains a clause that gives the employer the right to terminate the contract if the employee becomes unable to effectively render his or her services for a stipulated amount of time. For example, contracts often provide for an employer's right to terminate for "incapacity"—that is, if the employee loses his or her voice, becomes visibly disfigured, contracts a disease, or sustains an injury that materially detracts from or limits performance.

The key is to make sure that an employer cannot terminate you for incapacity unless you are incapacitated for a certain amount of time—for example, for at least four or five *consecutive* weeks in any one contract year. Optimally, this incapacity period will be longer—preferably eight weeks in any one contract year. It is also reasonable that a station should not be able to terminate a contract for incapacity if the injury or illness sustained occurs as a result of a work-related event.

The Morals Clause

A morals clause provides that if the employee commits an act or does anything that might negatively affect or reflect poorly on the employer or that tends to or does in fact offend a portion of the community, the employer can terminate the agreement.

In real life, whether or not a company will exercise the clause often depends upon the flagrancy of the offense and how important the offender is to the employer's ratings and profitability. The rule of thumb in *The New Age* is that if you bring in ratings, employers will do all they can to rehabilitate and save you. If you do not, and the offense is serious, you will be terminated—especially if the employer can save a salary.

The Indemnity Clause

In broadcasting you often rely on writers, producers, and reporters to supply you with information, and you hope that the material supplied to you is correct. But what if it is not, and you and the station are sued? Or what if you report or ad-lib something that offends someone, and the next thing you know, someone files a suit against the station and names you as a codefendant? Your best defense is to provide a clause in your contract stating that if you act in good faith and within the scope of your employment, you will be indemnified and held harmless by your employer (who should be insured) against any and all claims, suits, actions, damages, expenses, and awards in connection with any alleged wrongdoing. It is not always possible to obtain this language—but if you can, try to secure it. In any case, take comfort in the fact that I have not seen an instance where an employee acted in good faith and the employer didn't indemnify the employee for all of the employee's costs in connection with the claim or suit.

Please note that a number of the provisions that I have discussed above may not be attainable from certain employers. However, many, in some form or fashion, can be secured, and you should have them incorporated into your employment contract. Your efforts in this area will be well rewarded.

SECTION VII

The New Age Media and the
Multimedia Journalist

The New Media and *The New Age* Requirements to Be a Multimedia and a Multi-Skilled Journalist

Throughout this book we have discussed the broadcaster's need to get more with less and fewer. One reason that this is a necessity is that TV news viewership has been dwindling, which translates to less advertising revenue for the employer. One reason that news viewership has been eroding is that viewers—many of them younger—get their news from the Internet. Because of this very real competition for viewers, local news stations, network and cable news divisions, and programmers have adopted the strategy, "If you can't beat 'em, integrate 'em." As a result, in almost all news and programming operations, blogging, Tweeting, using Facebook, and appearing on radio have become an integral part of talent's daily duties. In *The New Age*, talent are required to be *multimedia journalists*.

Let's discuss some of the skills and duties that many on-air individuals are required to have and perform in *The New Age of Broadcasting*:

1. *Blogging and Online Marketing*: One essential duty of almost all on-air talent today is to blog about a story or material that you have already presented or will present on TV. This can be accomplished by:

   a. Writing and telling stories for or imparting relevant information via the Internet about material that you have *already* presented on TV;

   b. Expanding and/or further explaining the story that you have already presented on TV, and/or giving the Internet user various

means and links to secure further information about the story or
related subjects and material;

c. Introducing stories, material, and specials that you *will* present on
TV in the future. In essence, this communication is used as a tease
to secure the interest of the TV viewers and drive them to watch
you/your employer's newscast(s) or program(s); and

d. Writing, telling stories, and imparting information that will not
air on TV but is of specific interest to the Internet user.

Because individuals who seek out their news on the Internet are generally
younger, it is often beneficial for the talent to write or rewrite, and to tell or
re-tell their stories, in a snappier writing style that is more Internet-"YouTube"
appropriate. Additionally, because the talent is using the Internet, which is a
visual medium and full of eye-catching stimuli, it can be beneficial to more
effectively "sell" pieces with compelling visual and musical teases that will grab
the Internet user's attention.

In addition, when producing your online stories, in many instances, you
need to make them a bit flashier, with quicker edits, and more current music
than stories airing on TV.

The key here is to understand that when you blog, you are communicating
with and marketing your stories or information to individuals who are used
to receiving their information and communications in a different way than
the conventional television viewers do. Therefore, in order to be most effective, you must adapt your writing and marketing to the medium and to the
intended recipients of your message. In order to cast the widest Internet marketing net for your online stories, it is also helpful to post "hot teases" and links
to your stories on other Web sites.

What the need to blog also requires is that all talent become Internet and
social-marketing savvy. One major means to accomplish this is to know who
your New Media audience is, to know what their expectations are, and to meet
or exceed those expectations.

2. *Tweeting*: As this book is being completed, the use of Twitter is being
heavily adopted by viewers and broadcast journalists throughout the

United States. As discussed, Rick Sanchez, on his daytime CNN newscast, was one of the first anchors to effectively integrate Tweeting into his newscasts. As a result, he instantly connected with his viewers and obtained immediate feedback regarding the news and information that he had just disseminated or had planned to discuss.

Talent and producers can Tweet as an effective means to ask questions about a particular story, place, event, or individual, etc. So, Twitter—when used effectively—can serve as an extremely valuable real-time news and information source for talent.*

Besides securing immediate feedback, Tweeting can be an effective means for talent to be in contact with and establish a *New Age* connection with viewers by telling them what events and stories they have just covered, letting them know what stories or specials they will be covering, and sharing with them selected personal stories. (Please note the safety concern discussed below.)

Additionally, my colleagues and I at KLA have seen firsthand how having a substantial number of Twitter followers can be a material factor in attaining a coveted position, or in not securing one. In *The New Age*, it is quickly becoming essential for on-air talent to have a significant social-media following and presence.

One very important reminder is for talent to be extremely judicious and wise as to what information they Tweet. For example, Tweeting about what event you are *currently* attending—though immediate—can lead to unwanted individuals seeking you out while you are at the event, which can result in significant privacy and safety concerns. So be careful not to sacrifice safety for immediacy and connection. We know that many viewers are voyeurs—but they can live through and vicariously enjoy what you have experienced *after* you have experienced it and left the scene.

---

* For example, in April 2011, during the tornadoes in the South, Jeff Spann of WBMA Birmingham "tapped his 60,000 Facebook friends (and 26,000 Twitter followers) to help him track storms around the DMA in virtual real time" (Michael Malone, "Stations Commit 'Social' Faux Pas," *Broadcasting & Cable*, May 16, 2011, 22).

It is also of the utmost importance to be consequence cognizant when Tweeting (or communicating through any other social media). What this means is that you must make sure that any message or information that you Tweet does not in any way potentially jeopardize or damage you, your career, your employer, your coworkers, or an employer's sponsors. If there is any question as to how a particular message can be construed or interpreted, it is almost always best to err on the side of caution and constructive decision-making by *not* sending it out! Always remember: *When it comes to your career, you can do 100 great things, but one unthinking, well-known destructive move can negate all of the good that you have done and do serious harm to your career.*

3. *Facebook*: Like Twitter, Facebook can be an effective means of sharing information with viewers, connecting with them, and providing a valuable source of information.

4. *Personal Web Sites*: Many talents have spent the time and made the requisite economic investment to develop or have someone else design a personal Web site for them. When it comes to personal branding, building your business; sending out carefully crafted messages about who you are, what you have accomplished, and who you aspire to be; and establishing a very effective, personal connection with others— especially viewers—a personal Web site can pay great dividends.

Because personal Web sites are just that—personal—you can write or promote what you want, *within the parameters of sound judgment.* Once again, this can be an efficient means of securing new viewers, connecting with those who watch you and your newscasts or programs, and disseminating relevant information. However, do not risk your safety by trying too hard to connect with individuals by sharing personal information and thereby jeopardizing your well-being. Obviously you want to impart information to the public that enhances your employer and is consistent with the messages, tone, feel, and philosophy that your employer wants disseminated, so you need to take care with what is disseminated.

One very important point to always keep in mind is this: Whatever is on your Facebook page and whatever you Tweet are a reflection of you and who you are. I have known individuals who have lost career-making positions because of the highly questionable pictures and/or comments that appeared on their Facebook pages. Also, never put yourself in a compromising or negative position (even during parties with relatives and friends) that others might see, photograph, and display on the Internet. The damage to you can be irreparable! Always remember that almost everyone in *The New Age* has the ability to take a picture of you or videotape you *at any time*, so there are no private moments. Everything can be shot and disseminated!

Now let's focus on some requirements for *The New Age of News*. With news budgets shrinking over the past years, a new brand of journalist has emerged. Whether this talent is called a video journalist (VJ), a backpack journalist, or a multimedia journalist, the same skills are expected: the abilities to shoot, write, edit, and produce. *New Age* talent is required to be a true one-person band!

In local news, you see much more of the multimedia journalists in many smaller markets, for a myriad of reasons. First and foremost, there are not any unions that have jurisdiction of and control over who shoots, writes, and edits. Also, in small markets, with many hungry, up-and-coming journalists, it has been much easier to implement *The New Age* requirements, since the new recruits will do just about anything to secure an on-air job so that they can learn and grow.

Larger markets have more unions, and therefore there are more restrictions as to what talent can be required to do. However, at the time that this book is being finished, broadcasters' efforts in *The New Age* to get infinitely more with much, much less are in full swing and very visible. It appears that many, if not most, large-market stations and station groups are successfully fighting unions in an effort to mandate that station talent now shoot, write, and edit. Additionally, more and more stations are requiring talent to learn how to shoot and edit if they do not already possess those skills.

What is interesting in *The New Age* is that because it is essential for on-air talent to be able to shoot their own stories, photogs or shooters (photographers) have been given a tremendous opportunity and entrée to become on-air talent and to file stories themselves. I have also been told that if you can shoot and edit, both photographers and editors will respect you and your opinions a great deal more when putting your pieces together. Obviously, it is always beneficial when working with someone to speak their language, as well as to understand and respect what they do and where they are coming from.

So, for every positive reason:

1. having a rock-solid journalistic foundation;

2. gaining the respect of others;

3. understanding what others do and "the process;" and

4. being or remaining relevant,

it is essential that you learn to perform *The New Age* skills of writing, shooting, editing, and producing your stories.

What *New Age* News Managers Want and Expect from Talent

In the *New Age,* it is crucial that talent are naturally curious people; the desire to be a reporter must be a calling and a passion. Below are some specific things that news executives have told me that they need from their *New Age* talent:

1. The desire and skill to find or generate actionable, first-block stories and the ability to do top-drawer enterprise reporting;

2. The desire and ability to identify and cultivate top-notch sources;[106]

3. The ability to bring "differentiated" and better content to the station's or the network's newscasts;[107]

4. The ability to be an "A player" in terms of:

    a. researching

    b. writing

    c. reporting a story;

5. The ability to truly understand the New Media and its underlying

platforms, and how to harness and use all of this knowledge to the employer's and talent's very best advantage;

6. The highly coveted ability to establish an *emotional* connection with your copy or material, so that it translates into a comfortable, yet confident conversation with the viewers;[108]

7. The ability to own your material, so that you thoroughly understand the information that you are imparting to the viewers and can effectively ad-lib and/or answer questions about it if required; and

8. The ability to engage the viewer in a demonstrative way, because if you are excited about and engrossed in the information that you are presenting to the viewers, hopefully they will be connected as well.

SECTION VIII

The Psychology of Securing
Effective Representation

Representation

I am a talent representative. Therefore, in writing this chapter I will try to be as objective as possible. However, it is important to understand that I have had a unique set of personal experiences that strongly influence my thought processes and my perspectives on this subject.

Here are some key concepts that you might want to consider when attempting to choose the most effective representation for yourself.

Understanding

It is of great import that your representative thoroughly understand the broadcasting business and its inner workings. Your representative should understand the impact of the choices that you will be asked to make during your career, as well as the kinds of opportunities that the representative will need to create specifically for you. In essence, your representative should either know or have access to the information that will allow you to make informed and wise career decisions for the short and long terms. Here is an example.

The Story of the Ice-Skating Boot Versus the Rollerblading Boot

The following is a story about a long-time client of mine who was most recently a weekday anchor in Los Angeles. I first met her as a result of a San Francisco news director's glowing recommendation. She was an intern-writer at his station. To this day, her intern demo tape is one of the three best tapes of its type that I have received in my 29 years of being an agent.

Besides having a great tape, this individual was clearly very smart and had a great natural ease with the camera. Within weeks of getting her representation, she secured an overnight position in Sacramento as a writer and cut-in anchor. She was soon promoted to a full-time reporter, whereupon she signed a two-year agreement with her station. During the next year or so, I critiqued three or four of her tapes, and although she was growing quickly, I felt that she hadn't yet hit the stride that I believed that she would soon attain. So I held off sending out her tapes to prospective employers.

Then, one Sunday afternoon, about sixteen months into her two-year Sacramento contract, I screened her newest tape, and I was blown away by how comfortable and compelling her storytelling had become, by the way she engaged me, and by the way she filled the screen. She was unquestionably on her way to being great.

I immediately called her to share my excitement. I was now ready to introduce her to the top-10 market broadcasting world. For the remainder of the afternoon and early evening, I re-edited her tape so that I had a great montage of her stand-ups at the beginning, followed by her best live and packaged reports. With this, the viewer, within minutes, would see the wide range of my client's reporting skills.

On Monday morning I called general managers and news directors in the top markets and alerted them that a tape of a potentially great talent would be on its way. After a week or so, I had heard from stations in New York, Los Angeles, and Chicago, as well as from one station in Miami and one in Dallas, all wanting to fly my client in for an interview. After some extensive interviewing, my client felt that one station in Los Angeles, two stations in Chicago, and one station in Miami should remain in the running. She then asked my opinion as to which station she should choose.

I believe that my thinking and advice proved to be correct, and for instructive purposes, I repeat the information here.

First: Although my client was receiving interest and offers from excellent stations in top markets, what station executives saw on her demo tape was the *great potential* of a smart, extraordinarily talented woman who was half-Latina. However, as my client's advisor, I had to remain absolutely aware that my client had been on-air for only about sixteen months. And although her tape was good enough to make a deal with *Blockbuster Video*, she still had a great amount to learn. Therefore I didn't want to push her too quickly and thereby jeopardize her future growth.

Second: The stations that were interested in hiring my client were all network-owned and reputable. However, the station in Los Angeles and one of the stations in Chicago had one thing in common: I felt that both stations were, in the past, great in the courtship of some young up-and-coming broadcasters but did not follow through with real nurturing or support in the marriage. Therefore, a number of their younger, less experienced recruits fell by the wayside. They either never evolved into the talents that they might have been with more support, or they suffered major setbacks from which they had to eventually recover. As a result, I would rule these stations out, no matter how well intentioned and enthusiastic the news managers there were.

Third: This left the station in Miami and one station in Chicago. Now the choice became really tough, as Miami and Chicago are both great news markets. The station in Miami had a brand-new general manager, who I consider to be one of the very brightest, most evolved, and most humane mentors that I have met in all of broadcasting. He is a true inspiration and my dear friend. After a dinner with him and his exceedingly accomplished wife, my client immediately concurred with my raves about this individual. However, there were some problems with the Miami station. First, it had no news director at the time, as the previous one had left and no replacement had been hired. The station was also in turmoil and needed a complete overhaul—which would take place during the ensuing months. On the other hand, the station in Chicago was the dominant #1, with a wonderful on- and off-air staff that had been there for years. Continuity and high ratings reigned at the Chicago station.

Fourth: After recounting all of this, I then gave my client my answer and my reasoning. My recommendation was that she go to the Chicago station, notwithstanding the brilliance of my general manager friend in Miami and his more-than-obvious strong commitment to my client's growth.

I explained to my client that at another time, when a news director was in place, when all of the anchors and producers were hired, and the station was more settled, Miami might be the better growth venue for her—but not now. Besides, one executive producer whom she met in Miami said that he could see my client immediately doing the big story at 11 p.m. each night in order to increase ratings. This scared me, as I felt that ratings success should not be put on the shoulders of someone who had been on the air for such a short amount of time.

Conversely, the Chicago station had many seasoned veterans and didn't need any great new flashes to improve ratings or increase viewership. Their agreement—which they fulfilled in every way—was to bring my client along slowly but surely.

I then asked my client to picture an ice-skating boot. Generally, it is made of soft leather, with one characteristic being that if you move the wrong way or your ankles are weak, you can turn an ankle and sustain an injury. There is very little support. In contrast, a rollerblading boot is strong and keeps your foot firmly in place, so there is little chance of turning your ankle, even if it is weak. I then analogized the current state of the Miami station to an ice-skating boot, in that there would be little support or day-to-day nurturing for her at the troubled station, whereas the Chicago station, with its rock-solid internal news operation, would give my still green client all of the support and protection that she would need as she began to compete in the highly competitive Chicago news market.

My client agreed with my advice, and she accepted the Chicago station offer. Within months, she was excelling as a reporter, and within a year and a half, she began anchoring. Soon thereafter, she secured a regular anchor position there. Step by calculated step, she grew.

The moral of the story is that when deciding on what your early moves should be, you should not be seduced by quick fixes. Keep the big picture of your career in mind. Make sure that you go to stations or programs that will give you the support and nurturing that is appropriate for your stage of development. Early flashes and subsequent crashes are never pretty. Do not go too fast, too soon.

I am very proud of the advice that I gave my client here, because I understood her stage of development and what she needed. *You should seek and retain a representative that has the knowledge and the wisdom to help you to choose your moves wisely.* And remember, rollerblading boots are great until your ankles and your skill level are ready for softer, more supple ice-skating boots.

The Short- and Long-Range Views

I believe that the best representative for a given person needs to have in mind the long-range view of that person's career, as well as their own long-term relationship with that person. For example, an agent must be willing to counsel a client to take a lesser-paying position because it is in the best long-term interest of the client, even if it means the agent must forgo a larger commission. Similarly, agents often get kudos for having clients who make big-market or much-publicized moves. The agent must be able to put the career of the client ahead of what may bring him or her more positive publicity. If, for example, a client would be best served by having an additional local-market experience before accepting a network position, the agent should put the client's long-term best interest ahead of her or his (and the client's) desire for immediate—but inappropriate—gratification and applause.

I could argue that already successful and well-respected firms would be less likely to need to compromise a client's career for their own good. However, at the end of the day, I believe it all comes down to the agent's character and whether the agent has a true long-term commitment to the client.

Executive Access and Knowing Your Client

If you have aspirations of moving up in market size, going to a syndicated program, or working for a network, it is desirable to find a representative who has a successful track record for marketing talent in those specific arenas. Additionally, with aggressive marketing, you will ideally have numerous employers interested in you, which will enable you to employ the all-important asset of leverage when you and your representative negotiate your deal.

Obviously, it is of the utmost importance for an agent to understand what makes you special when marketing you to others. For example, here is a story that had a great conclusion—because I knew what made my client unique.

> Years ago, we took on the representation of Julie Moran—not
> from a demo tape, as was our practice, but from a commercial

picture, a stellar résumé, and a wonderful in-person meeting. It was at that meeting that Julie's intelligence, extraordinary sparkle, texture of soul, and old-soul humaneness were clearly evident. Her very impressive background included graduating Phi Beta Kappa from the University of Georgia, being an All-American college basketball player, winning the Miss U.S.A. Junior Miss title, and possessing a thorough knowledge of basketball and other sports. She also appeared to have great character and strong values.

Two of Julie's goals were to become a major network sports broadcaster and to have a prominent role on a program like *Entertainment Tonight*. Within a few weeks of our association, an on-air position at Movie Time˙ became available. She tested for it and got it. From that position Julie garnered some invaluable daily on-air experience and a demo tape with which to market her.

Months later, a major sports opportunity opened up for a woman at the NBC Network. We were told that the prerequisites for the job were breakthrough talent and prior local, cable, and/or network sports experience. Notwithstanding the fact that Julie didn't have a prior sports-broadcasting background, we submitted her demo tape. The network's response was: "She's got the talent, but how can we hire someone with no sports broadcasting experience for this job? Thanks, but no thanks."

The orthodox route of submitting our client's demo tape didn't work. It was time for an *out-of-the-box* approach. I took a day or so to think things through. I knew that Julie had a thorough knowledge of sports; she just needed the opportunity to show it to the appropriate individuals. Unfortunately, the person who would ultimately make the decision didn't think that a meeting with Julie would be worthwhile. This was coupled with the fact that this high-ranking executive

---

* Movie Time was the forerunner of E! Entertainment Television.

was someone with whom we had no prior history or working relationship. But I decided to try my plan anyway.

I called the executive and identified all of the people whom our company had brought to his network, as well as to other networks and syndicators. I did this in hopes that it would establish my credibility. Before I had finished giving my full list, he acknowledged my eye for spotting breakthrough talent. I then said that I was positive that if he had a one-on-one meeting with Julie (who was based in Los Angeles, while he was based in New York), she would win him over with her sports knowledge. I would bet my credibility and my future relationship with him on it. I then offered to send him a first-class round-trip ticket to Los Angeles if he would agree to sit down and have a meal with her. If he didn't hire her, I would have paid for his ticket; if he did like her, I would be reimbursed.

I could tell by his reaction that I had gotten him to seriously acknowledge my strong belief in my client. The unorthodox nature of my approach worked. He said, "Ken, I can't accept your proposal, although I do like the effort. But here's what we *can* do. I'm going to be in Phoenix next week. How about having your client fly down and meet me there?"

I instantly accepted the offer on behalf of Julie, and once again reinforced her thorough sports knowledge. The next week they met. Three days later, Julie was offered the very prestigious network position.

Two factors played major roles here: One was that I *knew* my client and her abilities well, and I understood that if she met the network executive in person, she would dazzle him; and the other was that I needed to step back, get another perspective, and find an unorthodox and creative approach that would shake up the unfavorable status quo. In this instance, I found it.

The Julie Moran story points out at least three essential criteria for choosing a representative:

1. Do you feel that your potential representative knows who you are and what makes you special, or that he or she will take the requisite time to do so? Knowledge of a client is essential to securing optimal marketing, counseling, and contract-negotiation results.

2. Does your agent have access to the necessary potential news and/or programming employers for whom you might want to work? (We will discuss this below.)

3. Is your representative a creative, big picture thinker and marketer? This quality is even more essential in *The New Age*, where marketing is not just vertical, but also *Multi-Platform* horizontal, involving many diverse media.

Representing Your Unique Values and Goals

It is of equally great importance that your agent understand you, your values, and your goals. It is up to you and your agent to initiate conversations about what your goals and values are, and how they may change over time. It is important to be aware that as people grow and have different experiences, their expectations and goals may be modified, especially in *The New Age* of *Multi-Platforming*.

By understanding who you are, your representative is better equipped to correctly and effectively represent who you are to others. Clients often say that being represented is sometimes a passive position, because someone else is out there marketing and speaking for them. You will be a lot better off, and you should feel more secure, if you know that your representative understands and is able to effectively articulate who you are and what you aspire to achieve.

Achieving the Desired Outcome

Once again, if a representative *understands* you and what you want to achieve in the short and long terms, you and your agent should have a much better chance of achieving desirable outcomes and results.

Access and Track Record

It is of utmost importance that the representative you choose has access to information about openings that currently or will in the future exist, and about what kinds of positions can be created for you. To do this, your representative needs *access* to the news managers and program executives who will potentially hire you. There are also specific agents who have a reputation for having a keen eye for identifying and representing top talent. Therefore, in many instances, these representatives' client demo tapes will be viewed before others—which, of course, can be a distinct advantage for their clients.

There are also certain representatives who have developed long-standing positive relationships with news directors and network or program executives.¨As a result, these representatives may be contacted to submit candidates for a position well before an opening becomes public, because a news manager or executive may want to quickly see who is available without conducting a more public search. Therefore, some positions can be filled without many representatives even being aware that a need existed and that a discreet search took place.

On the other hand, news directors, recruiters, and program executives will generally look at all DVDs and links that come in, and it doesn't matter who represents you or what that person's relationship is with the prospective employer. If the talent is good and a deal can be made, you will get hired. Since

---

** Long-standing relationships with employers can make a great deal of difference in at least two instances. First, knowing how to negotiate with a specific executive can pay great dividends for a client, because the representative knows how far they can push the envelope with a manager with whom they are familiar, as well as what attractive things are attainable for a client and what are the best means to attain them.

Second, a positive working relationship with management can be of great help, for example, when a client needs to be released from an employment contract. A number of times I have been able to extricate someone from a personal-services contract (without any ugliness or bad feelings) because I had a good working relationship with a manager and the company. I remember one client who had signed a five-year renewal of her network contract, and during the first year of that agreement, a career-making opportunity with another employer became available to her. Partly because of the network's very positive view of my client and partly because of my long and strong relationship with a network executive, he agreed to let her out of her contract so that she could accept the position.

A representative's long and positive course of dealing with a particular broadcast manager can absolutely work to a client's advantage.

it is generally the bottom line that counts, people will deal with the devil if they feel that they can hire someone who will increase ratings. And if they personally will not deal with the devil, they will get someone else on their staff to make the deal.

The Concept of the "General Practitioner" Versus the "Specialist"

Currently, there is a proliferation of news agents in broadcasting. Why? I guess that it seems like fun; it looks easy—it appears to be lucrative, and you need no special training or education to do it. Anyone—yes, anyone—can become an agent! I am truly amazed that broadcasters, whose profession it is to research stories and to search out the truth, so often do so little—or no—research on an agent's background, experience, track record, and access to information and to prospective employers. It is incredible how many beginning and not-so-inexperienced broadcasters just sign with the first agent who calls them because they are flattered or because they feel that it is the right time to have representation.

You know why bad things happen to good broadcasters? One reason is that they do not do their homework when it comes to themselves and what is best for them.

When you are beginning a career, many reputable agents can help you find "a job." Far fewer representatives, however, understand the concept and practice of *Choreographing* a *Multi-Platform* career. This is analogous to the difference between someone bowling and someone playing chess. There are a lot of bowlers out there. You roll the ball, and you (hopefully) hit the pins. Great! Similarly, if you are a bowler-agent, you send DVDs or forward links, you see what hits, and your client takes a job. Task done! However, there are very few master chess players out there. These are representatives who, in concert with you, devise a step-by-step strategy and a big picture game plan in which career move after career move is well thought out and made with a specific long-term goal and with the big picture of your unique abilities and heartfelt aspirations clearly in mind.

Arguably, bowler-agents are fine early on. However, as you begin to grow, a far more sophisticated and advanced career manager may be more appropriate.

Additionally, if you aspire to go to a network or to a syndicated show, there are only a very few agents who do most of the business with those venues, who know both the ropes and the key players, and who have access to the critical information that can materially enhance your career.

At a certain point, then, you may want to seek the help of a *specialist*, rather than a *generalist*, to *Choreograph* your broadcasting career. This is analogous to seeking medical help. If you have a cold, the flu, or even something a bit more serious, you may (initially) be perfectly fine if you see a general practitioner. However, if you have something more acute, you may be best served if you enlist the help of a *specialist*, someone who has a proven track record and is an expert in the field. Would you expect your general practitioner to perform neurosurgery? I think not! Therefore, one doctor or one agent may not fit all! *Do your homework regarding various representatives' track records for accomplishing what it is that you aspire to do.* If an individual successfully secured your desired outcome many times before, you may increase your chances of attaining your most cherished goals by seriously considering that person to represent you.

However, all of the most well-respected and successful representatives had to start somewhere. It was not until my clients grew, and they stayed with me, that I gained day-to-day access to top network executives, syndicators, and top-market news managers. I understood my clients, and they trusted my instincts—even if I did initially lack experience. And we have all grown together!

Roger Federer, Serena Williams, Rafael Nadal, and Venus Williams didn't have a major tournament track record until they had the chance to play on the center court of the U.S. Open or Wimbledon—and when they did, they rose to the occasion and eventually became champions. If you are talented, and you trust your agent and his or her instincts, you can grow together. Your talent, your agent's understanding of you, and his or her hard work and thoughtfulness regarding you and your career can equal great success. (Nevertheless, experience in the specific field and strong relationships do help.)

In selecting which individual will be the most effective representative for you, carefully weigh all of the pros and cons.

Understanding Revisited—Demo DVDs

It is key for your representative to truly understand what makes you special and what your strengths and your non-strengths are. This is true for at least three reasons. First, in putting together a demo DVD (or link) for you that shows the very best of what you can offer to a potential employer, your representative must know what you do well and must make sure that your very best work is presented on that DVD. Many people have said that I have a keen eye for spotting talent. Part and parcel of this aptitude is my ability to transcribe what makes someone special onto a DVD, so that their demo DVD sings and stands out above the rest.

It is also important for your representative to understand what a particular prospective employer looks for in a demo DVD. This can vary from recruiter to recruiter, so sometimes demo DVDs need to be tailor-made for the tastes of the specific recipient or the requirements of the position to be filled. In essence, the representative does target marketing. If a representative knows a recruiter's preferences and dislikes, this kind of marketing can often materially increase an applicant's chances of securing a desired position. Years of experience and familiarity with key recruiters can tangibly help a client. However, if someone puts a DVD together that most people feel is great, lack of experience with or lack of specific knowledge about a recruiter can definitely be overcome. I would say that knowing what makes a client special is more important than knowing what a particular recruiter wants—though recruiter familiarity is certainly an added advantage.

Finally, it is crucial for a representative to understand what makes you special when they counsel you regarding the most enhancing next position for you to take. Every talent is different. And different positions can affect different individuals in different ways. An effective representative must understand how a particular position can help or hurt a particular client, depending upon that client's strengths and non-strengths, in the context of the client's current stage of development and goals.

Contract Sophistication

Once again, a representative who understands your goals and values is in the best position to negotiate the most appropriate and enhancing contract for you. This contract should reflect and effect your short- and long-term goals and values. As we discussed above, having a representative with some experience, or at least access to what is attainable in a particular contract, with a particular employer, obviously can be very helpful in this endeavor.

Don't Coast: Make the Most of Your Client's Current Position

It is also of great importance that whoever you choose as your representative helps you to keep growing by regularly critiquing your work and seeking out and creating new enhancing opportunities with your current employer, or with other employers for whom your employer will allow you to render services.

Here is an example of my being able to enhance and expand a client's present and future career opportunities with his *current* employer.

Years ago, my company secured the representation of a very talented individual who was between jobs after a stint as a reporter and then as a host for a nationally syndicated program. We helped him to secure a host position on a cable network entertainment program. About two-and-a-half years into his contract, the O. J. Simpson criminal trial was about to begin. After a couple of conversations with my client, I called his employer to suggest that my client anchor the network's live coverage of the O.J. trial from Los Angeles. To the best of my recollection, here is what took place.

I opened my call by saying that it appeared that the trial might well be *the* entertainment and news story of the decade, and that if the network's main anchor didn't want to anchor all of the trial coverage from L.A., my client would love a chance to fill in. I went on to say that because the O. J. Simpson case was a huge entertainment story, my client would be the natural person to be involved in the coverage, as he hosted the network's entertainment show of record. I then respectfully explained that there might be some aspects of my client's background that some executives and other individuals at the network might not be aware of.

I began, "For example, did you know that my client was a practicing California attorney before he began his on-air career?"

The executive responded, "I didn't know that."

I continued, "Did you know that my client's first job in TV was as a legal reporter for KABC?"

Once again the response was, "I didn't know that either."

Now on a roll, I inquired, "And did you know that my client anchored the Monday through Friday morning newscasts at KCBS?"

He quickly shot back, "I knew that one! We love his anchoring."

Ready to ask for the order, I said, "So, because this is *the* entertainment and *the* legal story of the decade, I really believe that my client is uniquely qualified to have the opportunity to anchor some of your O.J. (trial) coverage."

The executive said that my timing couldn't have been better, and that he had just met with his main anchor, who had chosen not to go to L.A.—at all—to anchor the O.J. coverage. As a result, my client would be given a two-week tryout. After one week, we were advised that my client would anchor the O.J. coverage indefinitely. As it turned out, he anchored the coverage throughout the trial. He thereafter was asked to fill in on other news (instead of entertainment) programs. Because of this assignment, my client's persona had been changed and enhanced—tremendously—for the better. Soon thereafter, my client was assigned to anchor the Monday through Friday evening newscasts for his network, as well as their entertainment program of record.

Knowing your client, and seizing and creating appropriate *additional* opportunities with the client's current employer, can enhance your client immeasurably for the moment and throughout the rest of his or her career. Additionally, as we discussed earlier, during the time that we have represented such major talent as Mario Lopez and Samantha Harris, we have been creatively proactive in seeking out new *Multi-Platform* opportunities for them, so that they and their careers can grow. You want the same kind of career-growth aggressiveness from the agent that you decide to hire.

The Concept of Bulletproofing a Client's Choices and Contracts

One very important concept for your representative to understand, embrace, and implement is *bulletproofing* the career choices that you make and the contracts that you enter into as much as possible. What this essentially entails is your representative's ability to be keenly *anticipatory*, so as to strategically minimize the risks for you in the career moves that you make. It also involves protecting you as much as possible in the contracts that your representative negotiates for you.

The ability to effectively *bulletproof* your career requires great knowledge and understanding of the business of broadcasting. Having the requisite experience and reading this book should be quite valuable in enabling your representative to be sufficiently knowledgeable and anticipatory.

What Should Not Be in Your Representation Agreement

As we have discussed, clients often sign with an agent who turns out for various reasons not to be the right one or becomes no longer appropriate for the client. Therefore, the client should always avoid being obligated to pay a commission to a representative "forever" in connection with a particular job.

What I recommend to clients is this:

1. *Do not* enter into representation agreements that renew automatically. This way, every two or three years (at most), *talent* can decide whether

or not they want to stay with a particular representative without the risk of defaulting into continuous representation.

2. *Do not* agree to any representation agreement clause that provides that your representative will be entitled to a commission on any and all future agreements with a particular employer. Therefore, if a new employment agreement with your particular employer is entered into *after* the term of your representation agreement has expired, and if you are no longer represented by that individual or firm, you will not be obligated to pay a commission to your former representative in connection with that new employment agreement.

Once again, when it comes to representation, be a good reporter. Ask questions, get truthful answers, and carefully read and understand your potential representation agreement(s) *before* you sign them!

Continuing Creativity and Education

Throughout this book, we have discussed *The New Age Reality* that many broadcasting rules are changing, will change, or need to change. We have all heard that doctors, lawyers, and accountants take continuing education courses so that they are knowledgeable and comfortable with what is new in their particular field. In many professions, such education is mandatory.

For talent representatives, there is no required formal training. There are no mandatory continuing education courses to take. As a result, it is essential that the representative whom you choose hungers to learn what is new in broadcasting, so that he or she can inform you; wants to keep evolving, so that he or she enables you to evolve; and is a non-defensive, creative thinker, so that he or she is open to new ideas and new paths of growth that can empower you and your career.

What all this means is that hiring a talent representative is a very important step that requires a great deal of time, thought, and effort—and a number of focused conversations with the individual(s) whom you are considering to be your representative(s).

SECTION IX

The Psychology of Breaking into
Broadcasting and Developing
Your Career

The Various Routes to Take

Through the years, I have been asked many, many times by aspiring broadcasters, "How do I break into broadcasting? What's the best way?" In *Broadcasting Realities*, I suggested four possible routes.

Route 1: The Grad-School Experience

You attend a graduate school of journalism before you have any real newsroom experience. From this route you can acquire a great deal of valuable knowledge, and depending upon whether the school has an affiliation with a nearby local station or its own news operation, you can also get some very valuable, real-life experience and a demo DVD with which to market yourself. I highly recommend this as one of your routes.

Route 2: The Initial Small-Market Experience

You begin your development by getting an assistant, writing, producing, or assignment-desk position at a (very) small-market station and then graduate into an on-air position there.

In an extraordinary situation, you may be fortunate enough to start on-air immediately—without prior newsroom experience. This can occur if the market is small enough, if you have good timing and there is an opening at the station when you apply, or if a news manager there believes in you enough to create an on-air opportunity for you.

Route 3: The Initial Large-Market Experience

This route calls for you to secure a position—for instance, as an intern or as an assistant—at a high-quality, large-market station or news operation. Then, as time goes on, you can hopefully befriend a reporter, producer, or photographer there from whom you can learn. Optimally, these individuals will take you out in the field so that you can get some off-air reporting experience. Hopefully, you can develop a demo DVD of your work with which you will be able to market yourself and find your first on-air job.

Route 4: The Course or Private-Instruction Experience

You take a course or a set of courses in broadcast journalism at a college or university, from which you can generate a demo DVD of your work, or you work with a private instructor or coach who will help you to develop your performance or voice skills and who has access to individuals who will help you to produce, shoot, and edit a demo DVD. With this DVD, you can go shopping for your first job.

The New Age has presented at least three other routes to consider:

Route 5: Use Your Expertise

As we have discussed, another means of becoming an on-air talent is to use your expertise—legal, medical, culinary, fashion, financial—to get your initial on-air experience and demo DVD. Then, depending upon your skill level and aspirations, you can transcend your expertise and move on to anchor, host, or report for a local station, a broadcast or cable network, or a national program.

Of course, you can also stay in your area of expertise and ride it as far as it will take you.

Routes 6 and 7: The Photog Route

In *The New Age*, photographers have wonderful opportunities to become video journalists. So if you can shoot and you aspire to be on-air, become a "shooter" at a local station, and begin to file reports there. Who knows what will evolve? Conversely, if you are an aspiring talent, learn to shoot, and go out and report. When you have a compelling story that is well shot and well reported, take it to a local station. It can be the inroad that you need to secure a freelance or a full-time reporting position there.

Route 8

Become a contestant on a competition show, such as *The Bachelor, The Apprentice, The Amazing Race*, etc. From this experience you could receive enough positive exposure and a good enough demo DVD that you will be able to go on to host or be a correspondent on other shows.

For example, recently two charismatic and exceedingly bright and accomplished doctors, Natalie Strand and Kathy Chang ("Nat" and "Kat"), won *The Amazing Race*. They were so compelling and engaging on-air that I took on their representation, and I am very confident that they will one day host their own medical/wellness/lifestyle show.

Since different individuals have different aspirations, different financial and geographic constraints, and so on, one particular route is not appropriate or effective for everyone. Here are some perspectives.

For on-air individuals, I believe that Route 3 is an excellent means by which you can begin to lay a strong journalistic foundation. The reason: If you can spend about a year in a high-quality, sophisticated news operation, you will be exposed to *how* things are done by seasoned, highly skilled broadcasters and learn *why* they are done that way. Thereafter, when you work in smaller markets alongside beginning broadcast journalists and inexperienced or less-experienced management, you will have an idea in your mind's eye as to how things are done by the "pros." This big-market experience and big picture perspective can be invaluable in helping you to more quickly develop your news instincts, your news sensibility, and your off- and on-air skills.

Quite often, top graduate business schools require applicants to have a minimum of two years of practical business experience before matriculation. Their perspective is that with real-life business exposure and experience under your belt, you will understand more and contribute more to classroom discussions. In essence, you will have had enough exposure to real-world business issues to see and to appreciate the big picture of business once you are in school. I believe the same thing is true of broadcasting. By initially spending time in a high-level news operation, when you thereafter go to work in smaller markets, you will have a greater understanding and a big picture perspective of what is going on, what you need to do there, and how to do it.

Additionally, having an initial large-market experience will give you exposure and access to individuals from whom you can learn a great deal. Hopefully you can cultivate a mentor or two who will answer your questions, critique your work, and take the time to explain things to you. Many individuals who took this route as their first real-life broadcasting experience say that it is amazing how much they learned through osmosis—that is, from just being around top professionals in a good news-gathering organization. It set high standards for them to live up to throughout their careers. These individuals also believe that beginning their careers in a top-market station gave them the taste and hunger to strive to make it "back there" (to the large-market station) full-time, in the on-air and off-air position of their dreams. It gave them a realistic picture and a goal to shoot for.[109]

In contrast, if you start out in a small market, with no sophisticated news-operation experience, you will be surrounded and taught by, and exposed to, individuals who, for the most part, are as inexperienced as you are. As a result, there will be few, if any, great off-air and on-air talent to learn from and to emulate.

When I asked top news managers for their perspectives regarding the large-market route, the great majority thought it was the optimal way to begin a career. However, one news manager voiced the concern that if you start out as an intern or an assistant in a large market, and you get promoted there, because of union requirements and the generally high standard of pay, you quickly earn big-market wages. The problem, she says, is that "these young kids begin to make good money, and because they (often) live at home and have few expenses, they feel flush. So they do not want to go to some small market for a third of their wages and pay their on-air dues. Seduced by the big-market money, they wind up staying in the large markets, in off-air jobs, and they never go to the smaller markets to pursue their dream of being on-air." [110]

To these individuals I say, "Your career is a marathon, not a sprint. Don't sacrifice your dreams for a quick buck or a fast break."

You should also be aware that the routes I have outlined are not exclusive. When beginning your career, there are no hard and fast rules—just some tried-and-true courses. For example, you can have a Route 1 experience along with a Route 3 experience. That is, you can go to journalism grad school and then intern or work in a large market. You can also intern at both a small- and a large-market station before seeking your first on-air position. This, in many instances, is an excellent game plan.

Route 2 for many broadcast journalists is also an effective means by which to begin your career. You lay a solid foundation by going up the ladder, learning as much as you can as a writer, assignment desk person, producer, and so on before going on-air. You can make rookie mistakes and learn from them in small-market news operations, where errors and inexperience are more readily accepted.

Two issues are:

1. As I discussed earlier, a number of my clients started their on-air careers in relatively large markets because they lived or went to college there and worked themselves up to on-air positions at their large-market stations. The inherent problem with this apparent success is that you do not have the chance to make your many novice mistakes in the smaller markets, where they are more forgivable. In larger markets, you are competing with more-experienced individuals. You cannot afford to make many mistakes there, so you are inhibited from stretching and taking risks—because risk-taking can beget mistakes. Therefore, you have a

much harder time finding your comfort level and your true voice. As we all know, it is hard to find the groove and your "zone" when you are always uptight. It can be done, but it is a much tougher process.

The key is that in small markets, you can experiment with your writing, shooting, editing, packaging, and delivery; try things; grow; make mistakes; and regroup. This is why the small-market experience is so valuable to your development. Remember: It is not how fast you initially go, but how much in the long run you ultimately grow!

2. A second concern about starting your career in too large a market or ascending markets too quickly is that you may not give yourself the opportunity to try your hand at and develop varied skills, such as reporting *and* anchoring. For example, if you start in a large market as a reporter, and in time you decide that you want to anchor there, you will have had no prior anchor experience, and you will be competing with others who may have already developed their anchoring skills in two or three smaller-market positions. As a result, you are completely overmatched, and you may never get to learn to anchor in a safe and nurturing environment.

Later, I will recount a story about a client who was a noon anchor in a small market and was offered a five-year reporter position in Philadelphia. Had she taken the Philadelphia job, she almost certainly would have left the development of her anchoring skills behind, with the result that she would mostly likely have to go down significantly in market size in order to begin anchoring again (after having lost five precious years of anchor seasoning).

The key is to move up in market size with a *Choreography* and a purpose; not as a way to make you (momentarily) feel good about your career, or as an (often false) litmus test for you to determine how well you are currently doing. *Choreograph* your career for the long run, with intelligence and discipline.

The question of whether or not attending journalism graduate school is the optimal way to begin an *on-air* career elicits varied responses. Some news managers say that this move is not necessary, since "news is more of a trade than a profession. There are no tests to become a good reporter or an anchor. You get ahead if you're good and experienced at your craft." [111]

On the other hand, *all* of my on-air clients who attended graduate school felt that the education that they received was well worth the time and money spent! One individual said that the ethical and professional responsibilities of being a journalist that were instilled in her during grad school have been invaluable. She believes that laying a solid intellectual and psychological foundation when one is beginning any endeavor of importance increases your chances of success and fulfillment. This woman continues to receive kudos for her reporting at a network-owned station. Two others felt the same way about the ethical and other practical information that they received in grad school. One of these individuals is now a network anchor; the other is reporting in Los Angeles for a network-owned station.

All of the individuals with whom I spoke felt that having a graduate journalism degree on their résumé had significantly helped them at one time or another in the job-search process, because they were accorded more respect— if for nothing else than that they had made an effort to lay a solid journalistic foundation.

I have found that attending a reputable graduate school of journalism is a *very* valuable asset that draws positive attention from news managers. It will not get you a job—your demo DVD, your interview, and your personal qualities will do that—but it can certainly help and be a difference-maker, depending upon the position sought (e.g., at a network) and the particular employer's value system. It most certainly will materially increase your knowledge, it can help you to interview more confidently and effectively, and it may well enable you to make a more compelling first demo DVD. And who knows? If more individuals attended journalism graduate schools, maybe there would not be as many ethical and quality-control problems as there are in broadcast journalism today.

I am a proponent of attending graduate school if at all possible, because I believe that learning as much as you can about your chosen field, from individuals who have a great many invaluable insights and lessons to share, is *always* an enhancing and worthwhile experience.

If you aspire to be an executive producer or to be in news management, journalism graduate school, and the business and economic information that you can learn there, can be of tremendous value. A number of news directors who aspire to become network executives or local-station general managers have said that if they had it to do over again, they would have attended graduate school, or at least would have taken specific courses there.

In connection with Route 4, I would definitely recommend that you have a large-market (or at least some market) newsroom intern or assistant experience as well.

Finding Your First Job

I recommend at least three ways to find your first on-air position—any or all of which can be used together:

1. Send your DVD or link and your résumé to each station in every small market that is geographically desirable to you. Then follow up with phone calls. If you are not successful with this approach within a reasonable period of time, try to get some feedback on your DVD and/or résumé. If you can make beneficial adjustments, do so, and then widen the scope of your geographic search.

2. Call news directors ahead of time, set up appointments with them, and then take a road trip to meet some of them in person. Personal interaction can make all the difference in positively separating you from a crowd of impersonal DVDs, links, and résumés. A meeting can get you the job if there is one immediately available, or it can keep you in the news manager's thoughts when an appropriate position opens. If you are a reasonably good interviewer, I would suggest arranging as many personal meetings as possible. I have repeatedly found that positive personal interaction can go a very long way in helping individuals secure coveted positions.

When you interview, it is important for the interviewer(s) to get a strong sense of your passion for journalism, your work ethic, and your character. It is also important for news managers to know that you aspire to be the best writer and storyteller possible, that you are constructively competitive, that you are a team player, and that you are going to be an excellent newsroom citizen. And even if you aspire to be the world's best anchor, it is important to believe and to impart to the news manager that you are aware that the best anchors understand the context of the stories that they are telling, and therefore, your *first* goal is to be the best reporter possible. Anchoring can come in time.

3. Send your demo DVD and/or forward your demo link and résumé to consultants˙ who may show or forward your work to prospective employers who are their clients. Generally consultants can be increasingly helpful as you move up in market size.

The Question of When to Hire an Agent

This is a question with no simple answer. It really depends upon the talent and the agent.

First, as we discussed earlier, if you are considering hiring an agent very early in the process, do your homework carefully. It is important that you find a representative who has a track record for helping people develop careers, which, in part, requires that the agent have an ability and enthusiasm for effectively critiquing your work as you grow. As discussed earlier, broadcast journalists rarely receive critiques to begin with, and when they do receive critiques in small markets, the critiquing can lack big-market and big picture sophistication (no offense meant to small-market managers). Even if your small-market station hires a consultant to coach you, that consultant is coaching you to be

---

* Unlike agents who work for on-air or off-air individuals, consultants are hired by some stations to bring talented broadcast journalists to their attention. Consultants often perform additional functions for their clients, such as conducting research as to how to "fix" or improve newscasts, newscasters' performances, promotions, or graphics in order to secure higher ratings. Please keep in mind that although consultants can be of great help to broadcast journalists by exposing their work and résumés to potential employers, consultants' salaries are paid by and their primary allegiance is to stations and production companies—not to talent. Consultants do not work in all markets and, except in the most unusual circumstances, they only work for one station in any one market.

successful in Eureka, Paducah, or Redding—the specific market that you are currently working in. A sophisticated and effective representative can give you critiques that may help you to be more attractive to larger markets and a greater variety of markets.

A good agent can also give you big picture advice regarding your career. This, too, can be quite beneficial. An agent will likely not be effective in securing your first or even your second job, however, as many small-market stations will not deal with agents. And agents often are not any more aware than you are about what small-market positions are available. In fact, small-market employers can be scared off by agent involvement, because they assume that as soon as you show any sign of growth, your agent will pluck you out of their station and take you to a larger market and a more lucrative position. The station may also be reluctant to hire someone who secures an agent for their first or second job, as entry positions generally pay very little, and there is usually no negotiation involved.

I have found that unless an individual has an extraordinary demo DVD and background, it is usually beneficial to take someone on as a client during their second or third job. However, I can definitely point to a few cases in which I have represented individuals right from the beginning and we have done wonderful things together. In these unusual cases, I was able to secure career-enhancing first and second positions for them. But this was the exception, not the rule.

So, once again, the point at which you should retain some sort of representation, and what that representation's function should be, depend upon your needs and aspirations and the particular parties and circumstances involved.

Building a Foundation, Step by Step

A poignant line from the film *Field of Dreams* is, "Build it and they will come."[112] My take on this thought is, "Build a rock-solid foundation of journalistic skills, and the most attractive broadcasting positions and other sweet fruits of your labors will come."

For example, tennis star Roger Federer developed the forehand, the backhand, the serve, and the volley, as well as the quickness and the agility he needed to win on all surfaces and in all situations. By building an all-around foundation, he has been able to adapt to difficult, new, and unusual circumstances and to thrive. By mastering all of the requisite skills, he laid the foundation for *all-time* greatness.

The key to successfully mastering skills is to break things down into accomplish-able and master-able steps, and then to accomplish and master them. For example, in my athletic endeavors, one small victory often led to and encouraged other small victories. These, in turn, led to the confidence and the ability to extend myself and my talents, so that ultimately I was able to achieve larger and more gratifying victories. Success bred success, technically and emotionally.

The first time that I played an exhibition match against Arthur Ashe (the year before he became the #1 tennis player in the world), my goal was to concentrate as intently as possible and thereby hit (master) each and every one of my strokes to the very best of my ability. I believed that if I could indeed do this, the points, the games, and the match would take care of themselves. They in fact did. On that occasion, I was victorious.

When I began my business, I transferred my Arthur Ashe match philosophy to that undertaking by believing that if I could serve each client to the best of my ability, each client's success and fulfillment would come, then other clients would come, and ultimately the success of my company and my personal fulfillment would come. Step by mastered step, that is what happened.

If I were to teach someone a skill, such as tennis, I would teach that person one master-able component of a stroke at a time. I would have that individual stand just a few feet away, and I would toss ball after ball to the student, until he or she got it right, by taking mental and physical *ownership* of the step involved. We would then proceed to more difficult and more advanced tasks.

When beginning broadcasters ask me for the best advice that I can give them as they embark on their on-air careers, I say, "If you understand—truly understand—and, where appropriate, personally master the easiest to the most complex behind-the-scenes and on-air duties, then there is *nothing* that can throw you later on. By understanding and mastering the 'where,' the 'how,' and the 'why,' as well as the big picture of how everything fits together, you will have the requisite internal foundation to conquer the broadcasting world."

As we discussed earlier, I am a big proponent of beginning your news or programming career by attending journalism graduate school and/or working at a small- or large-market station where you can be exposed to and gain a hands-on education regarding every step of the news-gathering process. I would:

1. Continually work on and develop your writing skills and style. This is of great importance, as writing is quickly becoming a lost art! Listen to and study how more seasoned and accomplished individuals tell a story, craft their language, etc. Learn as much as you can about writing from those who deserve your respect.

   News luminary Burton Benjamin said the following regarding the fact that no matter what form news transmission and news programs take in the future, those individuals who can write will always be valued:

   "The good journalist is a treasure, and they will not be able to develop or clone him in a laboratory. The problem that television faces, in my opinion, is for the creativity to keep up with the racing technology. I do not care whether or not a story is coming to you via satellite, has been written by computer and transmitted by a correspondent with an antenna implanted in his head. If he can't write, he can't write—by satellite or by quill pen. If he can't report, he can't report. And all of the technology in the world can't save him. There is so much at stake today, that if we simply go with the technology, we are going to be in trouble. There was never a time when a reporter who can write, report, analyze, ask the right questions was needed more."[113]

2. Gain proficiency in as many areas as possible. Ask for opportunities to report both hard-news and softer-news stories. Conscientiously work on developing your live and taped reportorial skills. Tell the viewers compelling stories. The ability to write and craft a moving piece is an invaluable skill. Develop it. Try your hand at anchoring; see how it goes and if you like it.

3. Learn to shoot, edit, and produce.

4. Enterprise stories, and cultivate valuable sources.

5. Continue to educate yourself. Read books on the history of broadcasting, and learn how the most accomplished individuals in the field think and how they act in various situations. Understand your profession's roots and ideals and how broadcasting has evolved.

6. Objectively review your on-air work as frequently as possible. Identify the areas that need work and/or polishing, and figure out how to improve your product and performance. Also, take note of the things that you do well, and consciously integrate them into your on-air repertoire. Be your own coach.

7. Try to enlist the critiquing of well-respected consultants, news managers, producers, and on- and off-air individuals in larger markets. But remember, everyone has his or her own subjective point of view, and the things that they suggest may not be right for you personally, for what you aspire to be, or for where you aspire to go. One rule of thumb to follow regarding critiques is: If a comment about your work comes up often, you should probably give it due consideration.

8. Study what the most effective communicators do. See why they and their pieces and styles work. There are good things about most individuals in top markets that you can emulate in your own personal way. Try to identify what those valuable qualities are and integrate them into your repertoire.

9. As you grow, try to push the envelope, bit by bit. Try new (appropriate) things in writing and delivery. See if they work and enhance the effectiveness of the manner in which you deliver your message. Continue to keep growing, improving, and polishing.

10. Study and immerse yourself in the news. Read well-respected newspapers on a daily basis, as well as periodicals such as *Time*, *Newsweek*, and *U.S. News & World Report*. Watch programs such as *60 Minutes*, *Nightline*, *Dateline NBC*, and *20/20*.

11. When you're on-air, *be real*, true to who you are, and conversational. Talk (as opposed to "read") to me and thereby connect with me.

Attaining "Understanding" and "Ownership" of Your Work

Years ago, a story was told to me about a reporter who was assigned by his TV station to cover a serious accident. The story allegedly unfolded this way:

Upon arriving at the scene of the accident, the reporter quickly, and without great care, scanned the area. He then went on to do some other things—such as watch a baseball playoff game on TV—until it was time to deliver his report. As the reporter began his presentation, he did his trademark walk-and-talk routine, walking around the accident scene and directing the camera to various points of interest, while he flawlessly delivered the facts that he had memorized earlier.

When the reporter finished, the studio anchor advised both the reporter and the viewers that an unexpected development had just occurred. The anchor shared the development with the reporter and the viewers and then asked the reporter to "analyze how the new information might affect the situation." Upon hearing the question, the reporter immediately panicked. His brain apparently locked, and he couldn't speak—for what seemed like an excruciatingly endless amount of time. As the reporter had only surveyed the surface facts of the story, he didn't understand its essentials, and therefore he had no clue as to how to intelligently respond to the ever-changing situation. A moment or so later, the anchor nervously asked the question again. The reporter continued to stand there, speechless, staring blankly into the camera. Finally, he began to speak. However, to everyone's embarrassment, he began to regurgitate the memorized facts, word for word, that he had given moments earlier—and never attempted to answer the anchor's question.

As he did this, a nearly hysterical producer implored the anchor to segue out of the report and back to the studio as soon as possible.

The reporter was fired soon thereafter.

On the other end of the spectrum, there are reporters who pride themselves on attaining a *thorough understanding* of their material. They can deliver their stories during torrential downpours, amid gunfire, in the face of gale force winds, and with curve after unexpected curve being thrown at them. And through it all, they do not lose their presence of mind or their ability to creatively and effectively thrive when major changes or delicate nuances arise. By familiarizing themselves with and understanding the elements of their story, they can see everything in the insightful context of the big picture. These individuals are said to have *ownership* of their work. They have mastered the material and made it their own.

Having been in the news business for more than 29 years, I see examples at both ends of the spectrum every day. Some individuals take responsibility for and master their actions and decisions in a healthy and wise manner. Others, passively or destructively, do not.

We are all performers in life, as day in and day out we perform hundreds of functions. The reporter who froze was a performer who didn't understand the "why" and the "how" of the story that he was reporting on. He knew only the superficial facts. He didn't care enough to have a deeper understanding of the situation. Therefore, during a crisis period, when others with a more thorough knowledge and understanding might well have insightfully and adeptly responded to the anchor's question, this reporter was unprepared. He froze; he didn't know what to do or say; and eventually he ran for cover to his old script—literally!

Through the years, I have noted that a disproportionately large number of individuals who are great live reporters, anchors, and hosts received their initial broadcasting training in radio. When I asked two or three of these individuals why they are so comfortable in the face of the most frantic live situations, they essentially said the same things: In radio, since you have no prompter or script to rely on (or to constrict you), you just absorb the essential facts and then talk with the listener. You initially get the big picture, take ownership of the material, and then off you go. Because you are not relying on anything or anyone—if you are good—you develop the wonderful ability to ad-lib.

I often see beginning and seasoned reporters try to memorize every fact that they have learned and cram them all into their stories. The problem is that the communication of this memorization seems unnatural and non-conversational. Similar to the radio philosophy discussed above, the key to natural and effective communication on live TV is to absorb the essentials and then organically talk to us, share with us, and thereby engage us. Having a basic understanding of your material, and then taking ownership of it, is the way to do this.

The Sprint Versus the Marathon

It's Not How Fast You Initially Go, But How Much in the Long Run You Ultimately Grow

The Marathon

Careers should be viewed as marathons, not as sprints. That is, solid foundations should be laid and enhancing decisions should be made with the big picture and the long run of one's career in mind. And, although there are exceptions and caveats to this philosophy that I will discuss, I believe that true skills are developed, real success is measured, and wisdom is attained—over time.

The Big Picture

Years ago, I played in the finals of the Men's National Open Paddle Tennis (now Extreme Tennis) Doubles Championships against the #1 team in the country. The score was knotted at one set each. The final set was tied at eight games each, and we were in the midst of playing a tiebreaker. During the "breaker," one of our opponents, who was the best overall paddle tennis player in the country, mixed up his shots and his strategy a bit more. (He had the confidence, flexibility, and ability to appropriately change his strategy at the right time.) This caused us to be less effective than we might otherwise have been. They won the tiebreaker 7–5, and the title.

I had played as well as I could have hoped; I just needed to play some points more creatively. So, at 38 years old, after a couple of National Open Men's Doubles wins and a few second-place finishes under my belt, I decided that I needed to improve my game. I would study the national champions and see what I could learn about them and myself.

During the next tournament, I sat up in the stands and watched. It was fascinating. I saw things in the stands that I had never seen down on the court when I was playing against them. From above, I saw how one of my opponents planted himself so close to the net, that by lobbing the ball over his head, we could get his partner out of position enough, so that as a team, they might become more vulnerable. I gleaned all sorts of new possibilities and alternatives from my perspective in the stands.

At the end of a day of viewing, a thought about some of the broadcasters I know came to mind. I realized that some of the most talented communicators, with the biggest and brightest futures, were getting much too caught up with minor day-to-day job hassles. These problems were bringing them down emotionally. I realized that somehow they were not seeing the big picture. In the big picture, these skirmishes wouldn't have the impact of the smallest zit on an elephant's back. I often thought to myself, "God, these people have everything going for them. They just need to see the big picture of their careers the way that I do. They would enjoy the process so much more. They could also be more selective in the battles that they did choose to fight." I realized that because I was not fighting on the ground—day to day—as they were, but was instead, as their *Career Choreographer*, viewing their careers more objectively from the stands, I had a different, fuller, broader, and, in many respects, better perspective than they had.

The lesson was that far too often, while fighting our day-to-day battles, we never look beyond ourselves, or the immediate moment or situation at hand. I have seen and been involved in so many situations in which better perspectives and new spins and solutions could have been discerned and developed, if the individuals involved had just taken the time to look at and examine the big picture—that is, to step away from the heat and angst of the moment and calmly, creatively, and objectively study the situation that they are immediately involved in and the decision that they are about to make in the context of the long-term picture of their career.

The Marathon Versus the Sprint

It is crucial for broadcasters to look at their major decisions in the context of the big picture of their careers and to keep the perspective of the marathon versus the sprint in mind.

For example, many years ago, a client who aspired to one day be a host of the *Today* show was offered a five-year contract to anchor a national entertainment show within two years of beginning her news career. Upon receiving the offer, she was understandably ecstatic. When she asked my opinion, I told her that because she aspired to become a Katie Couric—that is, to successfully host a live morning news program—I felt that, although the entertainment position would move her to a national venue quite early in her career, in the long run that job would ultimately retard her great potential to secure the most coveted news positions—the ones to which she, in her heart of hearts, aspired.

I explained that what anchors often do on the entertainment program that she was offered is to read copy, over and over again, until it is perfect. Rarely is there live reporting, live interviewing, or going live with breaking news. These are just some of the skills that someone who wants to be a Katie Couric has to master. I believed that signing a five-year entertainment-show contract so early in her career would be ill-conceived, as she wouldn't develop the varied live skills that are prerequisites for the most coveted national news positions. As a result, in the big picture of her career, taking the entertainment position might well have been sprint-heaven for my client, but it also would have been marathon-suicide.

Another story. Years ago, a 23-year-old client of mine, who was earning about $18,000 per year as a weekend anchor in a small market, was offered a position as a general-assignment reporter at a network-owned station in Philadelphia. The station offered her a five-year contract, with a first year's salary of approximately $95,000, and $5,000 to $10,000 raises each year thereafter. My client, in sprint-ecstasy, said, "I'm so excited! Where do I sign?" To her surprise and disappointment, I said, "You don't." I continued, "You told me that your goals are to anchor and to report in San Francisco, or to be a main anchor in Seattle. If you take the reporting job, I have been told that you can expect to be a fill-in anchor two to three times a year. You will never grow to be a top anchor with so little regular on-air anchor experience. Five years from now, when you want to go to Seattle or San Francisco as an anchor, you won't be ready. My best advice is to forgo the reporting offer, and let's get an anchoring *and* reporting position at a good station in a market the size of Denver, Phoenix, Sacramento, or San Diego. Although, in all likelihood, you won't make $95,000 as a weekend or noon anchor in any of these markets, ultimately the skills and the money will come."

With some regrets, my client agreed with my perspective. One month later, she became a weekend anchor in Phoenix. Two years later, she became the weekend anchor at a station in San Francisco, with a starting salary of more than $160,000.

In hindsight, it is easy to see that we made the correct big picture decision by turning down the Philadelphia reporting offer. My client is now an excellent anchor *and* an excellent reporter, having worked on and significantly improved both of those skills in Phoenix. As a result, she now has the tools, and has put herself in the best position, to have a long and successful marathon run as an anchor and a reporter in the market of her choice.

One last story: A client with a world of potential was in a small market and was offered a job to anchor "headlines" for a national cable network. I strongly suggested that he decline the offer, as people who anchor headlines at the network generally do not do any day-to-day (or any other form of) reporting. You go in, read, and leave.

Once again, if my client was going to win the career marathon, he needed to have a strong foundation in *both* anchoring and reporting. It was much too early in his career for him to choose one skill to the exclusion of the other. He is now a weeknight anchor and reporter in a top market, and the networks have been calling him. Why? Because he has developed into a wonderful reporter, as well as a top-tier anchor!

Big picture—marathon—thinking can make all the difference in the world as to whether you fulfill your most cherished broadcasting goals—or you don't.

Crunch Time

The other day, a news manager of a television station called me. He said that he would be giving a client of mine, "Terry," a plum assignment that afternoon, which would showcase Terry's broadcasting strengths. This manager told me that Terry was one of three people who were being considered for a coveted national position, and that if my client was on his game and really showed his stuff, he, in all likelihood, would get the position. The manager finished our conversation by saying, "Kenny, I can't be any clearer than this: If Terry gets it right, his career is changed for the better from here on out. It's up to him. Starting this afternoon, it's crunch time!"

The last few minutes of a close football or basketball game are sometimes referred to as "crunch time"—a critical point during a sports contest, when the outcome of the game can go either way. Crunch times are those defining moments when individuals are faced with significant choices. They are our opportunities either to make wise decisions and enhance ourselves (and others) or to make poor and weak decisions, settle and sink, and be destructive to ourselves (and to others).

As someone who counsels individuals throughout each day to make the most positive and healthy career and life decisions, I have found the concepts of crunch time and defining moments to be particularly useful, effective, and visual.

I believe that not enough attention is paid to the fact that each of us faces crunch times—or moments of decision—many times each day throughout our lives. And although it is constructive and healthy to say that we must give 100 percent all the time, there are some or many defining moments in real-life broadcasting that can truly change the course of a career. These are moments when breaking news events happen—such as a bombing, the slaying of a public figure, a weather emergency, a war—and everyone is watching and everyone cares. These are your center-court opportunities to show your stuff.

I can think of many, many instances when proactive, constructive individuals identified an important news moment and then seized it. They tapped into their potential and their well-laid foundation, and they thereby raised the level of their performances to great heights. And many times these performances led directly to great career advancement and further enhancing opportunities.

But making the most of a breaking or important story is just one means of seizing a defining moment. Another way is to initiate great stories, and thereby create defining moments for yourself. I cannot tell you how often I hear news managers complain that reporters never enterprise stories or cultivate sources. They just take what is assigned to them. On the other hand, I am willing to bet that many of the most successful and well-respected reporters enterprised some or much of their best work.

SECTION X

The Evolution Imperative!
and a Closing Gift to the Reader

The Evolution Imperative!

I t is essential that throughout your career you keep learning, improving, polishing, adapting—in other words, evolving.

My dad had two major, highly successful and rewarding careers that spanned more than 80 years. As noted earlier, when he was "retired" at 66 years young by the department store chain that had employed him for decades, the emotional wind was temporarily taken out of his sails. But he continued to:

1. exercise and stay fit and active;

2. read appropriate periodicals, such as *Women's Wear Daily;*

3. visit clothing manufacturers, with whom he did business for years and with whom he hoped to one day work again; and

4. "comparison-shop" many of the top department stores to see what they were showing and what their customers were purchasing.

By doing all of this, my dad stayed current and relevant. He continued to learn and know everything about the business he loved. He continued to *evolve.* So when, at the age of 69, he was offered a position to train buyers of a new chain of stores called T.J. Maxx, he was relevant and ready! That position lasted nearly 30 years, until he retired at 98. Throughout that time, my dad continually counseled me to "always keep growing and keep learning."

Colin Cowherd, the extremely wise, insightful, and talented nationally syndicated sports-radio talk-show host, has time and time again cited tangible examples that prove and reinforce the reality that if you are not evolving, you become *irrelevant*. I totally agree with Colin's philosophy and have always counseled my clients accordingly. I also do my best to live my life and conduct my business in a manner consistent with this philosophy.

For example, approximately 22 years ago, I left my position at the William Morris Agency as vice president of news at the Los Angeles office and founded my own on-air agency. However, instead of focusing only on newscaster representation, I created a hosting division as well, as I felt that there was going to be a huge need and set of new enhancing opportunities for newscasters who would like to host, as well as for traditional hosts. Up till then, the competing news agencies had been focused solely on doing just that—offering news representation.

As time wore on and programming became more and more popular and profitable, having a hosting division turned out to be great for our clients and gave our agency a tremendous competitive edge regarding the servicing of our current clients and the signing of new ones. However, as more time passed and hosting became even bigger, the large theatrical agencies began to see the profitability of going into this area and they did—which put us at some competitive disadvantage because we didn't offer the commercial, literary, or production representation that the major theatrical agencies did.

Wanting to remain ahead of the curve, be relevant, and offer the very best and most wide-ranging representation to our clients, our company and I needed to evolve again. So I explored all sorts of partnerships and affiliations in order to grow and continue to offer our best to our clients. As I did this, competitors heard about my efforts and tried to spread the word that I was selling my company in order to retire. In fact, nothing could have been further from the truth. I was doing my best to evolve for our current and future clients.

Through the years, we have formed *strategic* alliances with various theatrical agencies and then with Octagon, which have given many of our clients the exposure and the wide range of ancillary representation opportunities that they, at different times in their careers, might need. It has been a huge success. Our clients have grown, and we have grown. And it has given us a tremendous competitive advantage over those news agencies that continue to focus on news only, as well as over other theatrical agencies that do not have our news and hosting experience, access to news executives at the highest levels, and *Career Choreography*™ mindset.

I am anticipating that many individuals who read this book will wonder and ask why I disclose some of our competitive advantages herein by explaining a good deal of what I know and the means by which I counsel. Here is my two-level response:

First, on a competitive level, just because someone knows some of what to do intellectually doesn't mean they can effectively implement the information. For example, on an intellectual level, many professional tennis players know how Roger Federer executes his forehand, serve, backhand, and volley. His competitors have studied tape on him endlessly. However, all of this knowledge doesn't enable them to play like Roger, beat Roger, or secure his extraordinary results.

Similarly, I believe that I truly know and understand what makes Matt Lauer the best morning show host ever! I am also crystal-clear that I, in my wildest imagination, cannot host like Matt!

As a talent representative and *Career Choreographer*™, I remain thoroughly secure in my representation abilities, my eye for identifying extraordinary on-air talent who are blessed to have "it," and my long, strong relationships and friendships with my clients, as well as broadcast executives, at all levels, in all areas.

Second, and far more important, I am passionate about the fields of news and hosting, and they, in turn, have been very good to me and my family. Writing this book is my opportunity to help *all* present and future talent—clients and non-clients—to grow and evolve, and that, at the end of the day, is why I love what I do! My life's mission is to see what "can be" in individuals and to help them make their potential, goals, and *Gold Ring Dreams* a reality. A *Broadcasting Reality*!

I love representing my clients, and I truly believe that if I continue to evolve and be the very best I can be, we will be together for a long, long time! So, let others grow. I hope that other talent agents learn from this book, as I continue to learn from others. This way, we will all be better and do our very best work for our clients.

I understand the merits of evolution and also that you cannot stop it! My goal is to make my best efforts to remain at the forefront of it.

Don't Lose Sight of "The Gift"

Throughout this book, I have presented a number of the pressing issues, tough conflicts, and harsh *New Age Realities* of broadcast journalism. However, as a talent, a news or programming executive, and/or a broadcaster, you must never lose sight of the access, the platform, and the power that you have to truly help your fellow man and woman by supplying them with the essential information that they need in order to intelligently and effectively live—and lift—their lives. This opportunity is a *gift*. It is the gift of being able to truly serve others. You are in a position of trust, with a gift to be made the very most of—and cherished.

Carpe diem!

A Closing Gift to the Reader

I would like to close this book with a second gift—my gift, to you, the reader:

I have done my best to make the broadcasting information that I have shared here important and relevant to you. You have my best efforts. However, with the passing of time, there will always be new and more *New Age Broadcasting Realities*. And at some point, *The New Age* will pass and give way to a new *Stage* of broadcasting. However, because change remains constant, there are three *Realities* that will *always* serve you well, no matter what *Stage* you are in: Keep evolving. Stay relevant. And never lose sight or touch with what your heart and gut are telling you is right.

My very best wishes to you,

Ken Lindner

The Ten New Age Career Choreography™ Commandments

*T*he *New Economic Reality* is having a tremendous impact on broadcasters. It is also playing a major role in almost all news and programming decisions that they make. In order to successfully navigate through this highly challenging *New Age*, here is what everyone in broadcasting must keep in mind:

1. In *The New Age*, employers need to get more with less and fewer. Therefore, they want to employ only "A Players" who bring their "A Game" to their jobs every day. So be an "A Player" and bring it!

2. There is a certain well-conceived, logical set of strategic steps that, when effectively implemented, will materially increase your chances of accomplishing your career goals and dreams. This is *Career Choreography™*. The key for you is to become the most efficacious *Career Choreographer™* possible.

3. What employers want and need from their on-air talent is for the talent to maintain a positive and lasting connection with the viewer. Your goal as talent is to establish this connection with the viewers and those who are on-set with you.

4. In *The New Age*, being totally exclusive to one employer and/or one job is outdated and shortsighted. It is now essential for talent to *Multi-Platform*. This will increase your visibility, recognizability, marketability, brand awareness, and income—all great things!

5. You must look at *Career Choreographies*™ very strategically and see who has alliances with whom, and who benefits from your growing and gaining increased, enhancing exposure. Do not be afraid to be creative, imaginative, and aim high ("Aspire higher!").

6. When it comes to your employment agreements, "You don't get what you deserve, you get what you [are able] to negotiate." So, at a time when talent is asked to accept lower salaries and/or less job security, it is essential that you very carefully and thoughtfully review, negotiate, and craft the provisions of your employment agreement—including the "boilerplate" clauses.

7. Just as broadcasting is a business for broadcasters, it is also a business for you as a talent. So perceive and run your career like a business, and continually and strategically enhance your biggest assets: you and your talents!

8. In connection with all of the career moves and significant career decisions that you have the opportunity to make, be sure that they are the very wisest ones possible as seen in the highly insightful context of what you most want in the big picture of your career and your life.

9. In *The New Age*, when the employer asks on- and off-air talent to make contractual concessions in order for the employer and its newscasts and/or programs to survive financially or thrive, the talent in essence becomes the employer's *partner*. As a result, this employer-talent *partnership* should allow the talent to ask for and secure contractual concessions in the areas of exclusivity, security, duty assignability, and vacation. These concessions will not cost the employer extra money but can materially benefit the employee. Always keep in mind that *The New Age* employer's needs and requests for talent givebacks have changed the rules for *both* the employer and for the talent!

10. Always keep learning, growing, and evolving. And never lose touch with what your heart and gut are telling you is the right path for you!

NOTES

Section I: Your Introductory Information

1. Meg James, "Couric Makes Time to Talk," *Los Angeles Times, Calendar*, June 7, 2011, D1, 12.

2. James Raney, "Running Nonstop, and It Shows," *Los Angeles Times, Calendar*, June 8, 2011, D1, 10.

3. Ken Lindner, *Crunch Time: 8 Steps to Making the Right Life Decisions at the Right Time* (New York: Gotham Books, 2005).

Section II: The Aims of News and Broadcasting during Four Key *Stages* of Broadcasting History

4. Ben Grossman, "A Self-Hating Journalist Comes Around (a Little)," *Broadcasting & Cable*, June 22, 2009, 6.

5. John Eggerton, "Spectrum: What Is It Good For?" *Broadcasting & Cable*, June 6, 2011, 12.

6. Frank Rich, "And That's How It Was," *New York Times Magazine*, May 18, 2002, 82.

7. Edward Bliss, Jr., *The Story of Broadcast Journalism* (New York: Columbia University Press, 1991), 10.

8. Ibid., 11.

9. Ibid.

10. Ibid., 11–12.

11. Ibid., 47.

12. Ibid.

13. Michael Gartner, "O.J. Circus? Blame TV," *USA Today*, October, 3, 1995, 11A.

14. Bliss, *The Story of Broadcast Journalism*, 460.

15. Richard M. Cohen, "The Corporate Tolerance of News," In Erik Barnouw et al., *Conglomerates and the Media*, 32 (New York: New Press, 1997).

16. Paige Albiniak, "Syndicators Weigh Another Eleven," *Broadcasting & Cable*, July 20, 2009, 4.

17. Paige Albiniak, "Getting Tough: Sign of Things to Come? CBS Lawsuit Over Failure to Pay Bills May Be Precursor as Stations Struggle," *Broadcasting & Cable*, June 22, 2009, 3.

Section III: *The New Age Realities*, Insights, and Strategies on Which to Base Your Career Decisions

18. Mary McNamara, "No One Does It Like Oprah," *Los Angeles Times*, Calendar, May 25, 2011, D1, 11.

19. Alan Berger, Creative Artists Agency.

20. Ibid.

21. M. Scott Peck, *The Road Less Traveled* (New York: Touchstone, 1978), 15.

22. Anthony Robbins, *Unlimited Power* (New York: Fawcett Columbine, 1986), 73.

Section V: *New Age* Broadcasting Issues to Contemplate

23. Walter Liss, President, Buena Vista Television.

24. Joel Cheatwood, Executive Vice President, Mercury Radio Arts.

25. Donald V. Browne, President, Telemundo Communications Group, Inc.

26. Walter Liss.

27. Daniel Goleman, *Emotional Intelligence* (New York: Bantam Books, 1995), 411.

28. Connie Chung, "The Business of Getting the Get: Making an Exclusive Interview in Prime Time," in *The Joan Shrenstein Center on the Press, Politics, and Public Policy* (Cambridge, MA: Harvard University John F. Kennedy School of Government), 8.

29. Ibid.

30. Ibid.

31. Stephen Brill, *Brill's Content*, August 1998, 124–132.

32. Ibid., 123–151.

33. Ibid., 123–124.

34. Kenneth Starr, in a letter to Stephen Brill, June 16, 1998.

35. Brill, *Brill's Content*, 123–151.

36. Ibid., 130–131, 133, 140–141.

37. Ibid.

38. Ibid., 136.

39. Ibid.

40. Floyd Abrams, guest on *The Charlie Rose Show*, Public Broadcast System, 6.

41. Maria Elena Fernandez and Scott Collins, "Jackson Media Frenzy Faulted," *Los Angeles Times, Calendar*, July 4, 2009, 1, 4.

42. Donald V. Browne.

43. Arthur Ashe, with Arnold Rampasand, *Days of Grace* (New York: Knopf, 1993), 6–9.

44. Ibid., 20.

45. Brill, *Brill's Content*.

46. Marisa Guthrie, "News Orgs Battle Wacko Jacko Claims," *Broadcasting & Cable*, July 6, 2009.

47. Ibid.

48. Ibid.

49. *Jerry Maguire* (Cameron Crowe, Director), TriStar Pictures, 1996.

50. Man Keung Ho, *Minority and Adolescents in Therapy* (New York: Sage Productions), 8.

51. Ibid., Part II.

52. Ibid., 12 and Part II.

53. Edward Bliss, Jr., *The Story of Broadcast Journalism* (New York: Columbia University Press, 1991), 327.

54. Bob Papper and Michael Gerhard, "About Face," *Communicator*, August 1998, 29.

55. Ibid., 30.

56. Ibid., 31–32.

57. Ibid., 32.

58. Ibid.

59. Dr. Martin Luther King, Jr., *Why We Can't Wait* (New York: Signet Books, 1964), 134–135.

60. Craig Robinson, Executive Vice President and Chief Diversity Officer for NBC Universal. August 16, 2011.

61. Paige Albiniak, Broadcasting & Cable, May 16, 2011, 16.

62. Ken Lindner, 48–Supp. 3.

63. Julie O'Dell, "For the First Time, More People Get News Online Than from Newspapers," http://mashable.com/2011/03/15/online-versus-newspaper-news, 1.

64. Ibid., 2.

65. Lauren Indvick, "Americans Consuming More News, Thanks to the Internet [STATS]," http://mashable.com/2010/09/13/news-internet-study/, 1.

66. Ibid.

67. Charles Buchwalter; Scott Collins, "Jackson Memorial Seen as a Landmark," *Los Angeles Times*, July 9, 2009, 1, 4.

68. Ibid.

69. Ibid.

70. Buchwalter.

71. Joe Flint, "Distracted Viewers Ditch TV Dramas," *Los Angeles Times, Calendar*, May 12, 2011, 1, 13.

72. Buchwalter.

73. Ibid.

74. John Lafayette, "Still Ahead of the Game," *Broadcasting & Cable*, June 13, 2011, 8, 9, 12.

75. Alex Weprin, "Network News: One Click Away," *Broadcasting & Cable*, July 20, 2009, 10, 11.

76. Ibid.

77. Jon Lafayette, "Fox Makes Multi-Platform Case," Broadcasting & Cable, May 9, 2011, 14.

78. Ibid.

79. Greg D'Alba; Jon Lafayette, "CNN Pitches Comeback Story," *Broadcasting & Cable*, April 4, 2011, 14.

80. Lafayette, "Fox Makes Multi-Platform Case."

81. Ibid.

82. Ibid.

83. Ibid.

84. Sanchez, Rick (August 2, 2011).

85. Lafayette, "CNN Pitches Comeback Story."

86. Sanchez, Rick, (August 2, 2011).

87. Cheatwood, Joel (August 2, 2011).

88. Sanchez, Rick, *Conventional Idiocy* (Penguin Books, September 2010), 24.

89. Ibid., 31.

90. Ibid., 30.

91. Ibid., 30.

92. Ibid., 26.

93. Op. cit., Sanchez, (August 2, 2011).

94. Sanchez, *Conventional Idiocy*, 5.

95. Sanchez, (August 2, 2011).

96. Michael Malone, "Stations Commit 'Social' Faux Pas," *Broadcasting & Cable*, May 16, 2011, 22.

97. Ibid.

98. Ibid.

99. Ibid.

100. Ibid.

101. Ibid.

102. Ibid.

103. Ibid.

104. Op. cit., Sanchez, (August 2, 2011).

105. John Ferriter, Octagon.

Section VII: *The New Age* Media and the Multimedia Journalist

106. Jeff Kiernan.

107. Ibid.

108. Ibid.

Section IX: The Psychology of Breaking into Broadcasting and Developing Your Career

109. Bart Feder, Senior Vice President, CNN Current Programming.

110. Cheryl Fair, Vice President and News Director, KABC.

111. Donald V. Browne.

112. *Field of Dreams* (Phil Alden Robinson, Director), MCA Universal, 1989.

113. Edward Bliss, Jr., *The Story of Broadcast Journalism* (New York: Columbia University Press, 1991), 469.

INDEX

CPSIA information can be obtained at www.ICGtesting.com
Printed in the USA
LVOW11s1021030616

491103LV00001B/41/P